Becoming Arab in London

Anthropology, Culture and Society

Series Editors:
Professor Vered Amit, Concordia University
and
Professor Christina Garsten, Stockholm University

Recent titles:

Becoming Arab in London

Performativity and the Undoing of Identity

Ramy M.K. Aly

PlutoPress
www.plutobooks.com

First published 2015 by Pluto Press
345 Archway Road, London N6 5AA

www.plutobooks.com

British Library Cataloguing in Publication Data
A catalogue record for this book is available from the British Library

ISBN 978 0 7453 3359 5 Hardback
ISBN 978 0 7453 3358 8 Paperback
ISBN 978 1 7837 1156 7 PDF eBook
ISBN 978 1 7837 1158 1 Kindle eBook
ISBN 978 1 7837 1157 4 EPUB eBook

Library of Congress Cataloging in Publication Data applied for

10   9   8   7   6   5   4   3   2   1

Typeset by Stanford DTP Services, Northampton, England
Text design by Melanie Patrick
Simultaneously printed digitally by CPI Antony Rowe, Chippenham, UK
and Edwards Bros in the United States of America

To Heba, Naila, Mounir, Sharif, Rania and Osama.

Contents

List of Illustrations

Series Preface

Anthropology is a discipline based upon in-depth ethnographic works that deal with wider theoretical issues in the context of particular, local conditions – to paraphrase an important volume from the series: *large issues explored in small places*. This series has a particular mission: to publish work that moves away from an old-style descriptive ethnography that is strongly area-studies oriented, and offer genuine theoretical arguments that are of interest to a much wider readership, but which are nevertheless located and grounded in solid ethnographic research. If anthropology is to argue itself a place in the contemporary intellectual world, then it must surely be through such research.

We start from the question: 'What can this ethnographic material tell us about the bigger theoretical issues that concern the social sciences?' rather than 'What can these theoretical ideas tell us about the ethnographic context?' Put this way round, such work becomes *about* large issues, *set in* a (relatively) small place, rather than detailed description of a small place for its own sake. As Clifford Geertz once said, 'Anthropologists don't study villages; they study *in* villages.'

By place, we mean not only geographical locale, but also other types of 'place' – within political, economic, religious or other social systems. We therefore publish work based on ethnography within political and religious movements, occupational or class groups, among youth, development agencies, and nationalist movements; but also work that is more thematically based – on kinship, landscape, the state, violence, corruption, the self. The series publishes four kinds of volume: ethnographic monographs; comparative texts; edited collections; and shorter, polemical essays.

We publish work from all traditions of anthropology, and all parts of the world, which combines theoretical debate with empirical evidence to demonstrate anthropology's unique position in contemporary scholarship and the contemporary world.

Professor Vered Amit
Professor Christina Garsten

Acknowledgements

I would like to begin by thanking all those who co-produced this research by sharing their time, memories, thoughts and lives with me. Without their generosity, curiosity and support this research would simply not have been possible.

I express the deepest gratitude to Filippo Osella and Katy Gardner for turning me into an anthropologist and always encouraging me to think in new ways. Also at the University of Sussex, Richard Black, Raminder Kaur-Kahlon, Simon Coleman, James Fairhead and Jon Mitchell all showed me exceptional kindness and support. Thanks are also due to Dr Khair El-Din Hasseeb, Director of the Centre for Arab Unity Studies (Beirut, Lebanon), who generously provided me with financial support to complete the PhD research on which this book is based. I am also grateful to Marie Gillespie, Soraya Altorki, Tarik Sabry, Naomi Sakr, Myria Georgiou and Christina Slade, who have always showed such confidence in me.

I could not have hoped to complete this book without the unwavering love and support of my family and friends. My mother Naila Ramez-Aly, my father Mounir Kamal Aly, my brother Sharif and my sister Heba have provided love, inspiration and support which I cannot hope to capture in words. I owe particular thanks to Rania Khadr for her support, patience, partnership and forgiveness; to Osama Muttawa whose friendship I cannot live without and for the countless hours of walking and talking through chapters, ideas and life; and to Wadah Abusin and Hani Mostafa for always lifting my spirits and being there when it matters most. Finally, I would like to express the deepest gratitude to Haroon Shah, who gave so generously of himself to see me through an extremely difficult experience and to David Castle at Pluto Press for being so patient and persevering.

The author and publisher wish to thank *The Arab Review* (London), *The Arab World* (London), Iqra Publishing (Tripoli, Libya), Getty Images (Hulton Archive) and *Sharq Magazine* (London) for permission to reproduce copyright material. Every effort has been made to trace copyright holders and to obtain their permission for the use of copyright material. The author and publisher apologise for any errors or omissions in the above list and would be grateful for notification of any corrections that should be incorporated in future reprints or editions of this book.

Introduction

In this book I explore the lives of young people born or raised in London to migrants from Arab states and some of the ways in which they '*do*' or achieve Arabness in London. I argue that Arabness, like all other categorical labels is best understood not as a form of authentic 'being' but as repertoires of 'doing', achieved through the imperfect repetition of culture over time and space. One is not born an Arab in London, instead Arabness is a process of becoming through acts, enunciations, objects, spaces, bodies and settings like *Shisha* cafes, 'Arabic nights', through 'ethnic self-portraits', dance and narratives that re-order and re-collect growing up in London.

I consciously choose to think about 'doing' and not 'being'. To look at acts one must accept their implication in both individual agency and determining structures, their instrumentality, temporality and the contingent and indeterminate meanings they generate. Asking what something 'means' involves assuming a position of deconstructive *différance,* while asking what something 'is' involves authoritative and willing construction. Deconstructive gestures are not, as some tend to assume, a sign of reticence or exasperating postmodern indeterminacy, they are perilous because they question and intrude upon the integrity of ideas that we consider normative, common-sense and sometime sacred.

Treading upon the tenuous space between formal ethnography of the 'other' and auto-ethnography, I begin with the personal, not simply as ritual ethnographic reflexivity, but because it provides an opportunity to lay bare the motivations behind this journey and introduce the notion of 'performativity' which is central to the analysis I present. My sister, who like myself, was born in London to Egyptian immigrant parents in the late 1970s had run away from home at the age of 24. Her departure was deeply painful for the whole family. There was an overwhelming sense of failure, borne largely by my parents who in my opinion had worked tirelessly and selflessly to raise us. In truth her departure had been a long time coming. She had a difficult journey through childhood and adolescence. The poor decisions and choices she had made were her own, the result of idiosyncratic dispositions and coping strategies; but on other occasions I watched as she failed to live up to the ideals and expectations of others, which could only have added to her spiralling self-destructiveness. To my discomfort now, I must admit to having taken part in the disapproving glances and remarks. I suppose what that disapproval referred to was a rather common and boring question 'Why couldn't she just be normal like everyone else?' Yet now I find myself wondering why we take such comfort and security from the anonymity that conformity provides? It is after all a wretched reflection of a social and psychological fear that stunts and circumscribes personhood.

A recurring theme throughout our childhood was my sister's failure to master and embody the female, middle-class, Egyptian, Arab and Muslim 'identities' (not necessarily in that order) that she was expected to grow into, or as Butler (1990) following de Beauvoir (1997 [1949]) would described it, she failed 'to do' or 'to become' those things. She was neither passive, feminine or studious enough, nor had she mastered the art of living two lives, one in and one beyond the home and family. She was unable to make those desires, aspirations and behavioural norms her own, ultimately casting her as an anomaly and unintelligible, drawing her into constant conflict with those around her. She had 'gone native' with what, at the time, seemed an incomprehensible and unhealthy appreciation of urban English working-class and Afro-Caribbean cultures, both equally unacceptable and horrifying within the family and the wider 'Egyptian community' in which we lived. The pressure not to make 'mistakes', the feeling of being constantly watched, evaluated, moulded and judged, were exacerbated by her role as a daughter, the symbol of honour, the ultimate measure of whether our parents had successfully raised us despite and in spite of the 'England' that surrounded us. She was of course not alone in her predicament; many others, sometimes quietly and at other times dramatically suffered the same fate.

The preconceived ways of being that had been chosen for my sister consistently eluded her both as performances and perhaps more importantly as aspirations. I recall how she always resisted, with the help of her stubbornly Afro-Semitic hair, my mother's weekly attempts to tame and straighten her wiry locks, to make her appropriately white and presentable in that subconsciously colonised notion of Egyptian femininity. Adding to her failure to perform and embody these roles in a bounded sense was the rejection of her own imperfect performative renditions. My sister's 'failure' to demonstrate convincingly that she was 'playing the same game' had serious implications that led to her estrangement and rejection by members of her family and her peers, giving weight to the argument that while ethnic boundaries may exist between so-called 'groups', there is 'no axiomatic rule which stipulates that the boundaries of selfhood and self-consciousness are less significant ... than those of the collectivity' (Cohen 1994: 74). Therefore in part what follows in this ethnography is an attempt to draw attention to the nuances and relationships between 'ethnic boundaries' and cultural content in the process of becoming a subject.

After an anguishing few months my sister made contact with my parents. Their relationship had changed irreversibly and for me the rupture in my family life brought questions, I had long asked myself but avoided answering, sharply into focus. I was living in Dubai when she left home; I had left the UK in an attempt to 'return' to an Arab world that I had never left to begin with. Nonetheless I always seemed to see it in those terms. Being born and growing up in London somehow seemed circumstantial, an accident of fate, as if being brought into this world in Hammersmith Hospital was some kind of cosmological mistake which I should spend my life correcting by following my roots deep into the ground to emerge in a redemptive space somewhere hot and dusty like Cairo. While my sister and I were both sent off into London to become Egyptian in all ways, our paths diverged early on. I was more of a conformist than she was. I had my own problems making sense of myself and feeling comfortable in my own skin. I couldn't help feeling that 'we, Arabs' and particularly females born or raised in Britain, were torn between competing ways of life: between the demands of our families and communities on the one hand and the wider society on the other, not being able to live a full life in either one or the other realms or indeed between them. The challenges we faced as the children of immigrants were described to me in books and newspaper articles as 'identity crisis' and 'culture clash', which for a while I was content with as explanations for my sister's plight and to a large extent my own (see Erikson 1968; Thompson 1974; Anwar 1976, 2002; Taylor 1976; Ballard 1979). But it was not long before it became clear how much these explanations took for granted and how little they offered in terms of 'identity' or 'culture'.

In the initial weeks of fieldwork I conducted interviews and informal meetings with 'Arab community representatives'. I attended meetings in Parliament and City Hall ranging from a meet-and-greet with the first 'second-generation British Arab' borough councillor to the meetings of parliamentary lobbying groups like the Council for Arab-British Understanding. These encounters all seemed to be framed within a highly formalised lexicon of local, national and international politics. Community 'leaders' were keen to emphasise the size of the respective national minority they represented, the strength of their relationships with local councillors or ministers, and the importance of the funding which they had received or were seeking to ensure the continuation of 'services to the community'. Local councillors stressed the need for more 'Arabs to get involved in politics' so that, on the one hand, they would be represented in British politics and, on the other hand, to ensure that Arabs were seen as an integrated and successful migrant community. It seemed that there were many people hailing the 'Arab community', calling upon it to play a more active part in the public sphere and to 'act' like a community. At the time at least, the 'Arab community' itself seemed largely absent, a fact that was often explained as being a cultural problem, a legacy of the repressive political cultures of the Arab states from which these different groups had come. There seemed to be consequences to the absence of the 'Arab community' as an active agent on the multicultural playing field. While some of these consequences were economic and political, they were overshadowed by a similar kind of failing as that experienced by my sister, a performative failure. In other words, a failure to *recite* the norm of the 'ethnic community' as it is understood in multicultural Britain. Failures in the performative sense, those that fall short of normative ideals through imperfect recitation, play a deeper role in the story of Arabness beyond London and multiculturalism. For generations now, 'Arabs' have carried the burden of failing to be themselves somehow, of betraying their glorious civilisational past, of becoming a vassal, occupied, impoverished and enfeebled nation.

Like many others I believed that the problems of the 'Arab community' and its constituent 'communities' were down to the fact that Arabs were an 'unrecognised' and 'hidden' ethnic group and, consequently, unsure of their status in Britain. In 2010 the Office of National Statistics (ONS) announced that the categories 'Arab' and 'Gypsy or Irish Travellers' would be included in the 2011 census. The news was met with 'full support' by the Muslim Council of Britain[1] but with consternation by the Sikh Federation which argued, among other things that 'the Prioritisation Tool'[2] did not indicate any policy or service specific demand or need for including an 'Arab' category in the census and that 'Arab' had been favoured over 'Sikh,' an 'officially recognised ethnic category,' as a result of 'predetermined conclusions'.[3]

Gerd Baumann lucidly argues that Britain's political culture:

encourages so-called minorities to strive for emancipation as if they were sports teams: They are approached as so-called 'communities,'

and politicians, the media and almost everybody else thinks of them
as tightly knit 'cultural groups' held together by the same traditions,
value systems, and history. It is perfectly clear that this is not true; but
this is the misperception under which they must hope to achieve civil
emancipation, as well as the misperception under which British state
elites try to 'help' them. (1999: 76)

As George Yúdice argues 'there is no point in blaming the victims who
wield identitarian politics; instead our attention must be focused on the
politics and structures that feed its reproduction' (2003: 49). 'Foundationalist reasoning of identity politics tends to assume that an identity
must first be in place in order for political interests to be elaborated and
subsequently, political action to be taken' (Butler 1990: 181).

I cannot recall or identify a time where I had decided that 'ethnic
identity' or 'ethnic community' were important; they seem to have been
notions that had always been there. It could be that I gradually acquired
this high regard for ethnicity by virtue of living in London, a city that is
aggressively promoted as multicultural but which is silently fixated with
ethnicity which is always 'under erasure'[4] (Derrida 1988, 2001; see also
Kramvig 2005). It was perhaps the initial acceptance of the self-evident
nature of ethnic categories and ethnic groups which entangled me in an
all too simplistic routine of labelling, reducing and reifying differentiated
experiences under convenient ethnic labels and the formal frameworks
of state population management (Foucault 2000). The state is not alone
in believing that social conviviality is achieved through what I understand
as 'ethnonormative' nomenclature, which sits just as comfortably with the
delusions of those who continue to believe, as a Sudanese parent in his
early 40s put it to me, that he had raised his children in London '100 per
cent Sudanese'.

While people consistently demonstrate an ability to overcome the
illusions of nationality, race and cultural incommensurability by loving,
living, eating, dressing, reading and listening across these false boundaries,
structures of subjection and institutional power demand that the
multifarious identifications that people enact be distilled into discrete
labels. The logic of the international nation-state system has sought to
subject people to its restrictive terms of reference, like the pervasive
image of a world political atlas depicting 'yellow, green, pink, orange and
blue countries composing a truly global map with no vague or "fuzzy
spaces" and no bleeding boundaries' (Tambiah 1985: 4; Trinh 1989: 94,
in Malikki 1992).

I aim to make deconstructive gestures towards the discourses that produce the problematic 'Arab [and/in/of] London'. At the heart of these binaries are nationalism and the sedentary logic of the state which proclaim that the dweller is positively assessed in relation to the migrant wanderer, who is seen at best as a distortion and at worst a threat (Clifford, 1997). 'Sedentarist assumptions about attachment to place lead some to define displacement not as a fact of socio-political and economic contexts, but rather as an inherent pathological characteristic of the displaced' (Malikki 1992: 33). Migrants carry with them the cultural and psychic paraphernalia of 'arboreal origin' to new contexts, ripe with the logic of boundedness.[5] The favouring of fixity over mobility, of 'roots over routes', relies upon conventional modes of subjectivity that constrain the possibilities of subjecthood within rigid and exclusionary boundaries (Gilroy 2000a; D'Andréa 2006).

The persistence of these foundationalist discourses is not simply the result of the messy world outside rational and empirical academia. As Baumann argues, the study of ethnicity routinely acknowledges the complexity of 'identities': yet when it comes to empirical studies of ethnicity, most students are given (or chose) topics such as 'The Turks in Berlin', 'The Berbers in Paris', 'The Sikhs in New York', or, in my case, 'The Arabs in London'. 'The focus is on national, ethnic, or religious minorities as if anyone could know in advance how this minority is bounded and which processes proceed inside and which outside that assumed community' (1999: 145).

It is here that I would like to distance myself from the notion of *identity*, a term which today 'now either stands for too much or too little' bearing an awkward theoretical burden (Brubaker 2006: 37–40). Judith Butler (1993, 2004) replaces the notion of 'gender identity' with the notion of 'gender performativity', arguing that gender is not an essence but always 'a doing' that produces the gendered subject. I will attempt to argue that Butler's approach to gender and performativity are an appropriate basis on which to think about the ways in which ethnicities are conceived and played out in settings like London. Like gender, the structures and social consequences of 'race', ethnicity, culture and identity are inherently discursive and performative, being the result of the 'stylized repetition of acts through time' (Butler 1990: 140). Butler's description of the ways in which 'the performance of gender produces the effect of an organising principle – an identity – that appears to cause [the] behaviour' (1990: 140) can, I believe, be used to understand ethnicity, culture and identity (and their progenitor 'race') in contemporary Britain.

My central argument is that there is theoretical proximity in the prc
of being 'raced' and 'gendered' as I present them in this ethnogra
do not seek to subordinate or understate other intersecting processes of
subjection like class, which I incorporate in my reading but which may
require far more consideration than I am able to give it here. My task is to
counter-expose the hegemonic norms of 'being raced' (making and being
made an 'Arab') and 'being gendered' (making and being made into, an
'Arab wo/man') and how these are informed by class in London. Looking
at what it means 'to do' Arabness in London provides opportunities to
look at the underlying normative and psychical structures that inform the
doing of 'ethnicity' in a particular setting.

To my knowledge, this book is the first detailed ethnography of
the cultural practices of Arab Londoners. Rather than filling me with
confidence this claim fills me with foreboding. How will the subjects of this
book, 'Arab Londoners', take to the fact that my approach is unconcerned
with showing them to be a 'successful minority' or a legitimate 'ethnic
group' with a project of cultural preservation? How will readers in the
Arab world react to the way I question the existence of any *a priori* essence
which might constitute 'Arab womanhood' or 'Arab manhood'? Or my
reliance and advocacy of the work of Judith Butler, whose scholarship
will no doubt be eclipsed by the labels which precede her – 'American',
'Jewish', 'Lesbian'. Abu-Lughod describes this as the multiple binds when
one writes for other, mostly 'western' anthropologists, but at the same
time is identified with and accountable to an 'Arab' audience both in the
diaspora and the 'Arab world'. Writing with these considerations in mind
involves a 'complex awareness of and investment in reception … [to
which] there are no easy solutions' (1991: 142). I expect that some will
see fit to cast me as a heretic, one of those Arabs from the diaspora who
has been tainted by western thought, whose being has been ruptured by
dislocation from the cosmological certainties of my 'culture of origin'.
It is only the open space of double-critique and *tajawuz* (transcendence),
introduced to me so lucidly by Tarik Sabry (2010, 2011), that provides me
with the thinking space or identification to make the claims in this book.
It is in this marginal intellectual movement within Arab Cultural Studies
that I place this work, and to which I address it.

Anthropology and ethnography cause me to assume an instinctively
defensive posture, the former for reasons of postcolonial suspicion, the
latter for postmodern concerns over representation. In response I adopt
auto-ethnography as 'both a method and a text' (Reed-Danahay 1997:
5). While I assert here that I am doing auto-ethnography, sometimes

described as 'anthropology at home', I am inconveniently neither western nor native and remain uncommitted about what or where 'home' is. I find the most useful description of this textual movement to be that offered by Marilyn Strathern, who sees auto-anthropology as 'anthropology carried out in the social context which produced it' (1987: 17).

Fieldwork quickly confronted me with the folly of assuming that my belonging to the 'Arabs of London' was uncontested or unproblematic; there are few assurances based on a shared urban geography, 'ethnicity', language or religion. The presumption of familiarity, of being with 'my people' or in 'my city' was supported by some interactions and shattered by others. We are always only ever members of a group in passing. The streets, settings, people and practices that I considered familiar were often given new and unanticipated meaning through the discourses and practices of others. The idea that a person has grown up discretely 'inside' an 'ethnic community' or even in 'London' overlooks the fragmentation of the city and the way in which people's perceptions and identifications shift over a life course, to say nothing of the effects of class, politics, language, education, religion and nationality on the construction of insider and outsiderness.

The adoption of auto-ethnography as a methodological stance allows me to make sense of the entangled voices of self and others that produce ethnography. Because auto-ethnography has come to represent so many approaches, some of them very autobiographical, it is important to be clear on how auto-ethnography is used and understood in this book (see Heider 1975; Hayano 1979; Brandes 1982; Strathern 1987; Denzin 1989; Lejeune 1989; Deck 1990; Pratt 1992; Van Maanen 1995; Reed-Danahay 1997). Saying that I use auto-ethnography does not mean that the 'data' lies between my ears, but that I acknowledge that as a participant and an observer I am visible, interacting, affecting and being affected. I consider auto-ethnography to be a co-production, where participants make themselves and their personal experiences available to a researcher who is affected and affects the nature of the narratives and experiences shared with her/him, and attempts to represent these and orientate them to address theory.

The most progressive aspect of auto-ethnography is its attitude towards affect and emotion. My early attempts to hide my emotional investment and interest in this research were challenged primarily by participants themselves, who often turned the tables on me and asked searching and personal questions. Auto-ethnography, as a broad reflexive textual movement, encourages researchers to treat the feelings of participants as of equal importance and relevance to their own, and to include their own emotions and experiences in the overall ethnographic representation. 'Applying anthropological research to selves and others ... problematises the essentialising of both' (Aull-Davies 1999: 34), and the task of producing a truly reflexive ethnography that accounts for the dynamics of interaction, apply to all anthropologists, regardless of their presumed or assumed position.

I set out to find people aged between 18 and 40 living in London with an 'Arab' background. Initially I had considered focusing exclusively on those born in Britain. However, I found that many of the people I met had been born or partly raised in the Middle East or North Africa. In many families there were siblings born in Britain while others were born abroad. Although the idea of being British-born and notions of 'second generation' had been important to the way that I had thought about the research in its early stages, I quickly put this concern to one side. This does not suggest that country of birth should be entirely discounted in terms of its potential meanings to some. Indeed, for many people with little actual experience of the countries their parents had migrated from, being born in Baghdad, Damascus, Cairo or Kuwait represented a key connection to their Arabness. However, in terms of how people socialised within this age range I could find no guarantees in the sociological typology of 'first' and 'second' generations, or the idea that being born in Britain might make you more British or Arab than someone who was born abroad.

When I went looking for young Arabs at the beginning of my fieldwork I found them almost exclusively in social settings like restaurants, *Shisha* cafes, parties and gatherings in particular locales. '*Shisha* cafes' seemed to act as nodal points in the city's landscape, providing day-to-day spaces where people could socialise. Cafe sociability (which I discuss in chapter 3) gave an everyday dimension to my fieldwork interactions. *Shisha* cafes were settings where I could hear different dialects in interaction, where different customs, mores and sensibilities were played out, and where weekends and holidays were planned, job interviews and exams discussed, football matches and wars watched, and the monotony of daily routines eased by smoking *Shisha*, playing card games and exchanging gossip. I soon found myself moving from interviewing people or hanging out in cafes to joining in with different social activities. According to who I was with this could range from a university Arabic Society dinner or evenings out at restaurants, bars and nightclubs. These settings offered remarkably rich insights on the ways in which people expressed their ethnicity, class and gender (discussed in chapter 4). I also consider some of the ways in which young Arabs in London choose to represent themselves visually in ethnic self-portraits, the subject of chapter 5.

Even though I followed participants to the venues and settings that they socialised in, for many there was a disconnect between what happened in these places and the idea that it reflected 'Arabness' or indeed the material of social research. At the heart of this unease was the notion that I was researching 'Arab identity in London', which seems automatically to have the politics of multiculturalism as its vector, so that the task of 'representing' Arabs appropriately should only involve research on formal community structures and the political projects of integration or ethnogenesis. In contrast, I argue that what we should ask ourselves is 'How is Arabness done in London?' However unserious these settings may appear to some, my fieldwork was not determined by idealised notions of studying an 'ethnic community', a notion I was quite attached to at the outset, but by following the way that people embellish day-to-day settings, activities, objects and identifications with meanings which allude to their fantasies of a 'centre point' or 'identity' (Abu-Lughod 1991; Baudrillard 1996; Clifford 1997; Dürrschmidt 1997; Hastrup and Fog Olwig 1997).

Interviews were naturally an important part of my fieldwork; I found that repeat in-depth and largely unstructured interviews were the richest. I was often struck by the emotional potential that interviews and relationships with 'participants' could generate. Recollections of discrimination at school, difficult family relationships, or multiple dislocations and migrations were often deeply moving and emotional for the narrator and of course reminded me of my own reasons for undertaking the research. Listening to the narratives of growing up in London (chapter 2) and sharing in the lives of others over an extended period of time was a deeply personal privilege, generating fragments of meaning and relationships far beyond a strictly scientific framing of fieldwork.

Since the early 1990s a small body of British research on different 'Arab' migrant groups and 'Arab migrations' as a whole has emerged (see Searle and Shaif 1991; Karmi 1991, 1994, 1997, 2005; Halliday 1992; Al-Rasheed 1991, 1992, 1994, 1996; Lawless, 1995; Nagel 2001, 2002a, 2002b, 2005; Singer 2002; Al-Ali 2007; Nagel and Staeheli 2008a, 2008b).[6] While this literature is extremely valuable we are still left knowing very little about Arab migration to Britain or how and why London became popularly described as *Asimat al-Arab* (the capital city of the Arabs). I therefore turn to the archive in chapter 1. In total I collected over 800 newspaper and magazine articles relating to Arabs in London and Britain, some dating back to the turn of the twentieth century, which I interrelate with ethnographic interviews. Through this historical reconstruction, which makes no claim to be comprehensive or authoritative, I attempt to identify some of the critical junctures in the making of Arab London. My concern with the written record extends beyond knowable events and incidents to the power of discourse. Local and global discourses of 'the Arabs [in/and/of] London' produce a cultural object ('the Arabs') that carries with it meanings, insinuations and implications that continue to affect the way that Arabness is performed today. Together, interviews, field notes, images and artefacts allow me to present a critical account of the doing of Arabness in London. I make no claim to be able to represent a knowable social whole, instead the ethnography I present is one constructed through particular narratives and discourses, certain kinds of historical resources and not others, and only some of the cultural practices and voices of an extremely diverse group of people.

The politics of 'positions' and 'representation' extends beyond a reconciliation with the methodologies of my adopted discipline, it fundamentally draws me into wider philosophical concerns about how to approach notions of 'gender', 'race', 'class', 'ethnicity' and 'identity' which have become key, yet persistently inconclusive units of analysis for anthropology, sociology, cultural studies and literary theory. I attempt to: 'shift from foundationalist and epistemological account[s] of identity' to those which locate the problematic 'within practices of signification' and permit 'an analysis that takes the epistemological mode itself as one possible and contingent signifying practice' (Butler 1990: 184). Indeed the way in which I have repeatedly suspended the term 'Arab' between inverted commas leads to basic questions that cannot be overlooked.

What is meant by or who are the 'Arabs'? Is it people who are Arab or just the states from which they migrate? Is Arabness about language and religion, politics and history? If so, whose? Is it sufficient to rely on the amorphous notion of 'Arab culture', or even the comforting plural 'Arab cultures' to construct this group? Many of these questions will be left unanswered because the type of trans-historical identification which Arabness represents cannot be tamed or foreclosed – it is a moving target. My project is not to define or defend it as a phenomenon, what I seek is an understanding of how this identification becomes discernible in the quotidian in all its complexity.

Everyday Arabness

As a contemporary lived experience, Arabness has been decisively overshadowed by the metanarratives of formal pan-Arabism. One of the main trials of Arabness as a notion is that it remains captive to Baa'thism, Nasserism, nationalisms, inter-Arab enmity and the unresolved relationship between religious and secular modes of social organisation. Any account of a collective Arabness cannot help but be mired in the ideological and political history of *Arabism*[7] and the spectre of Arab civilisational malaise. Rather than Arabness being theorised from the ground up, from lived experience, a move that would make the manifest complexity of Arabness inescapable; the characteristics of Arabs and Arabness are often defined by the actions of states and ideologically driven cultural formalism. This has led to an intellectual impasse where we instinctively think of 'Arabism' and not 'Arabness'. The difference in form that I present here has no function other than to allow for conceptual space to think about the everyday doing of Arabness and to allow lived experience to re-contextualise our understanding of political, ideological and material conditions.

While the formal pan-Arab ideologies and movements of the twentieth century have declined and given way to parochial nationalisms and pan-Islamism; pan-Arabism remains a cultural leitmotif, albeit one that is often characterised by resigned cynicism. The struggle against the colonialist policies of the Israeli state and the suffering of Palestinians under occupation has taken on deep cultural significance and has become an enduring feature of Arab solidarity within the region and in the diaspora. Less is made of the suffering of Palestinians at the hands of their 'Arab brethren'. Arguably what has been lost in terms of ideologically driven political projects has been gained through an ever-expanding shared public sphere among Arabic speakers. Cultural production and popular culture have typically taken second place to ideological debates in the historiographies of pan-Arabism and Middle East studies. Cultural production by Arabic speakers has been radically transformed; it is no longer based on elite consumption of a formal literary tradition but on multiple media and mass consumption (Ulrich 2009). The music of Om Kalthum, Fayruz and Sheikh Imam, the poetry of Shawqi, Qabbani and Darwish, the publishing houses of Beirut, the broadcasting and film studios of Dubai, Doha and Cairo, the Arab blogosphere, Arabic pop music, dubbed Turkish soap operas and franchised TV talent shows have arguably done more to create connectedness among Arabic speakers in different nations and locations than the Arab League, the Ba'ath Party or even the writings of

Sati al-Husri. The notion of an everyday Arabness affords legitimacy to those who experience it in their daily lives to see it as a poësis, a text which they not only recite but, importantly, one which they continuously write (de Certeau 1988).

Unprecedented migratory flows from the 1970s onwards have bought Arabic speakers from different nation-states together, both within the Middle East and beyond. These have added phenomenological layers to the idea of 'the Arabs', and throw into relief both the continuities and discontinuities of 'shared' Arabness. It is in a place like London that your grocer might be Lebanese, your butcher Algerian, your Arabic teacher Iraqi and your neighbour Egyptian; where capital flows from the Arabian Gulf can provide a British-born Palestinian the opportunity to work on the Middle East desk of a global financial management company in the City. As Miller would argue 'In a London Street' Morocco, Iraq, Syria and Sudan 'are no longer thousands of miles apart, but just a few doors away' (2009: 289). These urban centres become cultural sites where dialects, traditions, religion, politics, food and music are counter-exposed, not only in an introverted Arab–Arab fashion but within the context of local and global cultural, economic and political flows (see Fog Olwig 1997; Gardner and Mand 2012). 'Identity and culture … increasing look … vestigial rather than determinant of the order of things' (Miller 2009: 289).

Migration and transnationalism are changing the very idea of what or who the Arabs are and it would be wrong to assume that changes in Arab cultural production and public spheres affect what it means to be an Arab in the diaspora in predictable or authenticating ways. Speaking, reading and writing classical or even modern standard Arabic is no longer a prerequisite for seeing oneself as an Arab. Many British-born or -raised Arabs only have a cursory understanding of Arabic beyond the vernacular they have acquired in their home environments or through television and summer holidays. A young British-born Algerian or Moroccan may find the Arabic of Iraqi or Egyptian friends incomprehensible. Indeed, most of the interviews that I undertook were conducted in English even though they were ostensibly about Arabness. The erosion of linguistic commonality in the diaspora has been countered by the racialisation of Arabness and Islam in North America and Europe. These have become minority political 'identities' that sit in a hierarchy of racial, ethnic, cultural and religious 'identities', which all purport to represent an essence and sustain the fantasies of primordial bond or incommensurable difference. Indeed, in a global metropolis like London, Arabness can be as simple as not fitting into the 'White', 'Black' or 'Asian' categories by which populations are managed and made intelligible.

Assuming the existence of an Arab diaspora as a form of consciousness would be as misleading as assuming a matter-of-fact 'Arab' world or culture. 'The idea of diaspora tends to homogenise the population referred to at the transnational level' (Anthias 1998: 564). On what basis are migrants from over 20 countries grouped together under one ethnic category? How can one speak of 'Arab migration' to Britain when migration and settlement patterns suggest different national and subnational groups with specific political and economic causes for migration, which take place at different historical times, for people with different levels of education and different relationships to the Arabic language and 'pan-Arab' politics?

Nineteenth-century colonial capitalism led to labour migrations from Yemen and Somalia to Britain, twentieth-century postcolonial capitalism led to labour migration from Egypt and Morocco, while civil war, state failure and British and American neo-colonial wars in the late twentieth and early twenty-first centuries have led to unprecedented levels of forced migration from the region to Britain and elsewhere. What connects low-skilled labour migrants to the students and professionals from Iraq and Egypt who came to Britain to qualify as medical professionals and engineers in the post-war period? Do the thousands of Iraqis, Somalis and Algerians who fled from war, totalitarianism and sanctions, share a common experience with each other or with the sojourners and students of the Gulf region, whose material investment in London is so much part of the notion of Arab wealth in London? Did these disparate groups have any sense of a common 'identity' as 'Arabs' at the time or today? What of the gendered, generational, sectarian and class differences that cut across these groups and their corresponding notions of self, collectivity, nationalism, tribalism, sectarianism and history? If migrants from the Arab world identify with each other on the basis of language, politics or dispossession, on what basis do their British-born or -raised children identify with each other? Do Arabic-speaking migrants in London have anything in common or any connections with their counterparts in Paris, Marseille, Detroit, Bogota, Lagos or Sydney? Sabry (2005) draws our attention to the way that emigration has become part of Arab popular culture as generations of Arabs dream of, apply for and sometimes die for a better future outside the region; yet it remains the case that Arabs in the diaspora are often described (or describe themselves) as living *fil'ghurba* 'in estrangement'. No positive connotations have been affixed to *al-Shattaat* (Dispersion or Diaspora) as a way of being or a condition; it is only very recently that phrases like *Arab al-mahjar* (migrant Arabs) have started to be used in neutral or positive ways.

The questions that I pose do not seek to negate bonds between Arabs, they simply seek to substantiate those bonds, which are often taken for granted, or are clichéd and almost always based on the past and not the present. The search for coherence is bound to disappoint – 'diaspora is constituted as much in difference and division as it is in commonality and solidarity' (Anthias 1998: 569). In the rush to assert the existence of an 'Arab community' and to make the case for its political incorporation into multiculturalism, the extent to which we can speak of an 'Arab community' or 'Arab communities', and the discourses and practices involved in *doing* Arabness and what they might tell us about prevailing epistemologies, have been left almost entirely without interrogation.

Gilroy favours the notion of 'connectedness', which he believes can account for mutability and differences in a way that accounts centred on a 'nation-state/diasporic' binary or 'brute pan-Africanism' are unable to do (1993: 29–31). Connectedness offers the same promise for the way Arabness is understood. Arabness is often synonymous with Arabism, which is all too often polarised as either formal pan-Arabism or the total rejection of the notion of 'the Arabs'. I therefore take the perspective that Arabness is about connectedness and not about a political project or the ultimate sameness of 'Arab people'. Instead of presenting a unifying notion of categorical cultures like 'Black' or 'Arab', different places and contexts should be seen as constantly leading to a reiteration of Arabness in a web of interactions between the local and the global, a process which takes place as much in the diaspora as it does in the 'Arab world'. Axel suggests that 'rather than conceiving of the homeland as something itself that creates the diaspora, it may be more productive to consider the diaspora as something that creates the homeland' (2002b: 426).

A diaspora is 'diacritically shaped by means of political struggles with state normativities and indigenous majorities; and upon the tension between local assimilation and trans-local allegiances' (Clifford 1994: 307–08). But equally, for young Arabs in the diaspora alienation is not simply about the struggles for rights in the countries of their birth, it is to a large extent about acceptance of their versions of Arabness. I attempt to understand the way in which this connectedness is manifest in the day-to-day context of London, by looking at its imperfect recitation between structures of subjection which create injunctions that produce that which they name: 'Arab woman', 'Arab man', 'British Arab'.

Tresspassing: The Reach of Performativity

I take Judith Butler's scheme of gender performativity as a starting point from which a broader set of normative structures of subjection like race and class can be sequentially analysed. What does Butler mean by asserting that gender is performative? What relevance does gender performativity have for 'race'? And what does race have to do with Arabness in London? While these are questions that will be addressed at length with reference to ethnographic insight throughout this book, a basic overview is in order at this point. In what follows I seek to lay out the basic terms of Butler's notion of gender performativity, look at some of the main concerns raised about its use and suggest that performativity can be extended to processes of racialisation.

Simone de Beauvoir's proposition that one is not born but becomes a woman raises many questions for Judith Butler. If one is not born but becomes a woman, what is involved in becoming a woman? 'Who is the "one" that becomes and when do the discursive mechanisms of becoming arrive on the cultural scene transforming the human subject into a gendered subject?' (Butler 1990: 111). Butler argues that:

> gender is not to culture as sex is to nature; gender is also the discursive and cultural means by which 'sexed nature' or 'a natural sex' is produced and established as 'pre-discursive,' prior to culture, a politically neutral surface on which culture acts. (1990: 12)

By radically deconstructing 'sex' and 'gender', Butler shows 'gender' to be a cultural fiction, not an internal way of being that manifests itself externally as an 'identity' (see Lloyd 1999; Salih 2002; Salih and Butler 2004). Butler's approach is not concerned with denying the biological differences between male and female reproductive organs, hormones and chromosomes, rather she is interested in interrogating gendering discourses and the normative system of values and institutions that give particular cultural meanings and social consequences to those biological differences. Thus gender is the effect of:

> Acts, gestures and desire [which] produce the effect of an internal core or substance, that produce *on the surface* of the body, through the play of signifying absences that suggest, but never reveal, the organising principle of identity as a cause. Such acts, gestures, enactments generally constructed are *performative* in the sense that the essence of identity that

they otherwise purport to express are *fabrications* manufactured and sustained through corporeal signs and other discursive means. That the gendered body is performative suggests that it has no ontological status apart from the various acts that constitute its reality. This also suggests that if the reality is fabricated as an interior essence, that very interior is an effect and function of a decidedly public and social discourse ... an illusion discursively maintained for the purposes of the regulation of sexuality within the obligatory frame of reproductive heterosexuality. (1990: 173)

'A "performative act" is one that brings into being or enacts that which it names' (Butler 1993: 134), reflecting a specific modality of the reiterative power of discourse to produce the phenomenon that it regulates and constrains' (1990: 2–3). In *Bodies that Matter* (1993), Butler turns to the pre-natal ultrasound scene in a hospital where a doctor or nurse announces 'It's a girl.' This speech act permanently transforms the foetus and has consequences way beyond physiological categorisations. Almost immediately a set of names, colours, dispositions and charac- teristics are bought to bear upon this yet-to-be-born human, an instant where discourse tangibly precedes and defines subjectivity prior to birth. 'Femininity is thus not the product of a choice, but the forcible citation of a norm, one whose complex historicity is indissociable from relations of discipline, regulation, punishment' (1993: 232).

Fundamental to an understanding of performativity is the notion of the 'speech act' developed by John Austin (1962), who suggests that language is not neutral but that autonomous agent authors deploy performative utterances with which 'things are done'. Austin attempted to categorise speech into two types, constantive utterances which were pure or unambiguous and can be substantiated as either true or false (e.g. today is Monday), and performative utterances that are neither true nor false but create an effect or social action (e.g. The words used in sentencing a defendant, in marriage ceremonies, proclamations of war or declarations of independence). Austin believed that 'ordinary speech' was a form of pure or unambiguous communication that either succeeded or failed in its communicative task. In contrast to 'ordinary speech' he created a category of speech, which he called 'parasitic' or 'unserious' speech acts; these were parasitic to the ordinary use of language in day-to-day contexts. Thus, for Austin (1962), language when used in a poem or play involved a necessary ambiguity and therefore complications for what he considered to be the point of language – felicitous communication. Austin's work transformed our understanding of how we use language and spawned scholarship way beyond linguistics. Jacques Derrida (1982) took issue with Austin's notion that the non-serious is external to pure communication, instead arguing that what Austin describes as 'parasitic speech acts' were in fact the internal and positive condition of possibility for language itself. The communicative formalism in Austin's approach is not a million miles away from the views expressed by quite a few people during my fieldwork, that the sites I had chosen for participant observation were 'unserious' perhaps even 'parasitic' to the formal substance of Arabism.

For Derrida, Austin would never be able to subject language to taxonomical exactitude because of the essentially theatrical nature of linguistic action. As Bearn puts it:

> one can understand Austin's motivation, for once the theatricality of linguistic action is admitted, we may not be able to hide our eyes from the theatricality of action period … If iterability troubles the authenticity of signatures, it may also trouble the very idea of authentic action. Thus the most troubling consequence of iterability may be that nothing is simply authentic. Everything is also theatrical: every utterance, a performance, every action, acting. (1995a: 23)

By unravelling Austin's model of language, Derrida draws attention to the 'double writing' inherent in communication, removing the distinction between pure and performative illocutionary acts.

A brief comparison between Derrida and Bakhtin (often overlooked) may help illustrate these different approaches. Bakhtin's notion of 'heteroglossia' argues that every time we use language we are using the voices of others.

> The word in language is always half someone else's. It becomes one's own only when the speaker populates it with their own intentions. Prior to this moment of appropriation the word does not exist in a neutral and impersonal language (i.e. not in a dictionary) but rather it exits in other people's mouths, concrete contexts, serving other people's intentions. It is from there that one must take the word and make it one's own. (Bakhtin 1981: 293)

Bakhtin believed that language originated in social interaction and struggle and that these are always implicated in its use and meaning. In other words, 'our use of language is a struggle to create our own voices' (Maybin 2001: 64).

Derrida and Bakhtin's approaches are similar but diverge on the point of intentionality and authorial agency. While Derrida would probably agree with Bakhtin's depiction of language as always being drawn from past utterances and contexts and that 'phemes' are (re)cited in new and unanticipated ways, it appears that their agreement might end there. Derrida's understanding of intentionality, what Bakhtin would describe as 'making the word one's own', is that it is always within the frame of the iterability of a sign 'which cannot be contained or enclosed by any context, convention or authorial intention' and, furthermore, that these signs are 'cited, grafted and reiterated in ways that do not conform to their speakers' or writers' original intentions' suggesting that every sign carries the possibility of a communicative failure (Derrida 1982: 93–103).

Thus Bakhtin's 'moment of appropriation' comes with no guarantees because it is always subject to failure. In other words linguistic action, authorship and reception are uncontrollable. For Derrida the use of a word or sign inevitably operationalises all the possible meanings, uses and inter-pretations of that word or utterance. Iterability stands for the impossibility of 'rigorous purity', our mastery of language, our broaching of it, and simultaneously its breaching, that which makes its repetition imperfect, incomplete, unsuccessful and 'communicative failure' is central to the structure of language, blurring what it means to successfully communicate.

Butler adopts a Derridean reading of speech acts so that the reiteration (or repeatability) of (gendered) norms has an inevitable dualism. While reiteration is designed to reinforce and reproduce forms of authority, the imperfection inherent in repetition also makes it inevitable that the same norms will be re-articulated and transgressed. Thus even though the injunction to be a given gender is fundamentally based on a set of regulatory norms, the 're-iterability' of those norms necessarily involves 'failures', a variety of incoherent configurations that in their multiplicity exceed and defy the injunction by which they are generated.

Some of the interpretations of *Gender Trouble* (Butler 1990) have resulted in the reading that 'if gender is performative it must be radically free' (Butler et al. 1994: 32). However, Butler argues that although agency is located in the compulsion to repeat, the repetition of signification is a regulated process. Gendered recitations take place within the context of heteronormative hegemony which does not simply hold up certain ideals of gender and sexuality as normal, but also confronts subjects with risks and consequences in transgressing those norms and boundaries, some

of them social and psychological and others physical. If heteronormativity were natural, as many believe it is, why then does it require such
stringent policing? Far from being the un-natural opposite of heterosexuality, homosexuality is deeply embedded in heterosexuality's core; it is a
condition of its possibility. For Butler, regimes of normative gender and
sex are the result of a compulsion to mime particular notions of gendered
personhood; a melancholic project of cultural survival and social intelligibility that involves a complex set of culturally instituted identifications
and desires.

Responding to criticisms in *Feminist Contentions* (Benhabib et al. 1995),
Butler clarifies her position on agency and power and goes on to further
elaborate her position in *Excitable Speech* (1997b) and *The Psychic Life of
Power* (1997a), where she turns to Foucault's concept of *Assujetissement* and
Subjectivation, or 'Subjugation' and 'Subjectification', that seek to describe
the process of always being subjugated by power in the process of
becoming a subject. By choosing to opt for neither humanist autonomy
nor structural determinism, Butler places the subject between the two,
where the impossibility of perfect repetitions of heteronormativity
provides the opportunity for agency which, in itself, is neither a personal
attribute nor a formal object but 'only ever a political choice' (Butler 1993,
1997a, 1997b). Butler rejects the strong heterosexualising imperatives
that produce over-deterministic understandings of gendered structures.
So while she supports the idea that 'every speaking being is born into a
symbolic order that is always-already-there ... the status of that always-
already-thereness' should not be seen as static or foreclosed (Butler et al.
1994: 35).

Butler's discursive emphasis has drawn criticisms from anthropologists
like Cecilia Busby, who argues that while Butler's theory has potentially
interesting sociological implications, it is primarily framed through the
philosophy of language and is not focused on acts and gestures but the
discursive frame within which they are realised. For Busby, the notion of
gender performativity seems to lack relevance for the 'fixed sexed body'
among the Marianad in India. Busby points out that Butler's work pays little
attention to actual material practices or the materiality of bodies, which
are simply seen as an effect of power manifested through language rather
than practices (2000: 11–19). It is true that Butler is not an ethnographer,
but the very purpose of her work is to expose forms of discursive and
corporeal power, the stylised acts and gestures that produce the 'fixed
sexed bodies' that Busby sees in Marianad society. Busby's criticism is
at least in part reflective of a broader scepticism towards the discursive,

textual turn in social theory and anthropology. This reaction can be seen as early as 1993 in Geertz who writes that

> 'text,' is a dangerously unfocused term, and its application to social action, to people's behaviour towards other people, involves a thoroughgoing conceptual wrench ... the suggestion that the activities of spies, lovers, witch doctors, kings or mental patients are moves and performances is surely a good deal more plausible than the notion that they are sentences. (1993: 30)

These readings of the discursive and post-structuralist turns in social theory reduce the possibilities of this body of scholarship to the immaterial, so that 'discourse' (narrowly defined) is stripped of the implications and relationships to bodily techniques and material practices. Nevertheless, Busby's point is decidedly valid in the sense that if anthropologists are to deploy concepts like 'performativity', they must be ethnographically grounded and substantiated. To my mind performativity is very much at home in anthropology. I suggest here that by re-reading *Sex and Temperament in Three Primitive Societies* (1963) by Margaret Mead we may find one of the earliest ethnographically grounded expressions of the performativity of gender.

Re-Reading 'Sex and Temperament'

The unfortunate title of Mead's monograph (originally published in 1935) is more of a reflection on the lexical and disciplinary conventions of the time than the ethnographic representation itself. In *Sex and Temperament* (1963) Mead suggests that the Arapesh, Mundugumor and Tchambuli tribes of north-west Papua (New Guinea) have a fluid and variable set of beliefs and practices in relation to biological sex and its relationship to (gendered) temperament. After providing ethnographic accounts of each tribe's practices and beliefs around sex and temperament, Mead concludes that two of the tribes had no conception that men and women possessed innate gendered temperaments that were either oppositional or complementary. The temperaments, roles and expectations of men and women varied greatly between the three tribes, who also seemed to accept that there was no single or natural way of being a man or a woman in that they saw nothing untoward in the different gender practices of their neighbours.

Mead argues that these tribes show a suppleness and variability in their ideas and practices about sex and temperament, a situation which contrasts sharply with what she acknowledges to be (particularly in her later work *Male and Female* [1949]) a reified American culture that idealises and standardises men (as dominant, brave, aggressive and independent) and women (as vulnerable, passive, emotional and closer to nature). One of Mead's greatest concerns throughout the book is how in her society 'any deviation from the socially determined role [is seen] as abnormality of native endowment or early maturation' (1963: 22).

The language that Mead uses in her analysis is significant; in the quotes from *Sex and Temperament* that follow I have italicised those aspects of her account that bring her close to a performative reading of gender. Mead described her study as one that showed how the three societies had '*dramatized* sex differences' (1963: 17) and how, in each society, 'each sex, as a sex, [is] *forced to conform* to the role assigned to it' (1963: 14). Mead attributes fixed and forced conformity in *Sex and Temperaments* to:

> the existence in a given society of a dichotomy of social personality, of a sex-determined, sex-limited personality, [that] *penalizes in greater or less degree every individual born within it*. Those whose temperaments are indubitably aberrant *fail* to adjust to the accepted standards, and by their very presence, *by the anomalousness of their responses*, confuse those whose temperaments are the expected ones for their sex. *So in practically every mind a seed of doubt, of anxiety* is planted, which interferes with the normal course of life. (1963: 306).

In a strikingly proximate allusion to 'imperfect repetition', which Butler borrows from Derrida, Mead argues that those whose dispositions are seen as alien or deviant are never able to 'wear *perfectly* the garment of personality that his society has fashioned for him' (1963: 289). Mead dedicates considerable effort to explaining what she describes as the 'deviant', a category that we might describe within a Butlerian understanding of performativity as 'transgression' or those whose imperfect recitations of gendered norms make them socially 'unintelligible'. Mead's 'cultural deviant' (1963: 290) is:

> any individual who because of innate disposition or accident of early training, or through the contradictory influences of a heterogeneous cultural situation, has been *culturally disenfranchised*, the individual to

whom the major emphases of his society seems nonsensical, unreal, untenable, or downright wrong. (1963: 290)

Both Mead and Butler also present transvestism and drag (respectively) as sites where the normative structures of gender and heterosexuality are exposed. Butler's observations of drag were designed to expose the parody of genders and sexuality under heteronormativity; in a similar vein, Mead was interested in what transvestism revealed about processes and cultural institutions that produce the gendered subject and how those related to ideas about what we would call today 'gender identity' and 'sexuality'. Butler's writing on drag has often been read as casting drag as a radically transgressive state. Like Butler, Mead disagrees with this interpretation, arguing that 'without any contrast between the sexes and without any tradition of transvestisms, a variation in temperamental preference does not result in either homosexuality or transvestism' (1963: 294). For Mead, transvestism:

> is unevenly distributed over the world, it … is not only a variation that occurs when there are different personalities decreed for men and women, but … it need not occur even there. It is in fact a social invention that has become stabilized among the American Indians and in Siberia, but not in Oceania. (1963: 294)

For Mead and Butler the processes and injunctions that produce gendered subjects begin early in childhood. While Butler looks at the process of 'girling' in *Bodies that Matter* (1993), Mead suggests that 'The *coercion to behave like a member of one's own sex* becomes one of the strongest implements with which the society attempts to mould the growing child to accepted forms' (1963: 295–96). Mead sees a concerted cultural project behind the production of the gendered subject, with both corporeal and psychological consequences for those who are unable to recite perfectly. 'The burden of the disciplinary song is: "You will not be a real human being unless you suppress these tendencies which are incompatible with our definition of humanity"' (1963: 296).

> And so in a thousand ways, the fact that it is necessary to feel not only like a member of one's society in a given period, but like a member of one's sex and not like a member of the other, conditions the development of the child, and *produces individuals who are unplaced in their society*. Many students of personality lay these multiple, imponderable

maladjustments to 'latent homosexuality.' But such a judgment is fathered by our two-sex standard; *it is a post hoc diagnosis of a result, not a diagnosis of a cause.* It is a judgment that is applied not only to the invert but to the infinitely more numerous individuals who deviate from the social definition of appropriate behaviour for their sex. (1963: 304–05)

Mead goes further, and comes closer to the sequential reading I seek in this ethnography, suggesting that what she has learned about the production of gendered subjects is equally revealing of the way in which social intelligibility and subjectification involves being 'raced' and 'classed'.

> The arbitrary assignment of set clothing, set manners, set social responses, to individuals born in a certain class, of a certain sex or of a certain colour, to those born on a certain day of the week, to those born with a certain complexion, does violence to the individual endowment, but permits the building of a rich culture (1963: 317)

As she notes early on in *Sex and Temperament*, Mead was not concerned 'with whether there are or are not actual universal differences between sexes, either quantitative or qualitative' or with the variability between and within sexes, or with espousing a treatise 'on the rights of women nor an inquiry into the basis of feminism' (1963: 15). But this disclaimer does not stop her from concluding that social hierarchy and power are sustained on the basis of the ontological status of sex, class and race difference so that 'to break down one line of division, that between the sexes and substitute another, that between the classes, is no real advance' (1963: 321).

Margaret Mead's monograph, published 55 years before *Gender Trouble*, seems tantalisingly close to the ideas that structure Butler's exposition of gender performativity and even pre-empts the proximity of these processes and forces to those of race and class. While Mead's account lacks a coherent philosophical framework of the kind that Butler offers, Butler's work is equally free from any ethnographic or ethnomethodological grounding.

Like Butler, Mead does not seem to transfigure the gendered subject within a voluntary or humanistic frame. For Mead the reproduction of defined sex-gender norms is framed by 'anxiety', for Butler it is framed by 'melancholia'. Gendering processes are forceful, their transgression creates consequences and thus they demand conformity and cast everyone as potential anomaly, but none more so than those who deviate. Gender is 'un-natural', 'unreal' and 'untenable' for Mead; it is produced through cultural, bodily and psychological disciplining, coercion and violence. In both Mead and Butler, what are widely assumed to be 'gendered identities' or 'personalities' have no ontological status beyond the discourses and practices that produce them (although Mead does not use these terms).

Reactions to *Sex and Temperament* show clearly that the undermining of the naturalness of gender identity was considered profane. Some of Mead's contemporaries rejected the philosophical and political consequences of her account, others dismissed her fieldwork as unscientific and others still claimed that Mead's own bisexuality was the main motivation for her analysis. Although she had written assertive responses to some of the criticism, in the opening paragraph to the preface of the 1950 edition of *Sex and Temperament* Mead seems to have felt the need to step back from the radical potential of her ideas when she wrote 'This is my most misunderstood book … I have been accused of having believed when I wrote *Sex and Temperament* that there are no sex differences.'

Getting Stuck Between 'Performance' and 'Performativity'

I would argue that Margaret Mead's account, while not benefitting from sufficient theorisation, brings her closer to Butlerian performativity than it does to the anthropological literature on performance that stems from the work of Victor and Edith Turner or the sociological literature on performance which follows from Erving Goffman. The Turners' work on cultural performance was centred on the notion that social drama and cultural performances had a remedial and regenerative role, most pronounced during episodes of cultural crises. Victor Turner sought to distinguish his interest in symbolic and sacred ritual performance from the everyday contexts of performance that Goffman and Schechner were interested in (Turner 1986: 5–7). But by the time Geertz comes to comment upon the Turners' work in 1993, Turnerian social dramas are understood to occur on all levels of 'social organisation from the state to the family' (Geertz 1993: 28; see also Schechner 2005; St John 2008; Korom 2013).

An 'anthropology of performance' movement gathered pace after Victor Turner's death in 1983. Conquergood's (1989) account of the 'new anthropology of performance movement' reflects the enthusiasm and energy in an emerging field of research which appeared to offer a radically new approach to culture that not only re-articulated the time-honoured theatre analogy in social science, but also seemed to go against the established structuralist and functionalist traditions in social-anthropology. Conquergood articulates the conceptual terrain of the new movement in a way that helps us to understand the different approaches to culture, structure and agency in 'performance' and 'performativity' scholarship. He suggests that the 'anthropology of performance movement' can be understood through four key terms: *poetics, play, process* and *power.*

'Poetics' stands for the movement's concern with the 'fabricated, invented, imagined, constructed nature of human realities. Cultures and selves are not given, they are made; even, like fictions, they are "made-up"' (1989: 83). The fabricated and constructed nature of rituals, festivals, spectacles, dramas and narrative 'remind us that cultures and persons are not just created; they are creative. They hold out the promise of reimagining and refashioning the world' (1989: 83). 'Play', he continues, is related to 'improvisation, innovation, experimentation, irony, parody, clowning and carnival.' The 'appreciation of play has helped ethnographers of performance understand the unmasking and unmaking tendencies that keep cultures open and in a continuous state of productive tension' (1989: 83). The notion of culture as 'Process' in performance literature represents a shift – from cultural reproduction as mimesis to cultural reproduction as kinesis, or, put another way, a shift from seeing *social structure* to seeing *social dynamics.* To account for 'Power', Conquergood suggests that the emerging subfield ask questions like: 'how are performances situated between forces of accommodation and resistance? How do they simultaneously reproduce and struggle against hegemony? What are the performative resources for interrupting master scripts?' (1989: 84).

Through the analysis of spectacular events, ritual, public culture and different forms of media, the anthropology of performance tends to celebrate culture as a dynamic and adaptive phenomenon and seeks out moments of anti-structure and ambiguity. However, as Morris (1995: 586) and Kolankiewicz (2008: 18) note, critiques of the new performance theory and social drama soon emerged from within anthropology. Max Gluckman, Turner's mentor, was vociferous about the secondary importance of ritual studies, which should always come second to the neo-Marxist readings of social organisation (Turner 1969: 7). Geertz also criticised social drama for being applied too liberally so that 'vividly disparate matters look drably homogeneous' (1993: 28). Critiques of the performance approach also arose from within the emerging field of performance studies, most forcefully in the criticisms of feminist readings of performance (see Phelan 1988, 1993; Diamond 1989; Reinelt 1989; Schmitt 1990).

There are instances of conflation, dissonance and convergence in the way that 'performance' and 'performativity' are used and understood. Put in the most basic terms, while always being interested in social institutions and organisation, 'cultural performance' tends to suggest the existence of active subject agents and often alludes to a pre-discursive self. In contrast, performativity transfigures the subject as being constituted by being hailed (in an Althusserian sense) and then confronted with the injunction to recite hegemonic norms, creating a 'subject effect' (not a subject), a notion that can be traced to Foucault.

'Performance' is associated with both Goffman and Turner and is informed by terms like: 'frame', 'game', 'stake', 'masking' and 'unmasking', 'drama', 'play', 'irony', 'anti-structure', 'symbols', 'liminality' and '*communitas*', all of which play prominent conceptual and aesthetic roles. The focus of Turnerian cultural performance is, on the whole, the symbolic and ritualised aspects of public culture like rituals, rites of passage, festivals, spectacle and other special events, while in *The Presentation of the Self in Everyday Life* (1959) Goffman's performances theory is firmly rooted in face-to-face interactions.

In contrast, Butler's performativity focuses on those aspects of culture that produce the gendered subject through a heteronormative matrix that acts to police and prescribe social intelligibility. The tone of her articulation of performativity is very different, it involves: 'injunctions', 'subjection', 'forced identifications', 'melancholia', 'failure' and a 'struggle for cultural survival' and 'social intelligibility'. My understanding of Mead (1963) suggests that in both Mead and Butler we can read a Nietzschean battle between Apollonian culture and Dionysian individuality. As demonstrated earlier, for Mead, the cultural structures that produce fixed relationships between sex and temperament do 'violence to the individual endowment', but permit 'the building of a rich culture' (1963: 317).

To some extent these different positions and evaluations of cultural structures, their processes and their consequences reflect the lives and gendered perspectives of the scholars themselves. For example, Turner's work on rites of passage is overwhelmingly based on male rites and, as Bowie (2005) outlines, has been criticised by Lincoln, who argues that Turner does not account for the way that women experience rites of passage. 'At those points where the collective interests of women as women diverge from those of "society as a whole" these rituals not only serve the latter interest, but make it very difficult for women to struggle against them' (Lincoln 1991: 117). Maurice Bloch (1992) has also been critical of the way that Turner's work on rites of passage underplays the role of 'violence', 'rebounding violence' and 'conquest' in rites of passage and ritual which, he believes, act to maintain status hierarchies in society. It is no coincidence that the more critical perspective and positions on cultural structures and their consequences come from Mead and Butler, not least because of their own personal struggles with them.

Fundamentally these debates are not simply about terms like 'performance' and 'performativity', they are about structure and agency. The bone of contention for many anthropologists and sociologists considering Butler's work is the belief that Butler's performativity is anti-humanist and dismisses a subject actor behind the doing of gender. In a 1998 interview Butler explicitly distances her version of performativity from what she considered to be the theatrical donning and doffing of roles that she understood Goffmanesque performance to represent. This in turn has spurred Smith (2010) to assert the structuralist credentials of Goffman's theory, while Brickell (2003, 2005) has tried to interrelate Goffman and Butler in order to produce ethnomethodologically grounded readings of performativity. Personally, I do not read the same kind of 'subject agent' crisis in Butler's work. Butler's argument is clear enough, following Foucault, 'Subjectification' (Fr. *Subjectivation*) is the site of agency and resistance, and her rejection of the 'subject' is explicitly in relation to the pre-discursive gendered subject. The theoretical formulation that scholars offer reflects a particular trail of thought at a certain time in their intellectual journey. Butler has engaged in consistent response, clarification and modification of her ideas, indeed, ten years after the publication of *Gender Trouble* she acknowledged that 'performance' and 'performativity' will always be related in some way (1999d: xxvi).

It is common to read the terms 'performance' and 'performativity' together; sometimes they seem to stand for the same thing, at other times they are presented as diametrically opposed, but their meaning can only really be understood by recognising whether they are being deployed in a constructivist sense on the one hand or a neo-structuralist sense on the other. Other important indicators that can help navigate the various ways in which these terms are used are whether 'performance' and/ or 'performativity' are being used to describe the aesthetics of cultural performance (rites, ritual, theatrical and other forms of spectacle) or whether they are being used to understand speech acts and hegemonic discourses that produce gendered, raced, sexed and classed subjects.

Beyond theoretical puritanism, it has been the proximate yet antagonistic connections between these formulations that have been the most anthropologically productive. There is a considerable literature that tries to link the broader discursive production of sex, to the rites of passage and rituals that physically inscribe sex and gender (see Morris 1995: 577–79). Butler's performative scheme has also been influential in the anthropological study of sexuality and queer theory (see Weston 1993; Morris 1995; Boelstroff 2007; see also Lewin and Leap 2002; Donnan and Magowan 2010; Lyons and Lyons 2011). The entry of performativity in both a constructivist Turnerian sense and a neo-structuralist discursive sense has corresponded with a broader incorporation of postmodernism and revisions to the anthropological project itself, with fieldwork, participant observation and ethnography having to account for their own 'performative features' in what has been described by some as post-human anthropology (see Turner and Turner 1986; Morris 2007; Whitehead 2009).

More recent anthropological engagement with the notion of performativity has seen the emergence of performative readings of nationalism, citizenship and minority status. Schein (1999, 2000), for example, applies a combination of performance and performativity to analyse modernity and the links between gendering and minority politics in China. Feldman (2005) offers a performative reading of the processes through which the Estonian state is constituted through acts that both construct and regulate the boundary between the nation and the immigrant minorities. Hermann (2005) interrelates emotions, collective memory and the performative aspects of (theatrically) staged historical representation among the Banabans of Fiji. Others have tried to account for some of theoretical structures identified as structuring gender performativity, like Geller (2009), who has tried to reveal heteronormativity as a trans-historical process with traces in antiquity, while Eves (2010) builds on the long-standing anthropological literature on embodiment to interrelate Maus and Butler in order to understand the bodily movements, comportments and dispositions of Lelet women in Papua New Guinea.

In this ethnography I am engaged in a similar task of conceptual and disciplinary borrowing, bending and indeterminacy around the notions of performance and performativity. More explicitly, I hope to offer a sequential reading of performative gender and race (and to a lesser extent their intersection with class) among British-born or -raised young people who see themselves or are seen by others as *being* 'Arab'. I argue that the structures of Butler's performative gender are a sound basis on which to interrogate 'race' in Britain. I believe that the ethnographic material I have collected suggests that, to a considerable extent, one is forced to recite 'race' and identify oneself as a 'raced subject' in Britain. In other words, that one can only be socially intelligible in Britain by being the *subject of* and *subject to* race thinking.

Performative Race: The Injunctions 'To Be' Ethnic in Britain

There is a clear genealogical line from the purported displacement of biological racism to the notion of cultural incommensurability and finally 'identity', which remains a potent and permeating mode of social organisation and the subject of everything from moral panic to commodification. The slippage from 'race' to 'ethnicity' which Goldberg (1993) describes as 'ethno-race' has seen 'a focus on 'race' and racism superseded by a resurgent interest in 'ethnicity' and 'culture' as the locus for identity politics or, increasingly, simply 'identity' (Alexander 2002: 556). 'Ethnicity', 'culture' and 'identity' are the successors of 'race' within the context of British ethnic governmentality.

The discourses and practices around the notion of the 'ethnic community' are central in this system where 'communities' must parade their differences and showcase their foods, smells, clothes, traditions, colours and thus their distinctiveness in order to be recognised and incorporated into the consciousness of the nation. The idea of having or possessing an ethnicity, of being part of a group, is so embedded and naturalised that we see ethnicity and ethnic groups everywhere, effectively producing injunctions to identify ethnically. The injunction to be a given race and *to do* an ethno-racial identity is rooted in the need to be intelligible within this economic, discursive, semiotic and institutional system of meaning.

I would argue that British *multiculturalism* is but the institutional manifestation of a far more deep-seated set of discourses and practices that we might describe as 'ethnonormativity'. It is perhaps the misreading of multiculturalism as a benign anti-racist project that backfired in the face of the moral forces that advocated it, that has led to a sense of betrayal or anti-climax in Britain (see Kundnani 2007; also see Skellington and Morris 1996; Keith 2004; Sivanandan 2008; Dean 2009 [1999]). The coming and going of multiculturalism seems inconsequential because another set of policy terms will emerge to repackage and obscure Britain's unresolved postcolonial condition (see Hesse 2000; Gilroy 2006).

Concerns regarding race have been incorporated within the discourse of liberal population management, where they now play a critical role in the discourse of societal health, happiness and economic prosperity. The intersections of neoliberal governmentality and ethnonormativity mean that to be ethnic and accepted one must also be economically productive – for there seems nothing more abhorrent to this postcolonial malaise than those with different religions, tongues and degrees of melanin being an economic burden on Britain, even if they are British citizens.

Governmentality is not a sociology of government but an overall approach to the technology of power (Foucault et al. 2007: 117). One of the central characteristics of governmentality is its ability to socialise us into governing ourselves through the institutional and discursive practices of government in which 'truth is produced and consumed in social, cultural and political practices' (Dean 2009 [1999]: 18). I am not sure whether the thirst for ethnic recognition of so many shades and complexions is simply ironic or a testament to the persuasive tenacity of British ethnic governmentality.

It is only within a system of ethnonormativity that ethnic and racial diversity become transgressive achievements or radically paradigmatic. Like the misreading of drag in Butler's work on gender, cultural hybridity, racial diversity, being 'mixed-race' or 'hyphenated' are often fetishised as radically paradigmatic subject positions. However, if these forms of hybridity are to be seen as paradigmatic at all, it should be in terms of their ability to challenge ethnonormativity and not in the fetishisation of hybridity itself.

There is much to be learned about racial subjection by exploring notions of identification and desire, encryption, melancholia and a project of survival, which are the theoretical terrain on which Butler's writings on performative gender rest. Thus the pervasive forces of heteronormativity and ethnonormativity bring into being that which is named – 'Arab woman' or 'British Arab woman', and imposes a set of gendered and racialising norms, discourses and practices which must be recited, albeit imperfectly, for cultural survival and social intelligibility. 'The analysis of racialisation and class is at least equally important in the thinking of sexuality as either gender or homosexuality, and these last two are not separable from more complex and complicitous formations of power' (Butler 1994: 21).

Miron and Inda attempt to bridge the gap between performative gender and race by interpreting race as a kind of speech act, arguing that 'race does not refer to a pre-given subject. Rather it works to constitute the subject itself and only acquires a naturalised effect through repeated or reiterative naming of or reference to that subject' (2000: 86–87). 'Race' is largely absent from *Gender Trouble*, however in *Bodies that Matter* Butler considers Nella Larsen's novel *Passing*, which Keresztasi Treat suggests 'leaves the door open for making the leap from the performativity of gender to the performativity and ambiguity of racial identity' (2002: 188; see also Piper 1992; Smith 1994; Juda and Bennett 1998; Sanchez and Schlossberg 2001; Hubel and Brooks 2002; Knadler 2003; Rottenberg 2004a, 2004b; Williams 2004; Harrison-Kahan 2005; Belluscio 2006; Horne 2006; Elam 2007; Cutter 2010). However, while she draws parallels between 'queering' and 'passing', Butler stops short of discussing performative race or expanding on what she refers to as 'racialising norms' (Butler 1993: 130; see also Salih 2002: 92–93; Hubel and Brooks 2002: 188).

The analysis of racial *passing* (discussed in depth in chapter 2) in both film and literature has uncovered some of the interacting and intersecting modalities of power around race, gender and class. Discourse is a gateway onto psychic structures, cultural, corporeal and material practices and conditions. I take Butler's call for sequential and interrelated readings of gender, race and their relationship to class to mean that, contrary to the caricaturing of performativity, a focus on the modalities of power of discourse is not 'linguistic monism'. What might distinguish the analysis I will go on to present from the literature on *passing* is that, first, I do so by calling upon ethnographic narratives and not literature. While these are both types of narrative and text, grounding a performative analysis in ethnography may go some way towards addressing some of the concerns raised by anthropologists.

Second, I attempt to explicitly consider how to interrelate the schema of performative gender – identification, desire, mimesis, encryption and the project of survival – with performative race. A performative approach allows me to understand the influences that gender, race and class retain as structures of subjection while at the same allowing me to go beyond constructivist accounts of these social axes of power by giving them no ontological legitimacy beyond their discursive and phantasmic construction, imposition and the injunctions 'to be' that they create.

In the following chapter I begin the project of inferring performative race from performative gender by attempting to identify the discursive forces that bring Arabness into being in the local and global context of London. I ask: How have 'the Arabs' been discursively represented and imagined in Britain? What have been the critical junctures in the relationship between 'the Arabs' and London? In later chapters I will extend this approach by asking how these discourses relate to the way 'Arabness' is practised, perhaps *performed* by young Londoners today. Historical accounts sometimes offer the pretence of going back in time, 'restor[ing] an unbroken continuity that operates beyond the dispersion of forgotten things, which we often go on to infer' (Foucault 1984: 81). My motivations for this act of historical reconstruction are more to do with the disruptions of historical truth making. Archaeology, in a Foucauldian sense, is the processes of working through the historical archive to bring to light the discursive formations and events that have produced (in this case) 'the Arabs' in London. Yet in order to disrupt those objects that are inevitably created and bought into being by repeatedly being named, archaeology must always be subjected to the disruptions of genealogical analysis. I find this double movement useful for dealing with essentialism. Spivak argues that the essentialism required to 'speak' as 'a woman' or 'an Arab' is not inherently bad, it is strategically necessary. It is the way in which essentialised categories are applied that requires critique. Thus strategic essentialism of this sort should be distinguished from the use of 'positivist essentialism in a scrupulously visible political interest' (Spivak 1985: 205).

> Genealogy does not resemble the evolution of species and does not map the destiny of a people. On the contrary, to follow the complex course of descent is to maintain passing events in their proper dispersion; it is to identify the accidents, the minute deviations – or conversely, the complete reversals – the errors, the false appraisals and the faulty calculations that gave birth to those things that continue to exist and have value for us ... (Foucault and Bouchard, 1980: 146)

In turning to the archive I do not seek origin or ethno-history or 'the erecting of foundations'; on the contrary, following the path of descent 'disturbs what was previously considered immobile, it fragments what was thought unified; it shows the heterogeneity of what was imagined consistent with itself' (1980: 147).

1

Critical Junctures in the Making of Arab London

Every three days a thousand Arabs arrive in London for business, pleasure or something more sinister. (*The Times*, 22 August 1978)

The only way you could tell it was Paris and not London was that there were more Japanese and fewer Arabs. (*The Guardian*, 24 November 1990)

What is it that really makes summer in the city? ... It is Arabs: Arabs by the thousand, walking in the park, drinking coffee in the Edgware Road, emptying the shelves of the Marble Arch Marks and Spencer. (*The Guardian*, 24 August 1998)

'I'm Arab, but not that kind of Arab,' said Mo(hammed) who was born and raised in London to Egyptian immigrant parents. So which kind of Arab was he? The amorphousness of the term 'Arab' carries with it a necessary ambiguity, always holding the possibility of a communicative failure. 'Come on you know what I mean! The money, the cars, the sleaze, their clothes, I just don't like being associated with that.' Mo was referring to the way he wanted to avoid the summer rituals of Arab Gulf tourists in West London and all the insinuations that follow from it. Mo's day-to-day life sat in stark contrast to the indulgences of Gulf tourists in the city and yet in London he shared the label 'Arab' with them and all the meanings and intimations that have calcified around it. If we are to understand Arabness in London it seems sensible to begin with how it emerged as a way of being or being seen, how it has been represented and interpolated within the context of the city and Britain more broadly.

In the initial stages of my research the absence of an account of 'Arab London' left me with a sense of being out of place and an inability to situate the present. Yet equally, why should that 'history' be 'Arab'? 'Representations of the collective past hinge ... on the backward projections of current perceptions of identity; the past takes mental shape by being viewed as the breeding and testing ground of today's social collectivities' (Cubitt 2007: 200). The political act of labelling is involved in any historicism where complex and often incoherent events and meanings are cast into a coherent and seamless ethno-history. That necessary representational move should always be qualified by the recognition that the relationship between the past and the present is not one of causal stability. The tensions around Arabness as a socio-cultural, political and civilisational identification are far too multifarious to merely be assembled as evidence for ethnogenesis.

The cursory journey into what has been chronicled about the 'Arabs' in Britain leaves little room for confident claims of having a knowable object at its end, it can only provide a partial and necessarily incomplete account. This version of the history of Arab London is based on ethnographic accounts from migrants and young Arabs raised in the city; British immigration and naturalisation statistics (1960 to 2011) and hundreds of press reports and articles between 1924 and 2007 about Arabs in Britain. Together they provide insights into the complexities of Arab identification and the discourses that produce 'the Arabs' in London as wealthy and exotic, dissimilar and suspicious, dangerous and violent.

Struggles of the Homeland: Students and Activists 1924–73

The number of Egyptian students or young people, female and male, domiciled in England was surprising. They must have all been there, a jostling, enthusiastic crowd, bearing their tributes of flowers or waving the flags of independent Egypt … Saad Pasha Zaghloul accepted with a kindly fatherly smile the exuberant homage of his youthful fellow-countrymen as they surged around him … At last the pent up enthusiasm reached the vocal point. A woman student led the cheering and the room rang with the cries that have long been heard in Cairo streets and elsewhere: 'Long live Saad Pasha!' 'Long live King Fuad, King of Egypt and Sudan!' and many others less suitable, perhaps, on British soil than in the exhilarating atmosphere of Egypt … Young Egypt-in-exile, well pleased with itself, with its outing and shouting, melted cheerfully away. ('Egypt in London: September 23rd 1924', *The Near East*, 2 October 1924)

The jovial tone in *The Near East*'s account of the gathering of young Egyptian students at the Claridge's Hotel makes light of the tumultuous nature of Egypt's resistance to British occupation after the 1919 Egyptian revolution and during the interwar years (1918–39). Whatever didactic hospitality London might have offered students was underwritten by its inexorable role in British imperialism. At once a place where students and technocrats from the Arab *Mashreq* sought education and training for the benefit of their societies, and simultaneously the colonial metropolis from which the occupation, division and domination of the Arabic-speaking region was orchestrated. Students and intellectuals from the countries colonised by Britain increasingly took to anti-colonial activism in London during the interwar years pointing to what Césaire (2001 [1973]) described as the 'colonial boomerang', or the collapse of the comfortable separation between ordered and stable imperial metropolis and rebellion and resistance in the colonies.

By January 1925, the turmoil between Egypt and Britain had drawn the small student population in London into the fray. The government of British Prime Minister Ramsay MacDonald adopted a set of 'heightened security measures' in response to intelligence that Egyptian students in England were plotting to assassinate members of the British government.[1] Although Egypt's incorporation and adoption of formal political Arabism was yet to be complete at this stage, the incident was the first of its kind where Arabic-speaking students were framed as conduits of political violence in Britain; it would not be the last.

Pan-Arab nationalism or *Al-Qawmiyah al-Arabiyah* incorporated anti-colonial self-determination, regionalism and a secular, yet religiously informed, civilisational commonality among Arabic speakers. Although the notion of Arab commonality has a very long history, pre-dating Islam as a level of group identification, its contemporary expression has been intimately informed by European concepts of nation as well as its emerging concurrently with Kemalism and Zionism (Khalidi 1991b: 1364; see also Hourani 1962, 1970, 1981; Sharabi 1970; Choueiri 1989, 2001; Kayali 1997).

We only need to look as far as London for traces of these early articulations and expressions. In May 1933 the Arabic Cultural Association was founded in London. Diplomatic staff and leading Orientalists and Arabists from British academia and government were its principal patrons. The association was ostensibly non-religious and non-political in nature and sought to enhance the cultural life of the small Arabic-speaking community in London by providing lectures and dinners.[2] The following month (June 1933) *The Arabic World*, a weekly newspaper edited by Dr Mahmoud Azmi, an Egyptian academic and journalist, began circulation from offices in the Strand. In its opening article Azmi related the emerging vision of 'The Arabic World, its extent, its unity and its aspirations':

> The Arabic World, that stretch of adjacent countries reaching from the Atlantic to the Persian Gulf is made up of the following political and administrative denominations: Morocco, Riff, Algeria, Tunis, Tripoli, Egypt, Sudan, Somaliland, Hedjaz, Nejd, Assir, Yemen, Palestine, Transjordan, Syria, Lebanon and Iraq.
>
> In spite of the numerous frontiers dividing these peoples, the many political and economic regimes in force, the various European influences existing there, and the dual Semitic and Hamitic racial origin, the Arabic World constitutes a social and cultural unit born of a great historical event, owing its continued existence to an important and determining characteristic.
>
> When these countries were conquered by Islam they became endowed by a unique social system with a single language. There are certain differences in the manifestation of their social lives as there are in the pronunciation of their language, but these are mere differences of detail. In the course of 14 centuries they have kept and continue to keep an essential unity of conception: the Arabic language has retained and continues to retain unity of literary expression.
>
> To these elements, which until now have brought about the unity of the Arabic World, a third – equally important – has been added, namely, the reawakening national sentiment in all its forms and in its juxtaposition to the renaissance of Arabic culture to which every region is now contributing. And the addition of this third element, due to the rapid evolution of ideas since the Great War, has had a radical influence on the conception of the Arabic World. From religious unity, having pan-Islamism as its aim, the Caliphate as its symbol, it has turned to nationalism, with pan-Arabism as its end and Arabic culture as its medium.
>
> But if the awakened national sentiment in the Arabic World is universal, the cultural levels of neither the national nor the protagonists of the daily struggle are alike. Nevertheless the difference, though worthy of note, is not likely to diminish the strong tendency towards a united Arabic World, which is composed of three main groups – ethnographical, homogeneous entities – thus: (1) Northern Africa, excepting Egypt (2) The Arabian Peninsula (3) Egypt, Iraq and Sham (Syria, Lebanon, Palestine, Transjordan).

Reduced to realistic terms, these entities take on the following aspects: – In North Africa the struggle is against absorption by the French, Spanish and Italian colonists; In Arabia the tendency is towards sedentarism and modernisation of the national economy; in Egypt, Iraq and Sham there is a desire for stability through treaties of alliance with Great Britain and France.

Not one of these entities – not one country forming a part of these entities, though preoccupied with its own national aspirations – forgets for a moment the common bond linking it to every other country in the Arabic World. A glance at the newspapers of any one of these countries shows clearly to what extent the common bond exists.[3]

The Arabic World sought to present a corrective message of the region and its people to its British readership. The depiction of Arabs in the British public imagination was a source of unease for the small community of Arab diplomats, students and settlers in London at a time when Orientalism had become a fundamental component of Europe's colonial sense of self. Dr M.R. Zada, first secretary of the 'Arabian Legation' in London, used the opportunity of the World Conference Film Banquet in July 1933 to protest against the 'horrible misrepresentation of the characters, customs and institutions of the Orientals by the screen'. His complaint was sympathetically received by the conference and in response *To-day's Cinema* conceded that 'as the film medium becomes more and more of an international medium, considerations of the box office, as well as politics and good manners will make us overcome our temptation to depict Orientals in an unpleasant light'.[4]

British colonialism, Palestine and Orientalism were the main reference points for activism around Arab causes in London. Palestinian leaders had regularly visited London since the mid 1920s to lobby parliamentarians in the hope of changing British policy after the Balfour Declaration. As the Royal Commission prepared its report in 1935, Conservative MPs and peers who had fought alongside Arabs against the Ottomans during the First World War formed a 'pro-Arab Parliamentary Committee'. A prominent supporter of the Palestinian cause, Mr M.V. Morton believed that the British public had to be provided with information from the Arab perspective; his efforts culminated in the establishment of the Arab Centre in 1937. The Centre began producing the *Arab Centre Bulletin*, which was distributed to a mailing list of around 5,000 journalists, academics, activists and members of the Houses of Parliament.

According to Izzat Tannous, head of the Arab Office in London at the time, the Arab Centre played an important role in raising awareness of the Palestinian cause among Arab diplomatic missions in London, who in his experience were not familiar with the particularities of Palestine's fate under the British Mandate. The work of the Arab Centre and its staff in London eventually led to the securing of monthly contributions towards its running from the Egyptian and Saudi Arabian embassies in 1939 (Tannous 1988). As war broke out again in Europe both *The Arabic World* and the Arab Centre disappear from the historical record. Their importance lies in the themes that they present us with: Arab commonality in the 1930s was fundamentally political. Anti-colonial struggle, anti-Orientalism and the fate of Palestine were at the core of this identification. London and the interaction of Arabs with and in it were central to the forging of that solidarity.

In 1939 Egyptian, Palestinian, Jordanian, Syrian and Iraqi students formed the Oxford University Anglo-Arab Union (AAU) with the prominent Arabist Professor A.R. Gibb, later known as Faris Gibb, as its president. The AAU was the first student society in Britain that reflected the ideals of pan-Arab federalism.[5] In the post-war period the number of students from the Arab world studying at British universities grew steadily[6] and new organisations began to emerge to cater for their cultural and pastoral needs. One of the earliest examples was the Anglo-Arab Association (AAA) established in 1948. The AAA provided welfare and social activities to Arab students as a means of strengthening cultural relations between Britain and the Arab world.[7] Shortly after its inauguration, the AAA established the Anglo-Arab Students' Hostel and worked to raise funds for its maintenance by organising, among other things, 'Arabian Nights' fundraising events, a theme we shall return to in chapter 4 as an enduring feature of Arab student life in contemporary London.

The debacle of the 1948 Arab-Israeli war was an emblematic example of the underdeveloped notion of Arab collective action. Unity was rhetorically and hypothetically profuse and yet the mechanisms for its realisation were elusive, with disastrous consequences in Palestine. Monarchies around the region, particularly those in Egypt, Transjordan, Iraq and the Gulf region were heavily reliant upon their relationships with Britain, the colonial power that had installed or maintained them. For the ideologues and activists concerned with national and regional sovereignty, Arab monarchs were increasingly seen as an obstacle to national and regional emancipation and development. Over the course of the interwar years and the post-Second World War period, pan-Arabism experienced a shift from traditional monarchism to militaristic republicanism as a model of anti-colonial self-determination. However, the growing militaristic republican movement taking hold across much of the region, with its nominally secular and modernist ideology, only enjoyed a short-lived solidarity. Ideological and political differences over the substance of pan-Arabism, the role of religion and socialism, the extent and speed of unification and, importantly, who would lead, were all highly divisive. Furthermore, the hereditary monarchies of Iraq, Jordan, Morocco, Libya and the Gulf region – with their own notion of dynastic, tribal and kinship-based Arabism – maintained a complex relationship of apprehensive recognition of the newly empowered militaristic pan-Arab republican movement in Egypt and Syria. These differences resonated in London, where relations between Iraqi and Jordanian students and the governments that sponsored their education were strained by student support for Egypt's Gamal Abdel Nasser, particularly during the 1956 Suez crisis.

Despite the virulently anti-Nasserite and anti-republican policies of Nuri Said's government in Iraq, which had placed the country firmly in support of British interests in the region within the framework of the Baghdad Pact, Iraqi students across Britain took part in demonstrations against British policy over Suez. In response to the tripartite attack on Egypt by Israel, Britain and France, 50 Arab students at Oxford University led by Mr E. El-Mehdi (St Johns' College) boycotted lectures and tutorials. The renowned historian Dr W. El-Khalidi, a lecturer at Oxford University, resigned from his post, sold his home in Oxford and moved back to Jordan.[8] At Loughborough College of Technology 40 Iraqi students boycotted lectures and went on hunger strike for three days, while in London 300 Iraqi students took part in a sit-down strike outside their embassy.[9] The protesters submitted a petition urging the Iraqi government to put its forces under a united Arab command, sever diplomatic relations with Britain and France, withdraw from the Baghdad Pact and impose an oil embargo on the European belligerents.[10] Unwilling to engage with the students the embassy staff called on the Metropolitan Police to disperse the crowd, a move which reflected the gap that was growing between young Iraqis inspired by the pan-Arab movement and the British-installed Hashemite monarchy. Iraqi students in Britain supportive of Nasser were condemned as supporters of 'Egyptian imperialism' or 'agents of Nasser' by Iraqi monarchists and the British press. Known Ba'athists or Nasserites were targeted by the Iraqi authorities, who withdrew educational grants, subjected some to interrogation and intermittently requested the Home Office to arrange deportations of Iraqi student dissidents.

The ebbs and flows of the emerging Arab state system constantly framed relations between Arab students in Britain. A good example of how this manifested itself in day-to-day interactions is provided by *The Arab Review*, the magazine of the Arab Students Union (ASU) in Britain, which began publication in 1958. 'Our team', chronicled the review in celebration of its first ASU football team, 'is a symbol of Arab unity. It includes players from nearly all the Arab countries – Syria, Iraq, Palestine, Lybia [sic], Jordan, Kuwait, Saudi Arabia, Sudan and Algeria. We have no politics in our team and every Arab who can play is welcome'[11] (see Figure 1.1). The urge to imagine Arabs as fundamentally unified not simply by their culture but also by their politics meant that Arabism, an emphatically political identification, and the collective reference point for solidarity, had to be left largely without interrogation or debate because of its divisive and contested nature. The complications of Arab political incongruity were, and remain, a key theme in the way Arabness is imagined.

Figure 1.1   Members of the first Arab student Union football team in Britain 1958 – the original caption reads: Standing left to right: Khalil, Hassan (Capt.), Ghassan, Hashim, Farouk. Seated left to right: Fayig, Maan, Ibrahim

Source: The Arab Review, March 1958.

Despite the inharmoniousness of their political loyalties and outlooks, most saw Arab unity, whether under the guise of secularism or religious modernity, as a panacea for the realisation of their national, regional and civilisational redemption. Yet the pretence of a happy Arab family and the allure of rhetorical Arab unity effectively involved the negation of those differences or the disavowal of those who represented them. Thus to be an Egyptian Ba'athi, an Iraqi Nasserite or a Jordanian republican was not simply a matter of political dissent or opposition to the mainstream, in many cases it involved being subjected to totalising discourses of sedition on the one hand and persecutions, banishment or imprisonment on the other. Indeed, in the coming decades the different approaches to national and collective Arab 'destiny' would be violently played out in the streets of London.

The close relationship between educational scholarships and membership of ruling parties and movements meant that Arab student activism in London was often orchestrated by state-sponsored student unions. When Israeli Prime Minister David Ben Gurion arrived in London in 1960 he was met by a demonstration of over 100 Arab students at Heathrow airport. It was not only Israel and the West against which Arab students mobilised. In the weeks leading up to the 1967 Six-Day War, 80 Arab students demonstrated at Heathrow airport at the arrival of King Faisal of Saudi Arabia, greeting the monarch with pictures of President Nasser.

The 1967 war was a turning point for the way that 'Arab' political activity in London manifested itself. The failure of Arab armies to repel the Israeli assault and, moreover, to liberate Palestine over the preceding 19 years, finally convinced Palestinian leaders of the need for an independent liberation strategy. Central to the story that would unfold in London was the lack of consensus and clarity among the different Palestinian factions with regard to the rules of engagement with Israel and the international Zionist movement (Sayigh 1997: 211). Yasser Arafat's Fatah movement and the Popular Democratic Front for the Liberation of Palestine (PDFLP) formally declared their opposition to attacks on civilian targets outside the West Bank, Gaza and Israel. Yet hardliners within the Palestine Liberation Organisation (PLO) simultaneously acquiesced to the creation of paramilitary cells which operated primarily in Europe (1997: 211). The Popular Front for the Liberation of Palestine (PFLP) had a far clearer position and openly declared responsibility for the first attack on an Israeli El Al passenger aircraft (1968). In 1969 the PFLP embarked on a bombing campaign in London aimed at Israeli and 'Zionist-owned' businesses. In July that year a device exploded outside the Marks and Spencer department store on Oxford Street. In August of the same year, an explosive device went off at the Zim Israel Navigation Company offices on Regent Street. In a statement later that month Dr George Habbash the leader of the

PFLP claimed responsibility for the attacks and warned that 'there will be more fire and bomb attacks on Jewish owned establishments in London'.[12]

The spiral of violence and instability around 'Black September'[13] in 1970 led 150 pro-Palestinian and pro-Syrian demonstrators to gather outside the Jordanian embassy in London where they chanted slogans against the 'murderous fascist regime of King Hussain [sic]'.[14] Although the rhetoric was heated, the demonstrations were peaceful. However, the following year, the 'Black September Organisation' made a failed assassination attempt on the Jordanian ambassador in London. The incident was the first assassination attempt related to inter-Arab political hostility in London. According to the *The Times*, the Metropolitan Police conducted searches of 'Arab homes' in the Notting Hill area where the assailants had abandoned their car and escaped.[15] The reference to Arab homes being searched in response to assassination attempts and other acts of political violence became increasingly common in newspaper reports in years to come, and signalled the start of a process that would cast suspicion upon the small settled community of Arabs in London.

On 1 October 1970, hundreds of people gathered outside the Banqueting Hall in Whitehall. Women and young girls dressed in black led a funeral procession carrying pictures of a smiling Gamal Abdel Nasser and the flags of the United Arab Republic and Occupied Palestine. The procession ended at the Islamic Centre in Regent's Park with mourners reportedly reluctant to leave, milling around seeming to 'have nowhere to go and nothing to do'.[16] Collective Arabness was intimately informed and organised around political figures, causes and allegiances which were at times powerful enough to bring Arabs from disparate national contexts and political persuasions together, and at other times drive those same parties to open conflict and confrontation.

Apart from the settlement of Yemeni migrants in South Shields, Sheffield and Cardiff at the turn of the twentieth century, it is difficult to point to any significant Arab settlement in Britain up to this point. Iraqi monarchists and members of the Assyrian minority fled to Britain after the 1958 'Free Officers' *coup*. The subsequent 1963 coup and the 1968 purges in Iraq also led Communists, Christians, Kurds and Nasserites to leave Iraq in greater numbers, with a small proportion coming to Britain (Al-Rasheed 1992: 539). Immigration and naturalisation data suggests a very low number of people of different Arab nationalities applying for or gaining British citizenship. Fewer than 200 people of Arab nationalities were granted British citizenship each year between 1960 and 1969. From 1968 onwards Iraqis became the largest Arab migrant group in Britain, with the highest number of applications for British citizenship. While Iraqi migration to Britain was largely motivated by political instability, the late 1960s and early 1970s began to see the arrival of migrant workers from Egypt and Morocco, most of whom came to the UK on temporary visa voucher schemes in the 'hospitality and catering' industries. Nonetheless, as none of the Arab states joined the British Commonwealth, large-scale labour migration to Britain simply did not take place.

Indeed it may have been the small size of the migrant and settled population that intensified the points of contact and interaction among Arabs in the city. Now in his mid 70s, Nader migrated to London from Egypt in 1969. He had intended to study but soon fell out of higher education and into employment at the Embassy of Kuwait. He explained how, in his initial months as a student in Britain, London provided more opportunities than his native Cairo for learning about the various shades of political, ideological and cultural Arabness.

> I must say that coming to London made me learn a lot. I lived with an Algerian and a Palestinian at first and I met Ba'athists, I never knew what a Ba'athi was when I was in Egypt. We met these people at the General Union of Arab Students in Collingham Road. We met left-wing ideologues and Ba'athists. They reminded me of the Socialist Union back in Egypt. They talked a lot but had very little activities. There were debates and discussions but, for me personally, my personal experience was that I learnt more about these different political positions and people by interacting with these people socially. Those Ba'athists are very ideological, almost fanatics. And the names – Michael Aflak and all those people – we learnt about them here in London not Cairo. Even though I was involved in political activism in Egypt we didn't know much about these figures or movements.

For many Arab migrants there appears to have been a clear distinction between their physical and economic embeddedness in Britain and their social and political embeddedness in the Arab world. Even for the most long-standing Arabic-speaking migrant group in Britain, the Yemenis, the struggles of the homeland consistently trumped the processes of settlement in Britain. This is well illustrated by Abdulgalil Shaif, Chairman of the 'Yemeni Community Association' in Sheffield:

> The first thing that Yemenis here wanted to do in 1971 was to support the revolution [in Yemen] and learn all about it. They could only

learn in Arabic. So the first information and lessons that they gained in working-class consciousness and organisation was not about the struggle here in Britain. It was about how the Yemenis organised the revolution back home. That was what taught them how to organise themselves as working-class people first of all, and then they applied that to their life and experience here in Sheffield. But they didn't learn about working-class struggle and development in Britain. They were divorced from that, and that was part of the racism they faced. If local working-class organisations had helped to give them an education about organisation, about taking power, it would have integrated them into the movement and they would have developed with that. But it didn't happen that way. The British trade unions and working-class organisations didn't bother reaching them, so they took their inspiration from their struggles in the homeland. (Searle and Shaif 1991: 74)

The divorce referred to by Shaif is noteworthy and we may add to it that, by and large, the causes to which Arabs in Britain were attached had little resonance with the British public or political establishment. There were attempts by Arabs settled in Britain to reach out to the broader public, but these were few and far between, and overwhelmingly focused on the Arab-Israeli conflict at a time when Britain was unequivocally allied to Israel both culturally and politically. After the outbreak of the Yom Kippur War on 6 October 1973 the General Union of Arab Students in London placed adverts in British national newspapers calling for donations for the reconstruction of villages and towns destroyed in Egypt and Syria during the war. On the seventh day of the war, Arab Londoners took to the streets marching on the Israeli and American embassies.

What seems like a passing incident from the historical record was put into ethnographic context during my fieldwork when a British-born female interviewee of Egyptian origin was astonished to identify her parents in the photograph below, her mother standing in the foreground holding a poster that reads 'Remember Palestine' (Figure 1.2). It was a poignant reminder of the way in which archaeology and genealogy can help in understanding points of continuity and discontinuity in the doing of Arabness in London. Thirty-three years after the photograph was taken, my interviewee – just as her parents had – gathered with thousands of others in London to demonstrate, this time against the Israeli war on Lebanon in July 2006. The same causes, the same protest routes and, in many cases, the same chants resonate across generations of Arab immigrants and their children living in the city.

Figure 1.2   Arab demonstrators with pro-Palestinian banners march on the Israeli Embassy in Kensington, London, 14 October 1973

Source: Chris Djukanovic, The Hulton Archive, Getty Images.

In November 1974 a British Airways flight from Dubai was hijacked. Twenty British hostages were on board and one of the conditions of their release was that the British Prime Minister Edward Heath express regret for the role that Britain played in the establishment of the State of Israel. Heath refused to meet the demands of the hijackers who later surrendered at Tunis airport. Days after the incident the Israeli prime minister Golda Meir visited London to attend a fundraising dinner organised by the Labour Friends of Israel group. The following day, pictures of Golda Meir weeping on Heath's shoulder at the dinner were published on the front pages of a number of national newspapers. In response to the front page photo Dr E. Mehdi who, as a student at Oxford in the mid 1950s had led Arab students in a boycott of lectures in protest at the Suez War, placed a one-page advert in *The Times* in the name of the Committee for Justice in the Middle East (Wednesday, 11 December 1974, p. 7; see Figure 1.3).

Although it makes few rhetorical concessions, the advert is notable for its attempt to articulate Arab concerns in the 'lobby' or 'interest group' genre using the logic of the British taxpayer's interests as its principal rationale. However, the economic impact of the Arab oil embargo became closely associated with the broader economic crisis in Britain and the

SHOULDN'T BRITAIN COME FIRST?

Every year millions of pounds of untaxed money under the charities act end up in Israel to support the Zionist movement. Once again this year Mrs. Golda Meir was here Fund Raising for the Zionist cause.

Once again Mrs. Meir was here demanding more sacrifice from a country already drained through world recession

More money from Britain to support the Israel war machine which is responsible for policing actions into neighbouring Arab countries and the indiscriminate bombing of Palestinian refugees.

More money to perpetuate Israel's military occupation of Arab Territories. More money so that more Jews can immigrate to Israel while 3,000,000 Palestinians are refused entry into their homeland.

A lasting peace in the Middle East can only be obtained by the full implementation of United Nations Resolutions on the Middle East and restitution of the full rights of the Palestinian People.

This is what Zionism has opposed for years.

Donations to Israel can only perpetuate the deadlock

ISN'T BRITAIN MORE IMPORTANT

Shouldn't British Money Remain in Britain;
To Build more homes,
To Improve Social Services,
To help Pensioners?

Shouldn't Britain come first?

COMMITTEE FOR JUSTICE IN THE MIDDLE EAST

P.O. Box 295,London N21 5LR

Figure 1.3   A campaign advert by the Committee for Justice in the Middle East
Source: The Times, 11 December 1974.

Sterling crisis of 1976, all of which led to an intensification of anti-Arab sentiment in Britain, where an increasing number of 'anti-Arab' incidents and attacks were reported.[17]

Apart from reinforcing the image of the region and its people as being violent, anti-Semitic and unstable; the 1973 war and the subsequent oil crisis that gripped Europe and North America also produced the oil boom of the mid to late 1970s. The extraordinary revenues and wealth generated by the Gulf oil-producing states in this period quickly found their way to London, adding a new layer of meaning to the idea of 'the Arabs' in the city; Arabs were not only violent but also undeservedly wealthy.

London for Sale: Playboy Princes and 'The Petrodollar Invasion'

The steady flow and growth of Gulf investment in London is one of the pivotal features of the Arab economy in the city. Although London is a global financial hub, Britain's role as surrogate father of the fledgling Gulf sheikhdoms was instrumental in drawing Gulf investment to the British capital in the late 1970s. In the early nineteenth century the Arabian Peninsula took on strategic importance for Britain in the quest to physically contain competing colonial powers, secure merchant shipping from piracy and establish telegraphic communication routes with India. Britain signed a series of treaties with the maritime tribes all along the east coast of the Arabian Peninsula in 1835 and went on to incorporate British arbitration of disputes between the rival tribes, followed by a series of treaties of 'Peace in Perpetuity' in 1853. What became known as the 'Trucial Coast' came under the control of the Indian Political Service stationed in Bushehr on the Persian side of the Gulf, which appointed British 'Political Agents' as advisers to tribal leaders along the coast. In 1892 'non-alienation bonds' were added to the existing treaties, which in practical terms gave Britain control of the fledgling sheikhdoms' access to the outside world with the exception of Oman (see Rabi 2006).

Britain encouraged the separation of the sheikhdoms from both the Ottoman Empire and Persia by bestowing titles and power upon tribal leaders that far exceeded those offered by the Sublime Porte. One by one, tribal leaders rebelled against Ottoman rule and applied to the British for dependency status (see Troeller 1976: 8). Britain was the first to legitimise the conquest of al-Hejaz by Ibn Al-Saud in 1924 and helped cement his rule by bestowing the secular title of 'King' upon him through the Anglo-Saudi Treaty of 1927 (Monroe 1981; Leatherdale 1983; Ayubi 1995; Al-Enazy 2009).

The discovery of oil in the east of the peninsula in 1938 would add an economic dimension to what had previously been a strategic geo-political colonial relationship. In turn British businesses benefited from a privileged position in relation to oil concessions. For the newly independent states and emirates of Kuwait, Bahrain, Qatar and the United Arab Emirates, statehood and independence coincided with the oil boom, and London, which had played a central role in the rise to power of their ruling families, was a natural location in which to deposit and invest their newfound wealth. The fabled metropolis that had provided the early trappings of statehood was soon to become the home-from-home of *Khaleeji* (Arabian Gulf) elites and ruling families (see Joyce 2003; Davidson 2007).

The arrival of tourists and the growth of *Khaleeji* investment portfolios in London are significant for two reasons. First, up to this point the Arab population of students and settlers in London came almost exclusively from non-Gulf Arab states which, at the time, were relatively 'westernised' in state orientation as well as being ethnically and religiously mixed. The western attire of Arab students, migrants and settlers from non-Gulf states allowed most to blend into the growing cosmopolitan mix in London. In contrast, early *Khaleeji* tourists were highly visible, their waving robes, veils and traditionalism corresponding more closely to the powerful aesthetics of exotic Orientalism (see Figure 1.4). Largely seasonal and transient in their visits, *Khaleeji* tourists aroused curiosity, and the extravagant spending and disreputable sexual behaviour with which they were to become associated, added another strand to the already potent image of Arabs in Britain as militants and terrorists, as well as providing a regular source of intrigue for gossip columnists and chroniclers of the bizarre in the British press.

Figure 1.4   An Arab family in South Kensington, London, 25 March 1976
Source: *Evening Standard*, The Hulton Archive, Getty Images.

Second, *Khaleeji* capital and tourism provided an important and consistent source of employment, and therefore income, for the settled Arab migrant population in London, many of whom became and remain employed as bankers, journalists, embassy staff, fixers, agents, restaurateurs and drivers for *Khaleeji* embassies, businesses and families. It is the growth and stability of these capital flows and tourist seasons that has done most to distinguish the Arabs of London socio-economically and perhaps socially from their counterparts in continental Europe.

By the mid 1970s, both British and Arab newspapers began to take note of the growing portfolio of Gulf property acquisitions in London. Some in Britain maintained that investments from the Gulf would create an expectation among Arab states that Britain would take a lead role in the formulation of an independent European foreign policy that would be more considerate to Arab political aspirations in the region, including possible arms deals with Egypt and Syria.[18] Panic ensued as 'petro-dollar investors' sought to acquire major companies and trading groups. Arab Gulf investments were seen as either insidious or a threat to 'national interests', with some commentators characterising them as a 'petrodollar invasion' or discussing them in terms of 'aggressive Arab interests'. Economic conditions in Britain, and the country's intimate relationship with the newly independent Gulf states, made London a particularly attractive setting for investment, medical treatment and tourism from the Gulf. The looming economic stagnation and high inflation in Britain soon dispelled any reservations Harold Wilson's government had about the political implications of Gulf investment in Britain, which was soon recognised as vital to keeping the country's head above water economically. In contrast to London, continental markets were perceived to be less exposed to the consequences of the 'petrodollar invasion'.[19]

Linda Blandford's 1977 book *Oil Sheikhs* devotes its first chapter to an account of London 'for sale', with free-spending, oil-rich Arabs 'off-loading' their 'petrodollars' in a period of 'Arab fever'. Blandford suggests that, 'If one had to pinpoint a moment in time when London realised that it had become the Arabs' new home-from-home, it was the day in August 1975 when airing mattresses appeared over the window-sills of a £300,000 mansion in the Boltons' (1977: 11). *Khaleeji* ruling elites began acquiring properties in Knightsbridge, the embassy quarter in Mayfair, Eaton Square, the Boltons, Grosvenor Square and Rutland Gardens. This was accompanied by a huge presence in the most exclusive hotels in the Park Lane area each summer. Entire floors would be taken up by one family and their entourage of servants. Middle Eastern restaurants in the vicinity of these hotels would reportedly send men carrying steaming pots and trays covered in tin foil to cater for the tastes of the *Khaleeji* clientele. Fleets of chauffeur-driven cars waited patiently for the moment when their clients would emerge from hotels and department stores in Oxford Street and Knightsbridge, scenes which remain a regular feature of summer in West London to this day.

The behaviour of (some) male *Khaleeji* tourists in London began to draw criticism from newspapers both in the Arab world and London. The damage that the insensitive behaviour of 'Oil Shaikhs' (sic) was causing to the image of 'the Arabs', not least those living in Britain, was spelt out in *The Times* in August 1976.[20] Newspapers in Egypt, Libya and Syria were primarily concerned that vast oil revenues were being invested in the capitals of the ailing former colonial powers instead of the front-line states of the Arab-Israeli conflict, while Kuwaiti newspapers lamented the corruption of their youth in the nightclubs and casinos of London.

The spending habits of princes and sheikhs from the Gulf were reported to be the main reason for the massive profits being made by major gambling clubs and casinos in the capital.[21] British newspapers were particularly interested in stories of 'Arabs' losing hundreds of thousands of pounds on roulette and blackjack tables, and paying thousands of pounds for sex in the capital. The excesses of prominent figures like the reluctant King Khalid Ibn Saud propelled the stereotype of the high-rolling, womanising and cash-laden Arab to the fore of public imagination (see Figure 1.5).

Figure 1.5 Libyan cartoonist Mohammed Alzuwawi caricatures the behaviour of male *Khaleeji* tourists in London 1977

Source: From the Alzuwawi collection, *Antum [You]: Social and Political Cartoons 1973–1983* (Tripoli, Libya: Iqra Publishing, 1987).

London also became a medical hub for *Khaleejis'* as the health service infrastructure in Kuwait, Qatar, the United Arab Emirates (UAE) and Saudi Arabia was still basic. The consulates of Gulf states in London opened 'medical section(s)' which were tasked with arranging the treatment of officials and citizens. Private hospitals, like the Cromwell Hospital in Kensington, the London Clinic in Harley Street and the Wellington Hospital in St Johns Wood, began to cater for this new market, providing culturally sensitive services, including interpreters, Arabic menus, gifts for the patients during Eid and eventually Arabic TV.

The trend in the early 1970s, when a small *Khaleeji* elite were buying major London landmarks and real estate portfolios, gave way to property sales in London to a new *Khaleeji* merchant class in the 1980s – less extravagantly wealthy in comparison, but no less determined to own houses and flats in London. The emergence of this new *Khaleeji* middle class also drew the attention of the British Council, which began to covet the Gulf as a lucrative market for universities and summer schools in Britain, designing courses to cater for the specific 'economic development needs' of students from the Gulf.[22] Up to this point the Arab student population in Britain had mostly come from the countries like Iraq, Egypt, Syria, Jordan and Palestine. However, the spending power of students from the Gulf states and the abundance of scholarships provided by *Khaleeji* governments changed this. The *Khaleeji* education market was not only vastly more lucrative than the rest of the Arab world but it was also seemingly free of the ideological baggage and militant politics of the Arab students from republican and front-line states in the Arab-Israeli conflict (see Figure 1.6).

Overall the discourses and imagery around *Khaleeji* tourists frequently cast them not as noble savages but as excessively wealthy and crass savages. The fascination with the *Khaleeji nouveau riche* in London and the growing economic influence of the Gulf on the British economy would not overshadow but sit side by side with the image of 'the Arabs' as terrorists, as a wave of Arab-on-Arab political violence gripped London and grabbed newspaper headlines.

The 'Stray Dogs' in London: Political Purges 1977–89

Even though relations between Arabs in London were marked by the tensions of the emerging Arab state system in the 1950s and 1960s those tensions were by and large dealt with peacefully in London. This changed radically between 1977 and 1989 when rival Arab secret services engaged

Figure 1.6   Original caption reads: Two Arab students standing in front of an uninterested painter and decorator during a protest at the London offices of the Arab League against Syrian involvement in the Lebanon, 10 June 1976

Source: Dennis Oulds, The Hulton Archive, Getty Images.

in a twelve-year wave of political violence in London. The political purges and reprisals began with the assassination of the former North Yemeni prime minister outside the Royal Lancaster Hotel in April 1977[23] and ended abruptly with the murder of the Palestinian political cartoonist Naji al-Ali near King's Road in Chelsea in 1989.

Arab-on-Arab violence drew ever more public attention as the incidents themselves became increasingly spectacular. On New Year's Eve 1978 two Syrian embassy staff were killed when their car exploded near Piccadilly Circus, just metres away from crowds of people seeing in the New Year.[24] Days later, on 4 January 1978, Said Hammami, the PLO representative in London was shot and killed in his office in Mayfair.[25] On 9 July 1978 former Iraqi prime minister General Al-Naïf was shot and killed by two gunmen outside his hotel on Park Lane. In late July eleven Iraqi diplomats were expelled from the UK for the suspected smuggling of light weapons in diplomatic packages. Days later (on 28 July), a hand grenade was thrown at the Iraqi ambassador's car outside the Iraqi embassy at Queen's Gate.[26] The following month (August 1978) the PFLP claimed responsibility for a high-profile attack on a coach carrying El Al aircrew from their hotel in Mayfair to Heathrow airport; two people were killed and nine bystanders injured in the incident.[27] The dramatic Iranian embassy siege in 1980 only added to a long list of violent acts associated with London's Middle Eastern connections, turning public opinion against thousands of uninvolved 'Arab' migrant workers, students and tourists. Mr Ali Tarrabassi, a regular visitor to London from the emirate of Sharjah in the United Arab Emirates wrote a letter to the editor of *The Times* in May 1980, in which he described how he had experienced discrimination for being visibly Arab in London.

Sir, I am an Arab from Sharjah. I write to you very angry and upset about my treatment by some people here. I do not know why! Is it because of the Iran embassy siege or of the films?

The story is that I used to like to come to Britain with all my family. We love the parks and flowers, green places we do not have in Sharjah. Every year I work hard to have some money to come for holidays here with my wife and two sons, but this year I come with my wife only because she is ill. We decided immediately to come to Britain to see a doctor. We would never spend our holiday money anywhere but Britain.

No wonder we were upset when we met the immigration officer at the airport. He was bad to us, he keep asking us questions for 30 minutes. We were very tired, the long flight the waiting and my wife ill but he must know how much money we have and where we come and where we go. My English is not quick and when I did not understand he said to me and I swear it 'We have enough ill people here to see –, you go back and stay with your camel.' He never use thank you or please. British are very famous for please and thank you.

On Tuesday May 6th me and my wife standing on Baker Street waiting to go to the hotel. We cannot find a taxi we wait for a bus and at 3:30 bus No. 30 came. We were in a queue and as we were going on the bus the conductor said no to us. He said you are rich Arabs take a taxi and the people behind us went on the bus. Two people saw this, I was upset, we walk and my wife ill. Why, what happened to the British we never treat people like this in home?

I am going home to be with my camel but we leave depressed and upset, my wife never come out from the hotel since Tuesday. Why, we never hate you, why you hate us? Please excuse my English.[28]

The situation soon worsened as the Libyan regime began to purge what Colonel Gaddafi famously described as the 'stray dogs in London'. In February 1980, newspapers reported a 'Libyan looking man' setting fire to a Park Lane Arabic bookshop that had been distributing *al-Jihad*, the publication of the Libyan Islamic opposition movement. In April 1980, two gunmen shot and killed Mohammed Mustafa Ramadan, a Libyan dissident and journalist, near the Central Mosque in Regent's Park. Days later, on 25 April, Mahmud Salem Nafa, a Libyan lawyer who had lived and worked in London for five years, was shot and killed at the Arab Legal Centre on Westbourne Grove. On 26 November Ahmed Mustafa, a Libyan student, was stabbed to death, allegedly by a 'Libyan hit squad'. After being missing for three days his body was found in a council flat in Manchester. In what seems to have been a reprisal attack, a firebomb exploded at the offices of Libyan Arab Airlines in Piccadilly on 28 December, but there were no injuries and little damage. The purge ruthlessly targeted any suspected opponents of Gaddafi's regime, however marginal the individual may have been. Eighteen-year-old Sanoussi Latiwish, a Libyan student living in London who was suspected of being in contact with the exiled opposition, disappeared in early April 1981; his decomposing body was found in suitcase in a field in Cambridge a month later.

At the same time that the Libyan purge was taking centre stage in the British press, other forms of political violence continued to occur around the settled community. On 3 June 1982 newspapers reported that 'an Arabic man' pulled a submachine gun out of a bag and fired at the Israeli ambassador as he left a party at the Dorchester Hotel. The four accused of his attempted murder had come to the UK in 1980/81 and registered as students. During their prosecution they were accused of being in contact with the military attaché at the Iraqi embassy, who was thought to have supplied the weapons for the assassination attempt. The incident was used by Israel as part of its *casus belli* for invading Lebanon in 1982.[29]

Beirut had traditionally been the publishing capital of the Arab world, however the Lebanese civil war, which began in 1975, and the 1982 Israeli invasion led a number of *Khaleeji* owned regional newspapers titles and publishers to relocate to London, which soon become the Arab world's most prolific and prestigious newspaper publishing centre. Indeed, London had not only become the home-from-home of *Khaleeji* elites and newspapers but also of exiled opposition movements from almost every Arab country who used the city as a refuge and a base for their activities and publications.

In the early hours of the 11 March 1984 an explosion occurred at a London newsstand selling Arabic newspapers on Queensway in Bayswater. A few minutes later a second bomb exploded at L'Auberge, a Mayfair nightclub owned by a Lebanese man and frequented by Arabs. Around 120 people were in the club at the time and 23 were injured in the ensuing fire. Shortly afterwards a third bomb was found and defused in a controlled explosion on Kensington Road. A fourth bomb exploded hours later at another newsstand on Queensway. On the same night two bombs exploded in the Whalley Range district of Manchester, where a number of Libyan families lived. The first was planted under the car of a Libyan exile while the second exploded in an apartment block and injured a Syrian couple and their child. Another bomb was found and defused the following evening at the Omar Khayyam nightclub on High Street Kensington.[30] The following day the Metropolitan Police provided armed guards to a number of key Libyan exile figures.[31] On 13 March a 44-year-old Libyan businessman Ali El-Giahour and three others were accused of the bombing spree in London. According to Anthony Ellison, Mr El-Giahour's solicitor at the time, he was well known in UK dissident circles and he was coerced into showing Gaddafi loyalists places where dissidents gathered and where the newspaper stands that sold anti-regime newspapers and periodicals were. El-Giahour was released on bail after spending time on remand at Brixton prison pending his trail, but four months later his decomposing body was found by police in an apartment in Marylebone with multiple shot wounds to the head.[32] A month later the ten-day Libyan embassy siege took place in which WPC Yvonne Fletcher was shot and killed. The string of incidents drew the small settled Libyan community into the fray as school children and teachers at the Libyan school on Glebe Street in Chelsea were searched by armed police.[33]

For the thousands of residents and settled immigrants from Arab states and their British-born and -raised children, there was no respite from the catalogue of incidents orchestrated by a small group of agents and militants who lived and operated within their midst. However it is the discursive move from specific regimes, national contexts and struggles to the portmanteau term 'Arabs' that has made such an enduring and effective association with political violence both possible and indiscriminate. Anti-Arab racism was becoming an increasingly common feature of Arab life in London as playwright Karim Al-Rawi outlined at a conference on anti-racism organised by the Greater London Council in 1984:

> The Arab, when stereotyped is often amorphous. He is rarely defined too specifically with regard to nationality. He is part of a semantic field that encompasses harem, barbarism and fanaticism. The Arab is always very different than the stereotype of the Egyptian, the Moroccan or the Yemeni. These national images have their own specific connotations. They are more concrete and more positive than the image of the word Arab. This word has literally become the equivalent of the term 'Nigger'. (Edmunds 1998; see also Jacobs-Huey 2006)

The 1985 'Hindawi affair' is an apt illustration of the way in which the most callous acts of political violence took place in and around settled Arab Londoners. Jordanian Nezar Hindawi had lived in London for five years; his life in London mirrored that of hundreds of other Arab migrants and settlers who arrived at the same time. He briefly held a job at the London-based *al-Arab* newspaper. But the similarity ended there. Whether willingly or under duress, Hindawi like El-Giahour acted as an informer for the Libyan People's Bureau in London supplying the names, addresses and car registration numbers of regime opponents. He was also allegedly involved with the Syrian intelligence service in London.

On 17 April 1985 he placed a 3lb bomb, allegedly prepared at the Syrian embassy, in his pregnant Irish girlfriend's luggage. The bomb was intended to detonate at 30,000 feet over Austria but was discovered in Ann Murphy's luggage at Heathrow airport where she was due to board an El Al flight to Tel Aviv. Shocked and appalled by her boyfriend's contempt for her life and that of their unborn child as well as the 375 passengers on board, Murphy quickly identified her boyfriend to the police, who subsequently 'searched areas of London popular with Middle Eastern people, but concentrated on Bayswater which has a large Arab community'.[34] Meanwhile Hindawi was allegedly collected by his Syrian embassy contacts and spent the night in a safe house. Fearing that he would be killed for the failed operation, Hindawi fled the safe house and took refuge in a hotel owned by a Jordanian man in Earls Court. The hotel owner knew Hindawi's brother Mahmud, who worked for the Qatari Embassy's medical attaché and managed to persuade his brother Nezar to give himself up.

The Libyan embassy siege in which WPC Yvonne Fletcher died and the callousness of the Hindawi affair caused attitudes towards Arabs in Britain to hit an all-time low. In January 1986 *The Sun* newspaper ran a headline, 'Arab Pig Sneaks Back In', in response to news that a Libyan with a British wife and children, who had been deported in the wake of the embassy siege in 1984, had returned to live in Britain. Dr Adnan El-Amad, director of the Arab League Office in London, attempted to bring a prosecution against *The Sun* newspaper on the grounds that the headline was incitement to racial hatred, but the prosecution was blocked by the Attorney General who described the headline as 'intemperate, abusive and insulting, but not racist'. *The Sun* responded to the news by publishing a cartoon with the caption: 'Trouble, Now the Pigs Object to Being Called Arabs'.[35]

Political violence in and around settled Arabs in Britain not only set the terms of how they were to be represented in the British press but equally it informed attitudes towards their compatriots and other Arab nationals with whom they shared workplaces, schools, mosques, churches and social spaces. Ghazi, one of my interviewees, who was born in Tripoli (Libya) and raised in London during the 1980s, described how the purge of Libyan dissidents in London, and the tensions of Arab politics more broadly, affected his day-to-day life and his relations with other Libyans and Arabs.

> I remember at the time that our parents were quite careful about who we mixed with, particularly if they were Libyan. The community was relatively small and people knew each other, or of each other. Those who were close to or part of the regime were known and we were only allowed to mix with families who our parents thought were safe, those closest to us. Anyone else was treated with a degree of suspicion, and they would be treated that way until proved otherwise.
>
> We were effectively told to stay away from other Libyans as much as possible. Libyan students who were here on grants were expected to write reports about their fellow students and the violence kind of spoke for itself. At the time of the shooting in Regent's Park we lived just down the road, in St John's Wood, and I remember hearing the shots

and a bullet hit our car, the police took the car away to test the ballistics and stuff like that. I mean sometimes we used to just try and hide that we were Libyan, not that we were not proud to be Libyan, even after I got my British passport I always say I am Libyan; but it was a difficult period and unlike other locations, like Rome or Germany, where the regime had activists actively campaigning for Gaddafi, London was the base of the opposition movements.

I remember right after the embassy siege that Gaddafi made a speech calling the opposition movement the 'Stray dogs in London'. The whole environment was tense and we did whatever possible to avoid crossing paths with anything that might draw us into politics. But it wasn't only Libyans. I remember there was a Syrian school friend whose father was assassinated here in London, and my mother wouldn't allow us to go to Queensway and Edgware Road; of course we went anyway, that's where everyone was hanging out. They even wanted us not to invite him to birthday parties and get togethers in case there was more to come, of course that was impossible.

It was the same with some of my Iraqi friends, and all the INC [Iraqi National Congress] families would not invite children from families that were considered to be Ba'athists and vice versa, and for those who were not rich enough to be part of the political establishment. With some of my Iraqi friends their parents would tell them specifically which families should not be invited together at parties and celebrations, because they didn't want any trouble. In a way Arab politics played quite a regular role in our childhood and we knew it.

Other British-born or -raised Arabs from different nationalities had a similar awareness and experience of the consequences of Arab politics at a young age. Ayham's Iraqi parents were studying in Britain on (Iraqi) government scholarships in the early 1980s and were sometimes left with no choice but to take part in government-orchestrated and -sponsored activities during the Iran-Iraq war.

My parents weren't really politically involved but one way or another you had to be at the time. I mean they weren't activists or anything like that, but you had to be pro-government, you couldn't be part of the opposition. Having said that though, up until the end of the kind of PhD period, it did become fierce; you had to be more vocal and more pro-active … things like spraying graffiti on the walls with anti-Iranian slogans, things like that. My dad, I think he did it once and then he refused to do it after that.

It wasn't anything they wanted to do – quite the opposite. You had direct requests from particular individuals, I'm not going to name them – but he [Father] had to. He did it once and he hated himself for it. I remember once they had like an Iraqi national day party and the embassy had invited all the Iraqis to a big hall in Cardiff, and all families and parents and whatever – and what happened was they sealed off the hall and a guy came in and started shouting that all the women and children stay inside and lock all the doors, don't open the doors whatever happens, and then he called out all the men – I remember my dad running outside – and apparently there were three vans full of Iranians with baseball bats. I remember actually a huge fight broke out and my dad actually broke his ankle in it and a lot of damage was done on that day.

It was crazy back then ... after that incident my dad completely withdrew himself from any Iraqi involvement – politically especially, and as a result they stopped funding him. He funded the last couple of years of his research out of his own pocket by doing extra work on the side, extra lab work and any savings we had were used to finish the PhD – that's why my mum left early, 'cause we couldn't afford to stay here with him so she took us back to Iraq even though it was 1987 and the war was still going on. So, yeah, we kind of knew about all this stuff even though we were just like little kids! It has been, it's been a big factor in our lives.

On 22 July 1987 Naji al-Ali was shot in the head outside the office of the London-based Kuwaiti newspaper *al-Qabas* on Ives Street in Chelsea. Al-Ali had drawn thousands of cartoons in which he lampooned Arab, Israeli and western governments in equal measure and was reported to have received hundreds of death threats in response to his work. His murder appears to have tragically punctuated twelve years of intense political rivalry and murder in London, allegedly orchestrated by the Syrian, Libyan and Iraqi embassies along with movements like the PFLP and Abu Nidal. With the stereotypes of Arabs as violent and undeservedly wealthy well in place by the early 1990s, a sea change in Arab migration to Britain was about to take place.

War and the Making of British Arabs

Britain was a principal belligerent in both the 1991 and 2003 Gulf Wars, both of which led to a dramatic growth in the scale of migration from

Arab states to Britain and a change of its character. In the eight years between 1992 and 2000, 10,398 Iraqi nationals were granted British citizenship, almost double the number that had officially settled in Britain over the preceding 30 years. Up to the mid 1990s, Iraqi migration to Britain had mostly been a matter of student settlers and members of the exiled political opposition. Even though the decade-long Iran-Iraq war had claimed the lives of up to half a million Iraqis and a million Iranians, the conflict did not trigger migration to Britain on the scale of the 1991 Gulf War and the subsequent 'Oil for Food' sanctions regime. The number of Iraqis settling or obtaining British citizenship increased rapidly towards the end of the UN-sponsored sanctions regime and the build-up to the 2003 US/UK invasion which wreaked physical, institutional and economic ruin upon Iraq. In 2003 alone, over 14,500 Iraqi asylum applications were received, with almost 50 per cent of applicants successfully gaining refugee status or indefinite leave to remain. Iraqi migration stemming from the 1991 Gulf War and the 2003 US/UK invasion bought with it a marked change in ethnic and sectarian identifications of Iraqis in Britain, with an unprecedented increase in the number of Iraqi Shi'as, Christians and Kurds migrating to Britain.

A 2005 Greater London Authority study of the number of people 'born in the Arab world living in London' (based on the 2001 census) points to an increase of 240 per cent in the size of that group in comparison to its 1981 size (Finella 2005). The make-up of the group had also changed significantly over this period. While in 1981 Egyptian Londoners were the largest group, migration from Egypt and settlement in London was not significant between 1981 and 2001, with the number of 'Egyptian-born' Londoners actually falling by over 5 per cent. In contrast, the number of 'Algerian-born' and 'Middle East-born'[36] Londoners increased by 87 per cent and 344 per cent respectively over the same period. Although the growth in the Middle East-born group is largely attributable to Iraqi migration, it was also fuelled by an increase in the number of Lebanese, Palestinian, Syrian and Jordanian migrants, many of whom had lived and worked in Iraq, Kuwait and Saudi Arabia up to 1991 but were expelled or displaced as a result of the war.

The growth in the number of Algerians living in London, which has never been an obvious destination for Algerian emigration, is almost entirely attributable to the civil war that gripped the country during the 1990s (see Martínez 2000).[37] Between 1997 and 2004, over 7,500 Algerians applied for asylum in Britain with only 17.5 per cent being granted asylum or leave to remain. Young Algerian men made up the bulk of migrants and refugees and a large proportion went on to gain citizenship through marriage to British citizens.[38] Similarly the collapse of the Somali state in the early 1990s led to an unprecedented influx of Somali refugees and asylum seekers to the UK.

It is important to remember that a significant proportion of Iraqi, Somali, Sudanese and Algerian citizens do not consider themselves to be Arabs and in many cases are not Arabic speakers. The emergence of independent Arab nation-states in the twentieth century saw the emergence of an Arab state system in which royalist and republican regimes alike staked their claim to the Arabness of their nations. A commitment to the Arabic language and the 'Arab *Ummah*' (Nation) became standard characteristics of constitutions. It was not until January 1956 that Egypt formally became an 'Arab nation'. As Tibi notes 'however natural such a declaration may appear today, it was certainly revolutionary at the time' (1981:182). Some found themselves living in nominally Arab states, such as ethnic Kabilys, Amaziqs or Berbers from Algeria and Morocco, Dinka-speaking people of southern Sudan, Assyrians and Kurds in Iraq and Syria, or Maronites in Lebanon, many of whom continue to contest the imposition of what they see as a hegemonic Arab identity and 'Arabisation' policies undertaken in many of these states (see Hourani 1947; McDowall 1992; Tapper and O'Shea 1992; Jawad 2005).

The patterns of migration from Arab states to Britain established during the 1960s and 1970s, which were principally based on a small flow of labour migrants and student settlers, were dramatically altered by conflict in the Middle East and North Africa from 1990 onwards, after which the failure of national and regional state systems became the overwhelming cause of migration to Britain.[39]

Migration, Ethnic Counting and the Racialisation of 'Arabness'

Migration patterns from the Arab world to Britain have been under-researched. Attempts have been made to quantify individual national communities (e.g. Yemeni, Egyptian or Iraqi), however historically attempts to investigate 'Arab' migration to Britain have pointed to the absence of the category 'Arab' from ethnic monitoring data as an obstacle (see Halliday 1992; Al-Rasheed 1991, 1992, 1994, 1996; Nagel 2001, 2002a, 2002b, 2005; Karmi 1991, 1994, 1997, 2005; Nagel and Staeheli 2008a, 2008b). While initially it may appear that there is simply no official data on 'Arabs' it is more accurate to say there have been a number of instances where data have been collected but that statistics are highly fragmented, creating problems of consistency, comparability and availability. For example the Labour Force Survey collected data on the 'Arab' ethnic group between 1979 and 1991, yet the 1991 census, in which the ethnicity question first appeared, did not enumerate Arabs separately in its published data.

Furthermore, from 1992 onwards the Labour Force Survey stopped enumerating Arabs separately and the group was subsequently included in the 'Other ethnic group' category. It is often not clear why ethnic and geographical categories have been changed. The data collection exercises of different agencies have not always been 'joined up' and changes in the way data are presented are common from one exercise to another. Prior to the release of the 2011 census data in October 2013 I relied on Home Office 'citizenship and naturalisation' and 'asylum statistics'. Between 1962 and 2010 Home Office immigration and naturalisation statistics record 254,000 people holding an Arab nationality as having gained British citizenship. The largest national groups among migrants from Arab states in Britain are Iraqis (32 per cent), Moroccans (10.3 per cent), Sudanese and Algerians (both 9 per cent) and Egyptian and Lebanese (both 8.8 per cent).[40]

It is possible to identify three phases of migration and settlement from Arab states to Britain. The first begins with the arrival of a small number of merchant families from Syria and Morocco who established themselves in the Midlands in the mid-nineteenth century to benefit from the burgeoning textile industry. Towards the end of the nineteenth century Yemenis and Somalis arrived in London as dock workers in the Merchant Navy, which eventually led to the establishment of Yemeni communities in a number of industrial and port towns in Britain such as Sheffield, South Shields and Cardiff (see Halliday 1992; Lawless 1995; Al-Rasheed 1996; McGown 1999). From the turn of the twentieth century up to the late 1950s relatively small numbers of students and diplomats were drawn to London by the dynamics of colonialism and educational modernisation.

The arrival of economic migrants and political exiles in larger numbers during the 1960s and 1970s characterises the second phase. The available data suggests that most Arab citizens working and residing in Britain did not take up British citizenship even when they became entitled to it. It was not until the mid 1980s that Arabs living in London long term began to apply for naturalisation, because of the passing of the British Nationality Act (1983). The fourth and final phase takes place between 1990 and the present, which has seen the highest volume of migration and settlement of citizens of Arab states in Britain, largely as a result of civil war and conflict.

Based on (actual) volume, Arab migration to Britain should be considered a relatively recent phenomenon. Ethnicity data from the 2011 UK census enumerated the category Arab separately for the first time and recorded 230,600 people as having identified themselves as ethnically 'Arab' in England and Wales. This makes 'Arabs' the second smallest ethnic group in England and Wales, where they constitute just 0.4 per cent of approximately 56.1 million respondents. Despite the centrality of London to the Arab world and Arab migration, in inner and outer London the picture is equally modest, with those identifying as Arabs making up 1.3 per cent of the city's population or 106,020 people (ONS 2012; see Table 1.1)

Table 1.1   2011 Census: Arab ethnic group in England and Wales

Area	Total persons
North East	5,850
North West	24,528
Yorkshire and The Humber	21,340
East Midlands	9,746
West Midlands	18,079
East	10,367
South East	19,363
London	106,020
Inner London	50,821
Outer London	55,199
South West	5,692
England Total	*220,985*
Wales Total	*9,615*
England & Wales Total	*230,600*

Source: Adapted from Table KS201EW (ONS, 2012).

While these figures help to give a reasonably accurate idea of the scale and distribution of those who self-identify as Arabs in Britain, they only partially account for the ways in which British-born Arabs, as well as those born in the Arab world, have negotiated the 'ethnic origin' question in ethnic monitoring exercises prior to the inclusion of an 'Arab' category in the 2011 census. Caroline Nagel has produced the most sustained research on Arabs in London, reflecting similar concerns over ethnic recognition by the state to Madawi Al-Rasheed. Nagel has argued that Arabs are 'hidden' to British multiculturalism because of the enduring influence of the race relations paradigm, suggesting that Arabs in Britain were a 'White minority' (2001, 2002a). In contrast Yuval-Davis and Silverman (1999: 10) have suggested that they were sometimes included in the political category of Black. The divergence of these readings points to the ethnic and racial diversity of Arabs and the difficulties involved in trying to fit 'Arab' into the racial and colour-based conception of difference prevalent in Britain.

Al-Rasheed has argued that the 'ethnic origin' question is often confusing to people from the Arab world, as they are not White, Black or Asian in the way that these labels are understood in Britain. In her research on Arab demographics before the 2011 census, Al-Rasheed (1996) concludes that the majority of Arab migrants would record themselves as 'White', transposing conceptions of colour from their country of origin, citing a kind of misunderstanding among Arab migrants of the situated meaning of race, ethnicity and colour in Britain. I would argue that an equally important explanation is that self-identification as 'white' is not the result of misunderstanding at all but an acute appreciation of racial hierarchies in a particular context and their implications for access to resources. As Ignatiev (1995) demonstrates in relation to the Irish and Brodkin (2009) in relation to Jews in the United States, the adoption or incorporation of groups into 'whiteness' is often the result of the interplay of racial hierarchies and the political economy of exploitation. The allure of structures of whiteness afflicts middle-class and working-class migrants so that, while acknowledging their own racial and class subordination, moral, class and racial others are simultaneously constructed (see Bhatt 2003; Dhingra 2003; Ho 2003; Mitra 2008). I would argue that some Arab migrants to Britain may have sought to distance themselves from 'Black', 'Asian' and, where it was applied, 'Arab' categories in ethnic monitoring exercises, seeking instead to be counted among other 'white ethnics' such as Italians, Greeks, Cypriots, Turks and Spanish, possibly coveting what they consider to be a more palatable Mediterraneanism.

Al-Rasheed (1991,1996) has argued that, in contrast to their migrant parents, when confronted with the 'ethnic origin' question, many 'second-generation' Arabs select the 'Other-other' category, a point I was able to corroborate with data from the ONS Longitudinal Survey where 66 per cent of people who identified as Arab and were born in England recorded themselves under the 'Any other ethnic group' category while 15 per cent used the 'White' ethnic category, with a further 10 per cent describing themselves as ethnically 'Asian'. It is likely that, despite the inclusion of the ethnic category 'Arab' in the census, a significant proportion of those who identify with the Arab world will continue to identify with a number of other racial and geographic categorical labels. As Skellington and Morris (1996) note, ethnic monitoring and ethnically themed research into education and crime met with considerable resistance from so-called 'ethnic minorities' in the late 1970s and early 1980s. This early reluctance to identify ethnically for the purposes of governmentality suggests that people perceptively realised that the correlation of socio-economic status and educational attainment with race could only serve to further stigmatise them (see McDermott 1987). Racialised statistics are symptomatic of a broader racialisation of society. The way in which the category 'Arab' has been incorporated into the race relations paradigm and multiculturalism in Britain points to a process of 'racialisation' whereby a fluid and contested set of identifications and fragmented migrations from the Middle East and North Africa have hardened under the portmanteau term 'Arab', no doubt satisfying the aspirations and concerns of those most committed to seeing people through the logic of 'ethnonormativity' (see Murji and Solomos 2004).

Making and Unmaking 'Arab London'

As Keith (2005: 96) argues, comprehending the changing face of the cosmopolitan metropolis is partly a process of reconciling the way in which institutions at the heart of regimes of governmentality figure the racial imagination. The pervasive logic of ethnonormativity as a set of cultural values and beliefs, institutionalised by the state and lived by people, transfigures the landscape of the city into a patchwork of racialised and classed enclaves. The way in which ethnicity, race and class come to mark the city landscape has become a consistent theme in Urban Anthropology (see Hannerz 1969, 1983; Hirsch 1983; Wacquant and Wilson 1989; Anderson 1992; Massey and Denton 1993; Wacquant 1993, 1994, 1995; Portes and Stepick 1993; Goode and Schneider 1994; Gmelch and Zenner 1996; Low 1996, 1999; Hartigan 1999; Low and Lawrence-Zuñiga 2003; Breunlin and Regis 2006). Human geography has also made significant contributions to the way we understand the interaction and intersection of race, gender and class in cities (see Kobayashi 1994, 2000, 2008; Kobayashi and Peake 1994; Dwyer and Jones 2000; Pulido 2000; Berry and Henderson 2002; Mahtani 2006, 2014; McKittrick and Woods 2007; Johnston et al. 2007; Dwyer 2008; Brooke and Samura 2011).

In as much as race and class become structuring forces that mark the city landscape, Arab migrants and settlers in London have, like most other communities ended up seeing London in part through an ethnic lens where there are areas seen as 'too White', 'too Black' or 'too Asian'. On the whole Arabs seem to have avoided East London and South London and have settled mainly in central, western and north-western parts of the city. The highest concentration of Arabs exists in Westminster, Kensington and Chelsea and Hammersmith and Fulham in inner London; and in the boroughs of Brent, Ealing and Barnet in outer London. The most visible densities occur in an area stretching westwards from Camden through the northern wards of the Royal Boroughs of Westminster and Kensington and Chelsea, which have the highest density of people born in the Arab world and living in London. There is also a relatively contiguous band from the Borough of Hammersmith and Fulham towards the Boroughs of Ealing, Hounslow and Brent. This band of settlement corresponds quite well to the area between the A41 (heading north-west) and the A316 (heading west/south-west) and is particularly concentrated along the western corridors of London close to the A4 and A40.

In inner London, Edgware Road has long been seen as the centre of Arab life. It is perhaps better described as the road around which Gulf tourism has evolved, with its restaurants, *Shisha* cafes and, in its early days, the Victoria Casino. The flats and townhouses of *Khaleeji* elites are to be found north and south of Hyde Park and Kensington Park, with different areas, such as Mayfair, Knightsbridge and South Kensington, attracting different levels of affluence from the Edgware Road, Queensway and Bayswater. The Royal Boroughs of Westminster and Kensington and Chelsea also contain a substantial volume of council housing in which the bulk of inner London's 'Arab' residents live. North and west from Church Street market there is a concentration of council housing taking in Maida Vale and Royal Oak and parts of Kilburn. Just south of this area is Golborne (Ward) in North Kensington and Westbourne Park (North Westminster), areas best known for their concentration of Moroccan migrants. This zone of residential council housing gives way to suburban housing as you travel north and west between the Harrow Road, Queen's Park and Brondesbury, which appear to have mix of Iraqis, Lebanese, Egyptians and other Middle Eastern residents. A large number of Arab families also live in the far south of Kensington and Chelsea, in the area around the World's End estate and North End Road in Hammersmith and Fulham.

Further west, towards outer London, businesses and services are a good indication of the settled Arab population. Starting from Shepherd's Bush along the Uxbridge Road all the way to Ealing Common there is a dense clustering of Arab-oriented retailers, wholesalers, market stands, cafes and restaurants. Crossing the A40 at North Acton, Lebanese bakeries, cafes and food importers pepper this industrialised area that eventually joins up with the Harrow Road at Willesden.

In Acton, Arab families began to settle around the King Fahad Academy in the 1980s. As Arab services took hold in the area the Arab population grew considerably, settling in West Acton and Park Royal as well as pockets in and around West Ealing, Hanwell and Greenford. Along the A4, around the town of Hounslow, there is a fragmented Arab community living in the western half of the borough, and in the area around Feltham there is a significant concentration of Algerian migrants. Although Arabs seem to be concentrated in West London, areas like Finsbury Park in the north of the city, with its large Turkish, Greek and Cypriot communities, also contains large numbers of Algerians. Similarly, many Iraqis have settled in the area south of Richmond Park and in the northern neighbourhoods of Kingston-upon-Thames. As the ethnographic chapters that follow will go on to suggest, Arab London begins to have meaning as a place based on this type of ethnic zoning; but, equally, the practices of young people show that even within what are considered to be Arab areas, the time of year, nationality, gender and class continually add layers of meaning that mark the way in which these areas, spaces and places are understood and used.

While on the one hand the archive and ethnic counting by the state offer a better understanding of 'Arab' migration patterns as a whole, they equally unravel the imputed straightforwardness of Arabness. What Arabs have in common is a contemporary political history, a history that is replete with passing moments of exhilaration that are decidedly overshadowed by tragedy, loss, displacement, occupation, war and tyranny. The struggles of their respective homelands have brought Arabs in London together, but equally they have driven them apart through fear and suspicion. From the first records of the Arab student population in the early twentieth century, Arabs living in Britain seem to have been defined by Arab and Middle Eastern politics, rarely if ever being considered or considering themselves a 'settled community'. Although the acts and incidents chronicled here are connected to tangible individuals and regimes, the pervasive power of discourse makes them coherent under the sign 'Arabs', extending the application of these meanings to all those who identify with Arabness. As a result, Arabs have inevitably become stigmatised and reviled for their politics, their violence, their visibility and, in some cases, their obtuse taste for consumer spending. The significations that these incidents and stories retain their traces in contemporary social arrangements, experiences and discourses, and are to some extent a history of the present.

It is no wonder that I could find no coherent 'Arab community' in Britain, for the meanings that have been generated around Arabness in Britain alone over the last century are enough of a disincentive. These meanings eventually provide a knowable object, 'the Arabs' who are wealthy and exotic, dissimilar and suspicious, dangerous, violent and homicidal. The language of war, hijacking, terrorism, freedom fighters, hostages, sieges, plots, militancy and hit squads have become important in the repertoire of terms associated with Arabs. Jim White's expedition into Queensway in 1992 for *The Independent* demonstrates the way in which the evaluative accent attached to 'the Arabs' can be internalised and reiterated by young Arabs growing up in London. 'Five lads were sitting on high bar stools, chatting. They wouldn't give their names. "We're terrorists," one of them mocked. "No publicity." "Call us all Mohammed," said another, "the five Mohammeds, five guys named Mo."'[41]

Discourses are pervasive, inter-textual and powerful; meanings are encrypted into language so that, whether or not young Arabs are actually aware of the details of incidents in the way that Ghazi and Ayham were through direct experience, they are acutely aware that Arabs are considered to be (among other things) terrorists and rich, as part of the accumulated layers of meaning around the term of their 'ethnic' identification. These events, therefore, represent actual experiences for some while for others they are experienced through the pervasive power of discourse.

2

Learning to be Arab: Growing Up in London

In this chapter I consider how narratives of school reveal the incidents, settings and discourses that lead young people to recite situated versions of an 'Arab manhood' and an 'Arab womanhood' in London. I begin with narratives of the 1991 Gulf War as recollected by Arab Londoners who were at school during the conflict. These narratives reveal the phenomenological substance that connects local experiences and international conflict, and, in equal measure, counter-exposes the ways in which hegemonic masculinity and 'ethnicised masculinity' are (re)cited in situ. In the second part of the chapter I turn to narratives of becoming an Arab woman and consider how these reveal the modalities of being 'raced' and 'gendered' through specific incidents, acts and settings. The narratives of learning to be an Arab woman at school reveal Arabs in hiding and *passing for* other ethnicities, 'secret' lives based on false alibis, the demands of different forms of heterosexuality, and the ways in which Arabness can be experienced as both redemption and crisis. I argue that the accounts that young people relate suggest that becoming an 'Arab man' or 'Arab woman' is part of a project of cultural survival and social intelligibility, and that Arab identity is not an essence or a cause of behaviours and dispositions but an instrumental reaction to being hailed and subjected by social institutions, hegemonic gendered norms, national and international politics and media representations.

Narratives draw upon memories, but they are framed in the present and the narrators' sense of themselves now. Narratives are structured, inherently social and intended for public consumption (Gardner 2002: 31–32). They are stories that people tell in different ways to different audiences and in reference to different social contexts; they always seek to achieve a particular end. Listening is therefore far from a passive act, the listener affects the narrative itself and the different roles and plots that are emphasised or hidden (2002: 33). The ways in which the past is recollected, and 'self' and 'other' constructed, relies on a complex patchwork of memories of the everyday. It is not always the spectacular that defines our sense of self and the milestones over a life course; sometimes it is the passing incidents – conversations at the family dining table, the playground fight, a malicious remark from a peer or a teacher, the thoughts and feelings one has on the walk home from school, the testing and stretching of boundaries at gatherings of friends and family, news headlines of war, overheard telephone conversations with relatives. The stories that follow bridge the gap between the spectacular and the banal, drawing them together in the narratives of growing up in London and learning to be Arab.

I had not anticipated that the Gulf War would have such a prominent place in the narratives of growing up in London or in the process of learning to be Arab, yet time and again the war was a recurring feature of people's recollections of early adolescence. The Gulf War did not simply happen in a distant, dusty and forbidding Middle East, it was also played out in the daily lives of young people in London. These informal histories are a vital part of the project of understanding 'critical events from a pluralist perspective, so that we hesitate to apply closure too early' and ensure that the right to name and the right to organise memory and history are not monopolised (Das, 1995: 209–10).

The 1991 Gulf War is a point of convergence in the diasporic experience of living with Arabness in 'the West'. In 1991 the American-Arab Anti-Discrimination Committee set up a call centre to record the large number of attacks against Arabs in the United States (Peters 1992). On the other side of the Atlantic the tenuous position of Arabs in French society was again played out, this time as a result of conflict in the Arabian Gulf (see Silverstein 2004). The French press eagerly sensationalised the threat of a terrorist attack by French 'Arabs' and the 'Arab threat within France'. Michel Poniatowski the French Minister of Interior even suggested the 'mass expulsion of immigrants (read Arabs)' (Gross et al. 1996: 125). According to Silverman and Yuval-Davis (1999: 10) the postcolonial syntax – '*Maghrébins*', '*Communauté Maghrébine*', '*Beurs*', '*seconde/deuxième génération*', '*jeunes issus de l'immigration Musulman*' or '*Communauté Musulmane*' – was suspended as the terms '*jeunes Arabes Français*' or '*Communautés Arabes*' came into use, capturing a particular kind of 'other' and a particular kind of threat. Most literature on the Arab diaspora has paid little attention to the way in which Arabs living in Britain were affected by the war.

The War at School

> What do Hiroshima and Baghdad have in common? … Nothing yet.
> ('Jim's Gulf Joke Goes Down a Bomb'. *The Sun*, 4 January 1991)

Two days before the Iraqi invasion of Kuwait, a 31-year-old Syrian man who lived on Edgware Road, took 150 people hostage for 10 hours at the Tokyo Joe nightclub, a well-known Arab haunt in Piccadilly. Among the hostages were members of the Kuwaiti and Emirati ruling families.[1] The incident sat well with tabloid coverage at the time, which fuelled widespread fears that there were hundreds of Arab and Muslim would-be terrorists in Britain. 'WE SHOULD ROUND UP EVERY ONE OF THE IRAQIS NOW IN BRITAIN: BEFORE THEY ATTACK US ON OUR OWN DOORSTEP' read the headline of the *Daily Star* on 20 August 1990. The headline was not that far-fetched; between September 1990 and March 1991 over 160 Iraqis and Palestinians were deported from Britain. A 'security round-up' on 18 January 1991 led to over 150 'Arabs' being interned without trial.[2] The 'Arab detainees,' as they came to be known, were questioned by a panel known as the 'Three Wise Men'. They were refused the right to know why they had been identified as a potential threat or even which organisations they were alleged to have links with. The panel asked the detainees questions about the Iraqi Ba'ath party and the London-based General Union of Arab Students; they were also questioned about their attitudes towards Israel and America.[3] The detainees, some of whom had lived in Britain for over 20 years were also denied legal representation during their interrogation and the Court of Appeal refused to intervene to bring their detention under normal judicial standards. It was only the concerted effort of a handful of MPs that kept the plight of the detainees in the news and eventually led to their detention being subject to due process.

Newspaper reports in Britain suggested that Arab students were feeling the effect of the conflict in their day-to-day lives. At the School of Oriental and African Studies (SOAS) a Palestinian student reported 'I've friends who have been called "dirty Arab", and been told to "get out".' An Egyptian student at SOAS reported that the abuse she encountered was the worst in the two years she had been in England: 'On the tube a guy looked at me and said "Iraqi bastard", "bloody Arab".' The anxiety among the Arab student population in London was heightened by news that a Lebanese PhD student had been among those arrested in the 18 January round-up.[4]

Many of the Iraqis I interviewed had only been in Britain for a few years when the crisis erupted. With their sense of 'belonging' firmly invested in Iraqi nationalism and kinship ties, they were presented with a particularly difficult set of circumstances and emotions to navigate. The narratives of young men during this period are marked by the experience of violence and the masculine bravado of fighting. Masculinity and violence were salient features of the 1991 Gulf War as a whole. Linville (2000) and Straw (2008) argue that the Gulf War was an opportunity in both cultural and political terms to *re-masculinise* America after the defeat of Vietnam. By extension, the war was also an occasion for America and Britain to re-articulate their respective global roles and 'national identities' in the early days of a post-Cold War world. Simultaneously the values at the heart of the notion of collective Arabness – solidarity, unity, kinship and honour – were once again unravelled by the war. Between and from these seemingly oppositional recitations of 'Arabness' and 'Britishness' in the international state system came the situated recitations and survival strategies of British-born and -raised Arabs.

Learning to be an Arab Man

Haitham is half-Iraqi, half-Syrian. Born in Kuwait, he lived in Abu Dhabi with his parents until he was sent to boarding school in a London suburb in 1987. Haitham appeared to lean more towards his mother's Syrian culture: his accent, the food and aesthetic he loved were distinctly *Shammi*.[5] He often spoke about Damascus, its historical sites, shops and cuisine. Iraq was a distant memory; he had never lived there and had rarely visited, nonetheless his attachment to it remained important, perhaps coming to the fore because of his estrangement from it and not least during times of conflict. He was about to start his second year of school in London when the invasion of Kuwait took place.

> I had a really rough year, I was homesick anyway but I also just got into loads of fights. I was really sensitive to what was being said and when you saw people reading *The Sun* and all the headlines – it was difficult, anything could send you off. Of course I was the only Arab in my year. I was lucky because there was another half-Iraqi half-English guy, a few years older, and he used to look out for me. He was well liked in his year and a good sportsman so people didn't mess with him. But I got beaten up so much, I was quite small and whenever someone said anything I just went for it. The worst thing was that we had to do CCM, which is

like military training at school, you choose a service and you do training, night exercises and everything. The officers were fine, they were very respectful apart from the odd jibe, but everyone gets that – but it was the other students they really had a field day with me. They said they were going to bomb my house and other rubbish 'Iraqi bastard', 'Arab pig' and stuff like that.

Media discourses in Britain around the war clearly had an effect on the way that Haitham's peers constructed him as the embodiment of 'the enemy' who should be defeated not only on the battlefield, but at school. His recent arrival would have made it easy for his peers to associate him with 'the enemy'. Panayi has argued that in times of conflict 'the length of residence of members of the group receives little consideration' (1993: 5). A common repertoire across narratives of the war at school and the experience of difference more broadly among 'Arab' schoolchildren at the time is that of being 'the only Arab' in the class or at school. A central feature of the repertoire is the arrival of other Arabs (friends or peers) who engender feelings of safety and solidarity and play a central role in resisting violence and bullying.

Ahmed had lived in Britain and Iraq intermittently while his parents completed their higher education. The family returned to Baghdad in 1988 only to be forced to leave two years later when the prospect of invasion loomed on the horizon. After almost a year living in Libya, the family decided to return to the UK, where Ahmed picks up his story:

When we got back to this country, life became difficult for me especially … I was much more aware of politics and living in hardship and, um, I missed having the luxuries of Iraq. But when you live in this country and then you start hearing racist comment and they start to bully and make fights just literally because I came from Iraq [sic]. It was 1992 and so it was still fresh after the war and a lot of kids used to make a point of saying, you are from Iraq and you are a Saddam loyalist and this and that and the other, to the point that I actually became a Saddam loyalist because I thought 'You know what, if you are already categorising me as a Saddam loyalist when in fact I left because of him well in that case I might as well become a Saddam loyalist and piss you off.' I used to go into school with pictures of Saddam stuck to my books and folders. I became very Iraq patriotic, anybody who would speak about Iraq I would have a fight with to the point to which I had two friends of mine, one Syrian, one Sudanese, and we were the only three Arabs in the whole school but we were the most feared three foreigners in that school 'cause like in Iraq we have fights every day, in England it's not the same so we were used to like getting beats.

Ramy: Tell me about your friends.

Ahmed: They were called Noor and Mohammed. Noor's dad was a political dissident from Syria and, uh, they were Christian, he wasn't even Muslim or anything, and he was a friend of the family and his son happened to be my age and in the same school so we made friends. Um, he'd adapted more to the English way of life rather than me 'cause he'd been here much longer. He didn't have that gap in Syria; he'd never been to Syria. He was born there and taken away when he was 2 years old, whereas for me that period in Iraq changed me, I became much more Arab and Iraqi, I realise that. The Sudanese guy, he was just hard core Sudanese, he'd only been in the country for five years so he was fresh.

Ramy: And how did you three communicate? In English or Arabic?

Ahmed: In Arabic and that was done on purpose to piss everybody off. It became a fight, literally a daily fight where, if somebody made fun of me or attacked me, the other two would automatically get themselves involved. I used to support them, they used to support me. By the end of the high school year we had built up such a reputation that people actually started to respect us, not because we were Arabs or foreign but because we were just really good at fighting. But it wasn't nice because you always felt threatened you always felt … that's when I felt I can never be part of this country. Sometimes it was verbal sometimes it was physical. As an example, sometimes they would just walk past and make a sound like a bomb being dropped. That used to make me go nuts! But really the war was …

It changed everything; I was more pro-Britain before the war. When I was in Iraq I couldn't wait to leave, but when I did and I came here and I saw this reaction, I couldn't believe it and I became much more patriotic. I realised that Iraq wasn't as bad as I thought it was and Britain wasn't as good as I thought it was. Unfortunately due to the situation I couldn't go back.

Like Haitham, in the shadow of the war Ahmed was bullied at school for being Iraqi and responded to verbal and physical abuse with violence. In both narratives other 'Arabs' are central to this coping strategy. Ahmed's narrative gives him the opportunity to recite a particular understanding of Arabness which is not contingent on being Muslim or being of a certain race, but based on a code of loyalty framed within discourses of masculine militancy and collective defence. Importantly, he is keen to stress that English schoolboys were not as hardened as Iraqi schoolboys, an allusion to the centrality of violence in the making of 'real authentic men'. Willis (1977) argues that although 'the lads' are a subordinated group, their values and actions must be understood in terms of their own culture rather than as merely reactive to domination. In this case, exclusion stemming from the circulation of war propaganda in British schools might be seen as an aggravating rather than a determining factor. As Ahmed is keen to point out, he and his friends gained the respect of others at school not because they were 'Arabs' but because of their ability to fight together. 'Solidaristic masculinity' and violence are sites of recognition and respect among adolescent males more broadly (O'Donnell and Sharpe 2000: 43). Alexander (2005) argues (following Keith 1993, 1995) that 'much violence in urban contexts has to be understood as instrumental, rational and everyday … and as part of a performance of masculine power and resistance that carries with it its own set of rules and expectations' (Alexander 2005: 200). Although these insights are important we must be careful not to discuss certain types of masculinity as if they were biological imperatives rather than a socially instituted regime (see Connell and Messerschmidt 2005). Nonetheless, masculinity here is given an 'ethnic' gloss so that notions of 'Arab' loyalty and solidarity during struggle or hardship, a central component and expectation of Arab fraternity, can be recited in the narrative. A theme that recurs in Ahmed's narrative as well as in subsequent accounts is the way in which the three friends use their shared Arabic language to invert and resist the way they were marginalised by their peers, and to fashion their own level of solidarity, so as to wrest control over the boundaries between themselves and others at school.

Ahmed's narrative makes a connection between his experience of discrimination in the early 1990s and his feelings of 'belonging' today. When Ahmed's family returned to Iraq in the mid 1980s, Ahmed's 'Englishness' had been an important marker at school in Baghdad where he was placed with other students whose English language was more developed than Arabic. But his sense of Englishness was challenged upon his return to Britain a few years later, in his opinion as a direct result of the media constructions of the war and one of its main protagonists Saddam Hussein. Paradoxically, even though Saddam's war-mongering and totalitarianism had caused the family's dislocation, Ahmed found himself cast as a 'Saddam loyalist'. Unable to escape this label, he felt he had no choice but to appropriate it.

The forms of ascription and self-identification that take place through everyday interactions at school are not solely about deciding what category a person belongs to but also about mapping a system of meaning onto them and 'their group'. The simulated sound of a falling bomb and similar taunts may be considered banter and an unavoidable part of youth interaction in the context of war. However, as Back points out 'the danger of racist banter is that it can easily turn into more serious insults and even pave the way for lasting ill-feeling' (1996: 90). In this case the banter was intimately connected to actual death and destruction wrought on a massive scale, and was intended to simulate and affirm that violence.

In a very different school setting Jamal, who was born in Egypt but raised in London from the age of three, narrates his experience of the war during his time at the King Fahad Academy in Ealing where over 1,500 Kuwaiti students arrived in September 1990 after becoming stranded in London as a result of the invasion. As would be expected from a Saudi Arabian institution, the school administration made every effort to welcome the Kuwaiti students and, among other things, distributed 'Free Kuwait' stickers and pamphlets to students and staff. However, relations between the Kuwaiti visitors and the overwhelmingly non-Gulf Arab student population of Iraqis, Egyptians, Palestinians and Syrians were strained, particularly by discourses about the war and who, and which countries, were acting like 'real Arab men'.

Jamal: The war was such a laugh! It sounds bad but it was exciting! There were bomb scares [at school] – sometimes we'd get called at home and told not to come in and a couple of times the school was just evacuated in the middle of the day. We would all stand outside while the fire brigade and the bomb squad drove through the gates with sirens and everything you know to check the buildings. I think some of the older boys might have phoned in a couple of those to get out of class – they couldn't do anything about it anyway. Every morning we had our bags searched at the gates for bombs, and they gave everyone an ID card that you had to have to get into the building. And then there was the Kuwaitis, it was like an invasion, suddenly it was like the school was full of them – no one told us about it – it just happened. The thing is most of our friends were Iraqi – we didn't have Kuwaitis before the war. Being a Kuwaiti was like a cuss anyway – we thought they were all gay. They were like the Jews of the Arabs, you know tight. Anyway we hated them and we loved Saddam. They were giving out these 'Free Kuwait' badges and no one at the school wore them! There were enough fights between us and the Kuwaitis! We would shout 'Saddam Saddam' in the playground, in the gym, wherever really [laughs]. The teachers hated it but it just didn't stop – we didn't do it that much in front of the Arabic teachers 'cause, you know – but in front of the English teachers and the Kuwaitis – all the time, until some of them just gave up saying anything. We didn't understand the politics of it all but we just knew that it was Iraq vs. Kuwait and that Saddam was standing up to America – and most of us were with the Iraqis 'cause they were our friends you know. When he bombed Israel – that was – we just loved it – he had the balls to do it and to stand up to the Americans, he was a hero.

Ramy: But how would you explain that to someone who might be horrified that you were a Saddam supporter, why did you take the Iraqi side instead of the Kuwaiti? I mean the rest of the country was in support of Kuwait's cause.

Jamal: Even the Arabic teachers, they had to show that they were with Kuwait but really I bet a lot of them supported Saddam. At home, when you heard people talking about it, they all didn't like the Kuwaitis or the *Khaleejis* that much, like they were different, not as educated, they just had money. And worst of all was like getting the Americans and the British to like fight for them … what a bunch of pussies, *khawalāt* [gay]. Arabs getting a British or American army to kill other Arabs. How can you justify that? Basically, no matter what, like the ultimate. We just thought, like, what is Kuwait? It's just this little place that used to be part of Iraq and the British just created it – they just didn't want Iraq to have more power. They were afraid of Saddam and that's … like at school, who would you rather support the Kuwaitis or Saddam? Saddam of course! We didn't think about who was right and who was wrong, it was a loyalty thing. We're Arabs and we're supposed to be one country, and look what he did to the Israelis – he stood up to them too.

Ramy: What about Egypt and Syria? They were fighting against Iraq too.

Jamal: Yeah, but that was different. No Egyptian or Syrian or whatever would really deep down inside support that. It did make me feel bad, it was a bit embarrassing, your own country is taking part in it. But that made me love Saddam even more because he was a man and we really thought he would win and bomb the Israelis and Americans.

As Jamal and Ahmed's accounts suggest, the figure of Saddam Hussein provided a ready-made model of masculinity and Weberian charismatic authority. In this case, a figure through whom others experience and project notions of ethnicised manhood. Jamal, Ahmed and Haitham's accounts suggest that in the narration of the war as an event, and male adolescence as an experience, there is a relationship between the idea of 'being Arab' and a set of masculine behaviours and expectations. While particular expressions of 'ethnic' or culturally specific masculinity should be taken into account, Mac an Ghaill (1994) argues that schools are one of the places where boys learn how to be male, where boys are implicitly socialised into adopting particular notions of masculinity. Boys learn that there are different ways of being a male, some more valued and prestigious than others, and perhaps none as powerful and attractive as the use of physical violence against peers, both male and female. On the other hand Jamal and Ahmed's reconstruction of the war as 'fun', through banter and masculine bravado, is, in another sense, a coping strategy. Jamal is reflective enough to recognise that his identification with Saddam was motivated primarily by his concerns over 'loyalty', showing solidarity with his friends and minimising the damage of the 'shame' of Egyptian involvement in a war against a 'brother country'. Choosing Saddam over the Kuwaitis made more sense in an environment where masculinity or, as he puts it, 'having balls', was highly valued. Both Jamal and Ahmed's accounts point to the importance of boundaries of inclusion and exclusion marked by masculinity, fighting, bravery and loyalty, which Jamal and Ahmed show to be as important among Arabs as they are between Arabs and non-Arabs at school.

Jamal's account contains what Les Back (1996) describes as 'race-gender othering' in relation to the visiting Kuwaiti students and *Khaleejis* (Gulf Arabs) more generally. Back suggests that while shared values and images of masculinity can break down some racial boundaries, race-gender othering simultaneously constructs feminised others who do not adhere to or reflect those idealised forms. Kuwait's inability to defend itself against the Iraqi invasion, and the decision by Gulf states to host and endorse the involvement of 'non-Arabs' to resolve what was seen by many as an 'Arab' dispute, are the main reasons on which race-gender othering is constructed. Thus, Kuwaitis, and by extension *Khaleejis* are constructed as disloyal, feminine and not 'real Arabs'; in other words, they embody a failed Arab masculinity.

Gendering Narratives and Arabs in Hiding

It is interesting to contrast these male narratives of the war at school with an account by Roula, who had been in Britain for two years when the Gulf crisis began. Her parents were active members of the Iraqi

Communist Party and left Iraq when Saddam Hussein came to power in 1979, settling in Algeria where Roula spent most of her childhood. When the Algerian authorities refused to renew her father's work permit, Roula's family was forced to migrate. Originally they had planned to migrate to Canada but were encouraged to consider coming to Britain by close family friends who had settled in London. Roula and her family stayed with their friends in a North London neighbourhood when they arrived in 1989, before moving to Hounslow where Roula joined the local school in Cranford.

Roula: I was quite happy there but actually it was the time of the first Gulf War so I actually lived in denial of being an Arab. No one asked so I used to, at the time I thought, ok, 'If I'm asked I'm not going to say I'm not Iraqi' but nobody really asked. When I was finally asked where I was from and I told them I was Iraqi, from that point on I was known as 'the dirty Arab' … it was one of the reasons we moved to Queensway about a year later, because it was more of an Arab area. That was an ugly ugly era. I was 'the bad guy'; I was part of the country that had just been invaded. We were good when the Iran-Iraq war was on because we were fighting 'the bad guys'. In Cranford the Asians and Whites were equally racist. There were only a handful, four or five Arabs, and I never knew they even existed, they kept it quiet. I felt like I was the only one. It wasn't harsh bullying because I was quite a popular kid, but it's when you feel even your friends are pulling away from you, that's when you get really depressed – when there's only two people left walking home with you instead of 15; or when there are boys picking up your skirt and saying 'you smelly Arab'. A lot of people got it worse, like that guy who we were staying with in North London, he used to get beaten up because they thought he was a 'Paki', but when they found out he was Iraqi during the war it got a lot worse. He still has a complex because of it; he actually got beaten up daily and he's a big guy who looks like he could defend himself, but you can't when there are like ten people all trying to beat you up. He definitely still has issues.

Ramy: So, what happened?

Roula: Well my Mum and Dad were working for *al-Sharq al-Awsat* [a London-based Arab newspaper] and my dad quit because he said, 'Ok I'm not working for a paper that says these things about my country.' They were one of the few Iraqis who remained against Saddam and said what he was doing was wrong. He [father] said this is a *la'uba* [a game]. How can we say it's wrong for the Americans to bomb us and invade us if that, if Iraq is doing that, invading another country? You know this is the man [Saddam] we ran away from. Lots of people were against him [Father]: they said 'How dare you say this, he [Saddam] has changed, he is anti-American, *Battal al-Arab ba'ad* [the Arab hero now]. And my parents still … Iraqis are so political that if their friends for 20 years changed their political views they would literally never speak to each other again, and that happened to a lot of Iraqis. Like half of our family friends, since then I don't know where they are, because the parents would have an argument over the war and that would be it. It was just a horrible time … my parents both got really depressed, it was a real period of uncertainty.

Like Haitham and Ahmed, Roula employs the repertoire of being the 'only Arab' at school. Roula also points to an additional survival strategy, namely hiding or *passing* for another ethnicity, in her case sometimes 'Mediterranean' and at other times 'Asian'. In numerous interviews the strategy of *passing* for 'Mediterranean', 'Asian' or 'White' was common. Situated ethnic hierarchies determine the racial and ethnic categories chosen for passing. Most interviewees who referred to acts of *passing* preferred 'Mediterranean' to 'Asian' because it was perceived to be closer to 'Arab' culture and implied a desirable accommodation of East and West, modernity and traditionalism, White-but-not-White, European but not Northern European. Although structures or degrees of whiteness still play a role in this type of selection, it is important to recognise that whiteness is not automatically preferred. It can be actively avoided for its own set of connotations. In many interviews, even those who could easily pass for 'White' would often speak disparagingly of 'indigenous' others as 'White people'.

It is notable that Roula felt she had to hide her Iraqi and Arab identification for fear of recrimination and, as she suggests, the handful of other Arabs at her school did the same. The strategies of hiding, concealing or *passing* affirm the power of discourse on two levels. First they suggest that the negative discourses around 'the Arabs' have social and physical consequences that can lead individuals to explore strategies like *passing* for cultural survival. Second, as with other narratives of *racial passing*, the ability to pass for another race or ethnicity is always qualified by the enunciation 'I am Black' or, in this case, 'I am Iraqi' or 'I am Arab'. I will take up the theme of passing and hiding in more detail in other accounts of 'learning to be an Arab woman'.

Roula's understanding of national and regional politics is heavily influenced by her parents' political orientation. Their decision not to be taken in by the rhetoric of pan-Arabism and pan-Islamism espoused by the Iraqi regime in crisis clearly had an impact on her political attitudes. The 'Saddam syndrome' seems to play a central role in the stories of all Iraqis, whether they supported or opposed him. Saddam dominated everyday conversation in Roula's home so much that the family fashioned a 'Saddam box': each time the despot's name was mentioned a fine would be imposed. Roula's narrative style corresponds closely with Sangster's assertion that women's narratives are embedded in family life and relationships that shape their view of the world (1994: 89 see also Cooke 1994). In comparison to Jamal, Ahmed and Haitham's narratives Roula's certainly appears to support this assertion. Yet there is no self-evident rule that 'gender' should be seen in terms of a 'gender identity'. A performative approach does not entail a rejection of the idea that there are narrative styles that correspond to particular gendered roles. It is the ontological status of gender roles that requires disruption. Gender has a 'truth effect' that is achieved through the collective performative accomplishments of social actors and audiences that lead to gender acquiring the semblance of a substance or 'identity' which appears to cause behaviour (Butler 1990). In this sense, Roula's narrative of living through the war is a testament to her immersion and interpolation of gendered discourses and the corresponding modes and styles of gendered narratives, what Butler might describe as 'subject effect'. Butler offers an insightful addition to the debate on the theoretical difficulties with personhood. In *Gender Trouble* she postulates that the 'coherence' and 'continuity' of 'the person' are not features of 'personhood' *per se* but instead are 'socially instituted and maintained norms of social intelligibility' (1990: 17).

My reading of Haitham, Jamal, Ahmed and Roula's narratives points to questions about how one is 'raced' and 'gendered' at the same time, and not simply to the existence of racial and gendered 'identities' as causes of behaviour. Rather than obscure the forces and processes that produce these narratives by resorting to an amorphous notion of causal gendered and racial 'identities', these narratives are better understood as products of situated repetition and (re)citation of hegemonic discursive norms between structures of subjection. In the following section I explore this assertion by looking at how support for Saddam Hussein among young 'Arab' men in London is not about 'Arab culture' or 'Arab identity' *per se* but about reciting more universal ideals around masculine heroism.

(Re)Citing Masculine Heroism

The 'Saddam syndrome' offers an opportunity to look more carefully at the notion of the (re)citation of hegemonic norms and the influence of structures of subjection. Why did Jamal and Ahmed and many others identify with Saddam? Ghada Karmi attempted to explain 'why there had been so much support for Saddam among Palestinians' to the Royal Anthropological Institute in April 1991. Her contribution offers a good entry point to this exploration (Benthall 1991: 17; see also Karmi et al. 1993). Karmi suggested that support for Saddam was partly the result of the Israeli physical and cultural oppression of Palestinians, which had made the gestures and rhetoric of Saddam attractive. However, she also stressed that the 'Saddam syndrome' was related to the nature of the 'Arab family'. Saddam was a:

> symptom, when he falls, another will come to power, and there are numerous Saddam clones elsewhere in the Middle East … the main problem is that a system of authority is reproduced in the Arab family. This is epitomised by the Arabic word *Rabb*, which means both 'God' and 'head of the family'. In these societies people are socialised from early childhood to admire strong masculine leaders. 'The West' has bought technology and the trappings of change, but has not changed the basic structures of authority [in the Arab world]. (Karmi, reported in Benthall 1991: 18)

Karmi's contribution (if accurately related) shows the continued prominence of debates on modernity and (typically) its incongruity with 'Arab culture'. In her estimation, European modernity has been imperfectly emulated in the Arab world, which has failed to adopt a corresponding social liberalism. Karmi was heavily criticised by other (non-Arab) members of the panel, who felt that her interpretation reproduced stereotypical approaches to the Arab family (Benthall 1991:19). I tend to agree with those criticisms. If we were to put a fixed and reified 'Arab culture' or 'Arab family' at the centre of our attempt to understand this phenomenon, we could argue that: 'in Arab culture' honour relates to masculinity and the social implications of manliness; that shame is experienced when manhood is undermined or when female virtue is publicly questioned (Gilmore 1987). Or that of particular importance to 'Arabs' is the notion of 'bravery' and 'militancy', which are qualities that traditionally have been celebrated among the pastoral Bedouin of northern Arabia and have a deep connection to a tradition of raiding and warfare (Meeker 1979). Also part of the Bedouin code of honour, specifically in the case of males, is the premium on freedom, steadfastness and autonomy, whether in the context of family relationships or political power (Abu-Lughod 1988: 45–71). According to the Ibn Khaldun's model of historical development outlined in his seminal work *al-Muqadimmah* (see Khaldun et al. 1969) the core values of the Bedouin ethos are at the centre of a struggle between the '*Badu*' (Bedouin), where these culture characteristics and values are prominent and intense, and the '*Haddar*' (urbanites), whose sedentary lifestyles are expected to dilute the concepts of honour, shame, generosity and chivalry, bravery and militancy (1969: 91). Thus we are eased into the notion of a culturally defective modernity.

What makes Karmi's 'culturist explanation' problematic is the implied particularity and integrity of these values across time, place and context, which amounts to a biological inevitability through the vehicle of 'culture'. Karmi implies that the solution to the values that lead to the valorisation of despotic and patriarchal tyrants is the imposition or adoption of a 'true' or loyal European modernity in the Arab world. Her assertion is extremely troubling; despotism and patriarchal tyranny (and their celebration by some) are hardly exclusive to the 'Arabs'. Why are 'bravery', 'militancy', 'loyalty' and 'autonomy' coded as 'Arab' or 'Bedouin' instead of a feature of masculinity and power *per se*? And to which project of cultural denunciation and subordination is such a designation applied? After all, these qualities and ideals are equally part of the idealised 'western' man, leader or soldier, and are conspicuously a part of British and American narratives of war, history and national identity. Is it then understandable, legitimate or unthreatening to be 'gung-ho', to have a 'stiff upper lip', or to be self-interested and daring if you are 'western'? Are these values and the devastating consequences they have had for life, on a global scale, the result of western family structures? The 'God' in the 'Arab family' is a feature of a more universal (yet variable) and consequential ideology – masculinity and patriarchy. The styles and aesthetics that give contextual meaning to reciting masculine heroism are thus performative aspects of a far more deep-seated structure, and should not be understood as determining features or become the building blocks of cultural incommensurability. Indeed, the way in which young Arabs recite a situated masculinity is replete with references, practices and ideas borrowed from multiple cultural contexts (see Racy 1996). The inter-textual nature of these imperfect recitations, and the centrality of discursive and corporeal power in their performative force, should draw our gaze away from 'multiple identities' and towards a processual understanding of the project of survival and social intelligibility within hetero-, ethno- and class normativity.

On 5 January 2007 the grainy images of Saddam Hussein's execution appeared on *YouTube*, just hours after the fact. I received an SMS from Shams, a British-born Egyptian, his message contained a 'spoken word' response to the execution:

> They found blood on da shirt of da brave martyr where those savage animals hit with their shoes after he majestically and gracefully met his demise.
> Muqtadar da pussy and his heinous minions were there
> Imposing their justice, the biggest injustice it was.
> Saddam da true son and leader of Iraq died a martyr.
> And Iraq, under da influence of da mob, descends into the depths of hell.
> People remember Saddam.
> He was the only one truly capable of ruling Iraq.
> Now Iraq is in the hands of pussies and cowards.

When we met a few days later over coffee in Portobello Road, I asked him about the message

Ramy: Where did you get that poem from, who sent it to you?
Shams: Bruvs, I wrote it. That execution propa pissed me off, I just had to get it out you know.
Ramy: Who did you send it to?
Shams: Just a few people, sympathisers.
Ramy: Ok tell me about it.
Shams: I don't know, I just woke up vexed, it was a bit of a shock; cause it happened so suddenly and on Eid man, how could they, that's disgusting. Like when you expect someone to pass away, like someone old, it's not as bad as when you just wake up and someone has been knocked over by a bus or something, you know what I mean?
Ramy: Yeah, but it was on the cards for a while man, why are you upset about Saddam's death?
Shams: Because it was just wrong, he is a *Ramz Arabi* [Arab symbol] you know. It's not because I think he was a good leader, yeah he did a lot of bad shit, but look at the country now, it's fucked up. I was having this

discussion with Sari and this other friend a Yemeni *bre* [brother] and they were like 'the execution was right, it was justice' and I don't know what. I mean it got pretty heated and they were like 'why do you care?'

Shams's poem, delivered in West London *mestizo* vernacular in the style of the American Black and Latino 'spoken word' points to the situated nature of repetition. He recites traditionalist pan-Arab discourses, which have argued that Saddam, a 'strong-man', is the only type of man capable of holding Iraq and other Arab nation-states together. There is a complex distinction between the defiance of western hegemony that makes Saddam an 'Arab' symbol of militancy and steadfastness on the one hand, and the excesses of his brutal and authoritarian rule on the other. His refusal to be dominated despite the overwhelming odds is central to his mastery of the performance of masculinity. In contrast, his hangmen are constructed as feminised and illegitimate race-gender others *'pussies and cowards'*.

As Farzana Shain argues, support for Saddam Hussein among British Asians during the Gulf War was connected neither to Saddam's beliefs and cause, nor based simply on shared religion. Instead she emphasises the extent to which support was an act of defiance towards a British social structure that, she argues, 'systematically excluded them from its benefits' (2003: 22). The identification with Saddam Hussein by Ahmed, Jamal or Shams is not only about masculinity or recitation of norms but, in equal measure, is a form of resistance and rejection of inequalities and hegemony on both a local and global scale. Perceived injustices in global and regional (political) systems are powerful forces that have worked in favour of others, who have been vilified and pathologised in 'the West' for not recognising the 'world order' or the West's monopoly on international violence. What many political figures – ranging from Saddam Hussein, Hassan Nasrallah and Osama Bin Laden through to Winston Churchill, Richard the Lion Heart, Hernán Cortés, Hitler and Franco – share is both a bloody legacy and an ability to use rhetoric and action to cast themselves in terms of masculine ideals – defiance, steadfastness and autonomy – which consequently construct them as authentic, legitimate and worthy of respect.

Ahmed's account clearly demonstrates that racism and violence at school led him to use the unlikely figure of Saddam Hussein as a trope for his resistance in his own battle for autonomy and honour in the playground. For his part, Jamal's attempts to make sense of the war were motivated as much by maintaining friendships as it was on code(s) of masculinity, solidarity and heroism. And Shams's response to Saddam's execution seems in large measure to be based on his rejection of the continued domination of the Middle East by western powers. The Saddam trope is not caused by an 'Arab identity', but by the imperatives of hegemonic masculinity within the context of ethnonormativity. In these accounts, this takes place at a particular stage of a life course and in relation to particular historical circumstances where one is *subject to* and the *subject of* racialisation, violence, destruction, nationalism, inequality and subordination. The idealisation of a particular brand of masculinity and the practices of 'race-gender othering' evident in these accounts are as much part of *being a man* or being *one of the lads* on a racially mixed South London housing estate (see Back 1996) as they are part of learning to be an Arab man in London during the Gulf War.

In the following section I look more closely at how young British-born or -raised women learn how to be 'Arab women', or in other words how they are 'gendered' and 'raced' simultaneously as adolescents at school.

Learning to be an Arab Woman

In her account of growing up in Detroit in post-war America, Alixa Naff emphasises the role of her family in impeding her assimilation. 'There was nothing in Detroit to impede Americanization except what my parents placed in its path, namely the native traditions they bought with them from … Syria' (2000: 108). In his study of kinship and community among Arabs in Detroit Andrew Shryock argues that 'Everywhere the Arab immigrant families turn' they see values in the society in which they live, particularly those related to sexual freedom and individuality, encouraged at the expense of their own. Their collectivist sensibilities, their ideas about male and female, their ways of marrying and raising their children are consistently portrayed as backward and immoral. The result, for the newly arrived immigrants, is a classic double bind, where the family traditions that make 'us' superior to 'them' become the values that are used to stigmatise Arabs, particularly the children of immigrants who are forced to negotiate this terrain daily (Abraham and Shryock 2000: 112).

While the narratives that follow also see the family as an important factor in circumscribing and limiting the ability to experience similarity with the 'mainstream', they are also revealing of the role that broader discursive and corporeal boundaries have in creating lasting feelings of otherness. An important difference between the context in which Naff found herself in America and those I present from London is the prevailing institutional approach to racial, ethnic and cultural difference.

This is not to suggest that assimilation is better or worse than 'multicul-turalism' (which is a separate discussion). What I stress in this section are the concrete processes of subjection through the 'ethnic family', the biopolitics of the education system and the prevailing cultural logic of ethnonormativity as reiterated and recited in everyday contexts, discourses and practices.

For many children, schools are the primary contact zone where society beyond the family is experienced and where discontinuities between minority and majority, and indeed between different minority groups, are confronted (McDermott, 1987; Lave, 1988; Patthey-Chavez 1993). As Basit and Shain have shown, schoolteachers in some settings see the 'Muslim family' in terms of a 'cultural pathology' that is restrictive and oppressive. Conversely, there is a tendency to construct schooling and mainstream society as liberating environments of equality and freedom (Basit 1997a, 1997b; Shain 2003). A good example of this is Dahlstedt's (2009) analysis of the 'partnership' initiatives initiated by state schools to engage local ethnic 'communities' in Sweden. 'Immigrant parents' are 'measured' and exhorted to adapt to an imagined 'Swedish normality', in order to become 'responsible parents' and 'equal partners'. The education system is part of the technologies and institutions of governmental-ity, producing healthy, wealthy, happy and, in relation to the children of immigrants, integrated citizens. The ethnic home is often characterised as disrupting and undermining this process of socialisation and population management. The dualistic bind that is created by 'school vs. ethnic family' overlooks the way in which these structures (home, school and wider society) are experienced in concurrence with and not in isolation from one another in the everyday lives of young people. Here I argue for sequential readings of regulatory ideals and the institutions behind them, which together circumscribe intelligibility. In both cases the tendency to think in generalised and stereotypical terms about who and what 'Muslim families' are and what 'British society' is seems all too predictable.

Suad sees herself primarily as being Jordanian but has a mixed heritage, with Syrian, Palestinian and Jordanian branches in her family. Her parents moved to London in the late 1970s and she was born there. After graduating from university, she found a job in London's Arab economy at the Middle East desk of an investment bank in the City. One of our conversations took us back to her childhood.

Suad: My Dad and Mum they came to London and they didn't know anything about the education system, but I have done the whole thing

– Church of England, Roman Catholic, I've done International Schools that are non-religious and I did an Arabic Islamic school so I've done the whole sector.

Originally I went to an American convent school in Kingston, my mum and grandmother had both been to convent schools in Jordan so it was kind of a family tradition. The whole discipline thing was very important. Then I went to KFA [King Fahad Academy], then to ISL [International School of London] and then from the age of 13 I went to an English school in Surbiton, a Church of England school, until I went to uni. I was the only Arab in my class at Surbiton. I felt completely isolated so when I went to uni I was yearning to meet Arabs, I mean that was one of the first things you know. I was really sick and tired of English people who always judged me and treated me differently because I don't go out and get drunk, I always felt invisible, I didn't fit in.

Ramy: Really, tell me about that, why didn't you fit in?

Suad: Because everyone was English and we were 15-year-olds, like teenagers, and everybody was losing their virginity and getting drunk and sleeping over and going clubbing and I couldn't do that, and then I was bullied because of all that and, you know, so I've always had that issue. My parents weren't religious or anything, just socially conservative. I got to the point where I would just switch off and say, you know what? I'm not going to let that bother me. I was the only Arab girl up until 6th form, actually there was another Arab girl there but she denied it.

Ramy: Why would she do that?

Suad: Nobody thought that she was an Arab because she didn't conform to their stereotype of what an Arab is – she wasn't dark enough, didn't wear hijab and wasn't wearing Gucci, she was just normal you know. Maybe she didn't want to be different; but I mean her name was so Iraqi for me it was obvious; I think she just didn't want the hassle. Anyway in the 6th form three other Arab girls joined and we were suddenly like the 'Arabs' and it was all hugs and kisses. We all became so cliquey together because we had all gone to English schools; one was from Syria, one from Lebanon and one from Iraq, and each one had gone to an all-English school, so for us to all get together … and it was fun you know. I am still in touch with all of them you know. Finally I had someone to identify with, we all had the same problems, the same restrictions, we couldn't sleep over, we couldn't have boyfriends or drink, so it was great 'cause finally I wasn't alone. We would speak to each other in Arabic, which was cool, and it drove everyone crazy [laughs]. At English school, as long as there are other Arabs or internationals, it's fine.

Ramy: What if there isn't?

Suad: I don't know, but I mean I really didn't enjoy being around WASPs.

Ramy: What's a WASP?

Suad: White Anglo-Saxon Protestants. There were only a handful of 'ethnics' you know, like there were two Black girls in the school and they were known as the 'Black twins', that kind of thing. I used to think of myself as English. I always used to say I was English. And then because of the way I acted I think some people assumed I was English or at least half-English, that one of my parents was English, until one day a group of girls in my class, I'll never forget this, they said to me 'You are not English, you are not Anglo-Saxon, you are British', that really was like, it made me feel like nothing 'cause whatever I did wasn't good enough.

Like Ahmed, Suad narrates the making of her Arab ethnicity at school and her estrangement from Englishness as someone else's doing. The complex demarcations of inclusion and exclusion at school are directly related to the unresolved and contested meanings around national and cultural identification and belonging in Britain. Suad tried to embody the White, leafy middle-class suburb in which she lived, and mimicked what she considered to be a loyal 'Englishness' (see Cesarani 1996; Kumar 2003). Suad's narrative emphasises the extent to which she had internalised the notion that she was English or that her behaviour and presentation meant that she could convincingly *pass* for English. However, Suad's physical appearance, as well as her name, seem insurmountable obstacles to her passing for English. Her performative rendition 'is the effect of a flawed colonial mimesis in which to be Anglicized is *emphatically* not to be English' (Bhabha 1989: 320). The way in which Suad frames these experiences prompts a discussion of identification, desire and mimesis, and bears a strong resemblance to literary and cinematic accounts of racial *passing*. As Adrian Piper describes, even when *passing for White* is successfully achieved, the awareness that recognition and equality is predicated on such superficial colour identification is in itself a blow:

A benefit and a disadvantage of looking white is that most people treat you as though you were white. And so, because of how you've been treated, you come to expect this sort of treatment, not perhaps, realizing that you're being treated this way because people think you're white, but rather falsely supposing that you're being treated this way because people think you are a valuable person. (1992: 25 see also Ginsberg 1996)

Suad is quite clear that the Arab girl who concealed her Iraqi origin at her school was able to pass for White because 'she wasn't dark enough, didn't wear hijab and wasn't wearing Gucci'. The intersection of the modalities of race, religion and consumption (class) here seems poignant in terms of their correspondence to the analysis of *passing* in film and literature.

In relation to racial passing in films like *Pinky* and *Lost Boundaries*, Wald (2000) notes that the epistemological authority of the epidermal common sense of race and the White gaze are undermined while highlighting the visual epistemology through which race comes to be known. The Black–White opposition is unravelled only to set up a narrative predicament and its subsequent closure which re-stabilises the opposition. Thus, by 'brandishing the performativity of race … [these films] do not provide the key to its undoing as a strategy of social power' (2000: 95).

Furthermore, the resolution and re-stabilisation of race in early accounts of passing are often made in reference to class mobility, whereby the demonstration of particular middle-class notions of taste and cultivation ultimately secures passage into whiteness, a point alluded to in Suad's narrative. Within these cinematic and literary narratives a colonial mimicry of whiteness seems pervasive and consequently a particular configuration of 'identification', 'desire' and 'mimesis' seems to frame the characters and the process of passing. Wald finds that the end of the traditional accounts of *passing* from Black to White and 'refusing to *pass*' comes about at the same time as the erosion of particular forms of political, social and economic laws of segregation and discrimination. Passing is thus put in context not as a denial of the 'Black self' but as intrinsically tied to survival between particular structures of subjection and material inequalities (Wald 2000: 119). The use of a number of ethnicities for *passing* by young Arabs in London affirms Wald's analysis of post-passing narratives in contemporary Black popular culture. Danny Senna's novel *Caucasia* (2002) suggests that the relationship between identification, desire, encryption, mimesis and cultural survival is not fixed in a single configuration but is reconfigured contextually. Equally, it points to the way in which the coming of age of multiculturalism may have reconfigured racial, ethnic and religious identification only to maintain their reality as a way of ordering and organising society.

Passing in literature and film is one part of the 'designs for living' (B.K. Alexander 2004) in a particular context and, as such, both passing and the performances involved can be seen as part of a traumatised project of survival. Having said this, Sánchez and Schlossberg's (2001) volume on passing, sexuality, race and religion suggests that passing is not always a mode of survival and self-defence but can also be a radical playfulness, an assertion which should draw our attention back to the tensions and undecideability regarding performance and performativity. For Bryant Keith Alexander (2004), passing is at once the site of performance (an active engagement) and performativity (ritualised repetition of communicative acts).

> This is not the process of becoming but rather the state of being between two performance communities – the point of origin and the territory of desire – with the performance expectations of both communities serving as a mediator in a tentative feud (or maybe fraud) of identity – acceptance versus denial. For although performance can manifest the subject of its focus, it does not modify the materiality of embodied presence and the social investment in race. (Alexander 2004: 380)

Alexander's reflections on the performance of 'Black masculine identity' lays bare the complex terrain of this field of investigation as he attempts to deal with 'passing', 'cultural performance', 'performativity' and 'individual agency' all at once – terms which are laden with theoretical tensions. In the process he transgresses the disciplinary boundaries that have been set up as determining different positions on the riddle of personhood and, like Butler, relies on a Foucauldian discursive subject manifest by the circularity of power within a given context, and on Bourdieu and Wacquant (1992) who argue that the performance of the 'Bad Black man' role is not always reactionary, because it is a 'reaction' framed by the historic structuring of Black–White relationships. The narratives of the war at school are also set against the backdrop of the historical structuring of relations between 'the Arabs' and 'the Europeans', another instant where we must consider how 'the shadow of the other falls upon the self' (Bhabha 1990: 188).

Thus, for Suad, being unable to pass for English and being ascribed (what in her eyes was) a subordinate political Britishness, marked her ultimate exclusion and the futility of a certain kind of mimicry. Suad's dissatisfaction with being seen as British is interesting. It sits in contrast to the more recent suggestions that there is a broad acceptance of 'Britishness' by immigrants and their British-born children because of its reinvention as an inclusive (colourful and not colour-blind) citizenship-based identification and belonging (see Kumar 2003; Ware 2007). Contemporary Britishness now has its own socially instituted and maintained norms of social intelligibility with their own performative imperatives and performance repertoires. But before we take comfort from this development it is important to remember that Britishness articulated in this way confirms the boundedness of the categories it has come to relieve, in this case 'English'.

While Suad is quite explicit about the ways in which her peers emphasised difference in their relations with her, she was less willing to articulate the role that family values and structures had on her school experiences. So, using my own experiences, I asked her:

> *Ramy*: Didn't you create any space to play in? So that you could be part of the social scene at school a bit more. I mean I had to come up with all kinds of wild excuses just to try and have a normal social life and I still didn't have a 'normal' social life, but I still fought to create a bit of space.
>
> *Suad*: It was my parents, I mean my parents were so controlling and I'm the only girl in my family and, you know, I can't even come up with that stuff, I'm really bad at it, you know, and they can see straight through me. And I kind of, somewhere along the line in my life, I just gave up I was just like – ok, look, *khalas istaslimt* [That's enough, I surrender].

Naber argues that Arab American women are forced to negotiate the terrain between the discursive constructs of 'Arab virgin vs. American(ized) whore' (2006: 92). The culture of going out, getting drunk and having sex seems to be uncritically associated with 'English culture'. Of interest for the way we might understand performativity and heteronormativity is that the inability to 'do' or recite the behaviour associated with oppositional constructs like 'Arab woman' and 'English woman' becomes the basis for the construction of an essential identitarian difference. Suad resents the fact that she was judged negatively by her peers for not being able to take part in becoming 'a woman' in the same way as they did, and in this case both forms of womanhood are at least in part structured around different enunciations of heterosexuality.

Suad does not perceive the restrictions placed upon her by her parents as being rooted in religion, but rather in their social conservatism. One might argue that what she seeks to assert here is that these strains are not rooted in irreconcilable religious differences but in a 'social conservatism' that could be as British as it is Arab. I must admit that the way I question her attempts to reconcile these 'two spheres' frames the family as the more consequential force of subjection that must be evaded. She fails to do what many young people may opt for, that is, to create a 'secret' life based on false alibis. As Zainab's narrative will go on to show, the false alibi, often described as 'living two lives', can allow the subject to *appear* to recite the injunctions of divergent forms of 'womanhood' more completely, but does not resolve the strain that these competing structures of subjection create.

Zainab's parents are Egyptian and arrived in London in the late 1970s. She was born in London, attended all-girls schools and lived in the same neighbourhood in Ealing her whole life. She elaborates on the themes of 'living two lives' at Queen's College in Harley Street.

Zainab: That was the biggest eye opener. There was no uniform, they promoted individuality to the maximum and all the girls there were rich, they weren't middle class they were upper class. When I first went there I was like 'Oh my God, how am I gonna compete?' But it was ok, I just became me, there were a few Arabs but not in my class, they kept that quite quiet and I didn't really socialise with them anyway. I'm telling you that place was different, everyone was drinking and smoking, I didn't take part in that. It's so stupid but it was such a big deal. All the girls had done everything and I was clueless. Obviously some of the girls in my class were seeing guys and they were like trying stuff but I was still watching and observing. But when I got to the school I discovered, like loads of the girls were on hard drugs and they were like on the class-As and going to these clubs all coked up, very pretentious, always had the latest everything and I just found that … 'Oh my God'. But I actually loved that place 'cause I really became myself, but I never used to socialise with any of them at all, I knew I couldn't. I don't know how I managed it for two years, 'cause they were always going out late and I didn't even want to ask my parents. But I let loose in my own way. I was so sheltered. I just think that our generation is so fucked up … It was so difficult growing up, we all have these psychological issues. I was definitely clearly two different people, until now, not so much now because the two different people are becoming one person, but at school I was like 'Zainab who's Egyptian but she's …' The thing is like, when I was at Queen's, nobody knew my private home arrangements, they didn't know that my parents wouldn't let me go out or see guys and stuff, they didn't know all that, I didn't let anyone know that side of me … They saw the side of Zainab which was trying out this and experimenting with that. I used to make out that I had some Arabic party to go to so I couldn't go out with them, so they thought I was having this amazing social life, like this Oriental thing going on and that's how I made it out ... I was among all these girls who were just like ... so cool, what an amazing life they have, they meet people and I wanted to be ... I didn't want to show them that because I was Arab or Muslim it was stopping me having a social life. 'Cause that's basically, that's what it was. I wanted to show them that I was normal. I mean, that first year of college I fell out of character. I became someone who wasn't me, even my mum said that 'You know Zainab, you have never given us problems you are not gonna start now.' The thing was, loads of people, loads of our younger people they do stuff but they get caught. I never got caught so I could keep up the image of being the good Egyptian, Arab girl but at the same time try new things. So I was always the *misaal* [*Mithaal* – example/ role model] in our Egyptian crew. Yeah and loads of people were really *mita'adeen minni* [had a complex about me] 'cause they thought I was an angel, but I really wasn't, I just hid everything and never got caught. I know how to behave here and I know how to behave there. That's the difference between me and other girls, they just get caught. I mean it's totally normal, it has to happen ... to want to try things, like my parents can't say to me like, you know, you can't do this because you are not from this culture ... but you have to realise that I am, I am from this culture in a way, and I want to try this.

It's the whole double lifestyle thing and the fact that you are supposed to live ... like our parents expect us to live in this society and not be influenced by it. It's because of our parents, I'm gonna blame the parents. Not only, but they don't understand that it's impossible not to be influenced by this culture we live and breathe it all the time we watch it on the TV, walking in the street, it's always there and even if you've got the religion, even if you go to Egypt every summer, it's not enough, like if your parents tell you 'don't do this' you will go through a phase where, sooner or later, you have to try it. The thing is people have different thresholds; I had a very high threshold.

Zainab's reference to falling 'out of character' is an apt allusion to the theatrical nature of performativity between structures of subjection, but what she relates is not a carefree performance but one framed within the imperative of the project of survival and social intelligibility. The performative imperative has personal and collective consequences: 'our generation is so fucked up ... It was so difficult growing up, we all have these psychological issues.' What I find interesting is the strength of theatrical metaphors in the way she describes her situated recitation. Although she describes two lives, two different people in her narrative, I feel differently. For me it looks like one life and one person that recites competing injunctions to an assembled but mixed audience.

One Performance, Competing Structures of Subjection

Zainab and Suad both describe childhoods where their parents are gripped by moral panic regarding the society that their children are being raised in, often expressed through tight restrictions on the child's interactions both within and outside the school context. Important for the way we read gender performativity, Suad's and Zainab's narratives show the heterogeneity of the gendering process and the nuances of its structures. They are not straightforwardly subject to injunctions to be a 'heterosexual women', but further they must satisfy many types of 'womanhood' structured around female sexuality, where virginity and honour are idealised in one set of discourses and practices while sexual liberation as emancipation is idealised in another. Furthermore, it would be difficult not to see how these heterosexualising demands are inflected by ethnonormativity. Together with class these are the building blocks of identitarianism.

Unlike Zainab, Suad is not able to create the same kind of space for herself because she is unable to be untruthful with her parents. Zainab has to invent a fictitious social life that allows her to present herself (to peers) as having an exotic, separate and appropriate Arab life. She explicitly describes this as living 'two lives' or 'being two different people' and believes there are negative consequences of this dualism which, in her estimation, not everyone is able to manage.

Zainab squarely blames 'the parents' for this situation in her narrative. Though her frustration may on the surface be understandable, it should be seen within the context of the oppositional constructs of 'ethnic minority families' and 'mainstream culture'. Basit (1997) argues that 'teachers, social workers and youth workers who encounter Asian children often refer to the contradictions these children are thought to face by being trapped "between two cultures"' (see also Watson 1977). This vocabulary has become so widespread that many young people have adopted it because of the sympathy engendered by the ideas of 'illiberal ethnic cultures' and the 'trap' of cultural conflict (see Ballard and Banks 1994).

Indeed, Suad's narrative of managing the conflicting expectations of her parents and her peers is described as 'surrender' to her parents, a reference to ambivalent attitudes towards the family. As Shryock points out: 'Americans often describe the family as a source of stress, an obstacle, as emotional baggage … a context that one must get out of to be happy, successful and well adjusted' (Abraham and Shryock 2000: 590–99). Indeed, I had framed my own understanding of self, family and society within the 'between-two-cultures' and 'identity crisis' paradigms. These approaches have been widely criticised and yet continue to be influential as a common-sense 'identity'-based explanation for the challenges of negotiation that the children of migrants face. Brah (1996, 2006) Alexander (2006c) and Ahmed (2006) note that the 'between-two-cultures' and 'identity crisis' paradigms have been used (among other things) to pathologise immigrant cultures, construct static and over-determined cultural communities and frame youth struggle within a binary of ethnic family vs. society in a manner that underemphasises wider struggles like anti-racism. For me these narratives show that both parties in this binary equation (ethnic family and mainstream society) are equally implicated in structuring the possibilities of *doing*.

Although in other interviews Zainab's father played an important role as the main figure of authority in the family, in her narrative of school he is largely absent. Instead her mother appears, as 'the primary caretaker(s) … [and] powerful enforcer(s) of the rules and social embodiment of femininity' (Hatem 1999: 193). Women and mothers are crucial actors in the reproduction of patriarchy. While Basit argues that some South Asian girls in Britain might 'want more freedom, but not too much' (1997a: 36), suggesting a degree of autonomy in how and why they comply to particular gendered discourses, Hatem reminds us that 'compliance with these rules cannot be assumed but has to be secured either through consent or coercion, or a combination of both. One could not however exaggerate their [young women's] autonomy and/or power' (Hatem, 1999: 193).

Zainab's account shows that the performative renditions of the project of survival require discursive and corporeal skills and techniques. Essentialised ways 'of being' are policed and demand appropriate performances, and yet the imperfections of those performative recitations have tangible consequences that are both constraining and productive. It is between the discursive, corporeal and material structures of subjection that Zainab 'finds herself' – or, as Foucault would have it, subjectivity is based on subjection. Thus the notion that she is leading 'two lives' is dismantled not only because it is part of a repertoire of terms associated with the 'fixed yet multiple identities' but more so because they are not two sets of performances, in the doing of 'race', 'gender', 'youth' and oppositional constructions of heterosexuality, they are emphatically one.

Resistance to and the *transgression of* codes and norms are often celebrated as evidence of the radical voluntaristic agency of hybridity. But by thinking in terms of performance and performativity, 'agency' is transfigured as a result of the injunctions 'to be' and the inherent imperfection or idiosyncrasies of each person's performative renditions. Suad and Zainab show that they do not simply possess a 'gender identity' but that particular processes, interactions and discourses during adolescence began their respective journeys of doing 'Arab womanhood', indeed that journey is ongoing and subject to elaboration, reversal and reorientation. Their narratives suggest that, at that time in their lives, becoming an 'Arab woman' was in many ways about not becoming an 'English woman'. In practice, the processes of being raced and gendered are synchronised to create 'Arab women' and 'English women' as oppositional repertoires that cannot be bridged in practice without always being liminal to both. In other words the routinisation of stylised acts that are required to embody British Arab womanhood always involves inherent recitational failures which are sometimes grammatically represented by the enigmatic hyphens that signify the simultaneous making and unmaking of this 'subject position'.

Rather than having to choose between seeing these negotiations as either the result of life 'between two cultures' on the one hand or a radically paradigmatic cultural hybridity on the other, a performative approach helps account for the complexity of both structure and agency through the notion of Foucauldian *subjectification* and the inherently imperfect and unpredictable outcomes of injunctions 'to be'. This unpredictability or uncontrollability is well demonstrated by Noura for whom meeting other Arabs at school in fact unravels the assumption that Arabness is collective redemption in the diaspora.

Contested Recitations of Identitarian Authenticity

The tendency to frame these narratives within a genre of Arab victimhood or the counter-hegemony of minority cultures should be resisted. Noura's account highlights the different and contesting constructions of 'Arabness' she experienced as a 13-year-old when she and her Iraqi parents moved to Britain from Syria. Her initial encounters with 'Britain' and 'English people' were primarily through a school in south-west London which she described as 'one hundred per cent White and posh', 'cold and impersonal'.

Noura: I didn't stay long at that school, a couple of months later my parents moved into London and I changed to a school which was probably about 5 per cent English and the rest were from all over the world.... Oh it was wonderful, it was brilliant [laughs]. Basically I really liked the fact that there were lots of Arabs; I could see them, I could hear them and really it was mixed and it was my first experience of people from India or Black people so this was quite interesting 'cause I was observing a lot. That first day you know everybody asks you where you come from, because that's the done thing you know, everybody comes from a different place. The change from one school to another was great, it was exciting, interesting and I developed a fantastic affinity to Africans because they were the middle ground for me, I loved them. My best friends were from Africa and they bridge the two cultures so they are a lot more kind of neutral in their interactions and, you know, men and women, but they also have a lot of values and respect that we have and a lot of respect for religion. But they don't carry the ideas that Arabs have, the up-tightness of Arabs, and the things you begin to see when you are outside that 'Arab' environment. I think I always saw those things because of my family. What I found that was interesting was the whole cultural vibe that was going on. You had the Arab groups which tended to stay with each other, you had the English groups, the Eastern Europeans and they all just hung out like that. Some people did mix but they were more like the first generation British who had been here for a while and maybe only spoke English.

Ramy: And how did you deal with that?

Noura: Becoming an individual creates problems because if you made friends with people who were from your country they want you to be exactly the same as them in everything. You know if they are like *muhajabat* [veiled] then you have issues, you know, because I was like a real Arab girl not somebody who has grown up here with parents who are really religious. I mean I was more Arab than they were but they couldn't see that, they thought I was too English. Like some Iraqis who I met at school expected you to act in the same way that they do. Like for example I made some Arab friends, some Egyptians, some Lebanese but for example I don't really care if what I eat ... like I was eating something and this girl came up to me and said by the way that food that you are eating is not Halal but don't worry, God is not going to punish you because you didn't know. And I was like 'I really don't care.' ... I mean when you are young the picture is not complete. But my main problem was that I was culturally more Arab than them, I can read and write and dance and speak different dialects and they can't – but for them it was all about religious values and not cultural values. Growing up here with other Arabs you can't come out and say you don't believe in religion and it's particularly Arab friends that are uncomfortable with your opinions. But eventually you don't discuss it with people. So at school you had to manage all these different relationships and contradictions of like loving Arabs and being Arab but at the same time hating the kind of expectations and some of the values that people just expected you to be a certain way.

For Noura, Roula and Suad London's is in part understood through the mapping of a racial landscape with 'White areas', 'Arab areas' and 'multicultural areas' that represent different possibilities for their projects of cultural survival and social intelligibility. What is interesting about Noura's account is that the novelty and redemptive comfort of hearing and seeing Arabs in her inner-city school seemed to have quite quickly given way to the realities of negotiating her inclusion and intelligibility among 'Arab' peers. The values and norms that her British-raised Arab peers associated with 'being' or 'doing' Arabness were quite different from her own. 'Their' Arabness was framed within the relationship between 'being' Muslim and 'being' Arab, while Noura's was framed within a secular notion of Arabness based on language (reading and writing) and cultural performances (dancing). For her British-raised Arab peers Noura's disregard for religious observance made her unintelligible within their own understanding of what it means *to be* or *do* Arabness in London. Unable to accept Noura's recitation of a particular kind of (secular) Arabness, her Arab peers cast her as being 'too English' the opposite of 'being Arab' in their contextual discursive economy (see Sarroub 2005). Equally, Noura believed that she was a 'real Arabic girl' implying that her peers did not understand what 'real' Arabness meant or 'how to do it'. Both Noura and her peers seek to recite and reiterate authentic Arabness as strategies of social intelligibility within a school environment that is marked by the valorisation of ethnic identification. In both cases the imperfect repetitions are considered to be failures of 'true' Arabness. The deconstructive gesture here is to suggest that what we seek to understand are not 'identities' or ways of 'being', but inherently imperfect and unpredictable recitations, all with absolutist claims to identitarian authenticity.

Boyarin and Boyarin (1993; Boyarin 1996) have attempted to work with Butler's link between mimicry and the project of survival by arguing that the repetition and mimesis of 'non-hegemonic norms' is a mechanism of Jewish cultural survival in the diaspora. They argue that 'mimicry across a generational boundary is attractive, comforting even, but also, to differing degrees, and particularly as one reaches adulthood, a matter of felt need within contexts' (Bell 1999b: 151). For the Boyarins, 'felt need within contexts' takes place through transnational movements that bring those in the diaspora into contact with each other and with those from the homeland, with whom they share cultural codes, signs and practices, which requires the learning and the mimicry of culture (in Bell 1999b:152).

As Bell (1999b) argues, I believe correctly, the Boyarins' approach is too functionalist and concerned with cultural reproduction in a way that the mimesis in gender performativity is not. Indeed, the notion that Jewish or Arab 'culture' (or any other set of cultural norms) are counter-hegemonic seems to disregard the multivalent nature of discursive power. Ethnic minority culture itself is often an agent and structure of subjection and not simply redemptive resistance to western hegemony. I would argue that the Boyarins' characterisation of minority ethnic culture as necessarily counter-hegemonic is similar to the way in which subcultures have been romanticised. Post-subculture readings confront us with the assertion that we cannot simply assume that subcultures are counter-hegemonic by virtue of their position in relation to the 'mainstream' (Marchart 2003). The Boyarins' valorisation of diasporic Jewish 'culture' as radically counter-hegemonic overlooks the way in which the discursive and corporeal acts involved in *being* a 'Jewish woman' in New York or an 'Arab woman' in London, materialise the body, investing it with cultural norms, animating and contouring the subject (Butler 1993), in other words they are forms of race-gender *subjectification* too. We are far better off seeing 'minority' and 'majority' cultures as competing discourses and injunctions that seek to impress themselves upon those that they hail, rather than being hegemonic and counter-hegemonic.

Learning to do 'Arab womanhood' in diasporic contexts seems replete with communicative failures. Failures of the performative kind are not pejorative but an inherent, necessary and natural reformulation of structure in its reiteration. I return briefly to Zainab's account of a school entrance interview at the King Fahad Academy when she says:

> I can remember my mum shouting down the corridor '*Lauw sa'alooki bita'rafi lugha Arabiyah ulilhum aywa*' ['If they ask you if you speak Arabic say "yes"'] and in my head I was like 'Why are they going to ask me about cars?' [laughs].

Zainab's mother intended to refer to *al-Lugha al-Arabiyah*, the 'Arabic language', however Zainab understood '*Arabiyah*' to refer to the colloquial Egyptian for 'car' (vehicle). Derrida asserts that all speech acts carry with them the possibility of communicative failure and that their meaning can thus never be foreclosed. Here the mother's authorial intention comes with no guarantees and Zainab must learn what her mother meant in her own way. In a similar sense, Noura had to learn that Arab in London was different to Arab in Damascus. Seeing these interactions and enunciations through the lens of performativity show them to be contextually recited versions of Arabness that have acquired a naturalised effect through their recitation, a set of doings rather than a pre-given or stable ethnic and cultural 'identity'.

These narratives of school and adolescence demonstrate the way in which becoming an 'Arab man' or an 'Arab woman' is learnt through recitations of and between structures of gender, racial and class subjection. They provide important insights into the possibilities for a sequential reading of performative 'gender' and 'race'. Equally, they expose the terrain on which subjectivities are (re)produced and how they are related to psychoanalytical categories. Butler's readings of Freudian and Lacanian 'identification', 'desire', and 'mimesis' and melancholia are important features of how she elaborates 'heteronormativity' (Butler 1990, 1993). For Rottenberg, the difference in the way that '*identification*' and '*desire*' are configured in the schemas of 'gender' on the one hand and 'race' on the other represents the principal problem for the project of extrapolating performative 'race' from performative 'gender' (2004a: 444, see also 2004b). Rottenberg juxtaposes identification, desire and mimesis in Butler's gender performativity with Bhabha's approach to forms of colonial mimicry. In the colonial situation mimicry emerges as a strategy for the enactment of colonial power and knowledge whereby the coloniser demands that the other approximate, through mimesis, the norms of whiteness. In so doing the colonised do not 'represent' whiteness but rather repeat and imitate it. The non-White subject is simultaneously encouraged to live up to norms of whiteness while always being excluded from ever 'truly' embodying it (Rottenberg 2004a: 440).

However, Rottenberg's assertions that mimesis in relation to gender on the one hand and colonial mimesis on the other are inherently dissimilar seems to flatten Bhabha's work which equally sees imperfect mimesis on the part of the colonised as creating critiques which are disturbing for the coloniser. Suad, Zainab and Ahmed's miming of 'Englishness' seems to speak to Bhabha's assertion that miming whiteness, that superficial identification with colour, is more to do with the promise of a common humanity and recognition, a recognition that the colonial relationship places out of reach. Where one mimes whiteness, one may appear White, but will never be White enough or, as Suad puts it, however good her miming of Englishness was it 'wasn't good enough' (see Warren 2001).

In contrast, social systems marked by race, can also force subjects to identify as 'non-White', in other words to embrace their ethnic otherness while simultaneously compelling and encouraging the desire to be the enigmatic other (whiteness). The forced *identification* with being non-White is not coupled with a *desire* to be or live up to the norms of non-whiteness. Fanon describes this as 'the black man wants to be white' (1967: 9) and Hall confirms this, arguing that 'Blacks could gain entry to the mainstream but only at the cost of … assimilating white norms of style, looks and behaviour' (1997: 279). The appropriation of whiteness is not one motivated by 'desire' *per se* but by the need to be socially intelligible and to survive. Indeed the 'secret Arabs' or 'Arabs in denial' that Roula, Suad and Zainab all describe seem to want to 'pass for' non-Arabs in order to survive, in order to avoid associations with those who are invaded and conquered in the international order and consequently in the playground, or to avoid being stigmatised by the discourse of 'the Arabs' prevalent in Britain – violent, unstable, dark, veiled, bearded and undeservedly wealthy.

To date, attempts to use the notion of gender performativity and heteronormativity to inform an understanding of race, ethnicity and culture have been criticised for not mirroring the configuration of identification, desire, encryption, melancholia and the project of survival on which the idea of gender performativity is based. I argue that these critiques, although insightful, somewhat miss the point. The structures of racial subjection cannot, nor should they be expected to, mirror perfectly those of gender subjection. The sequential readings of 'being raced' and 'being gendered' that Butler calls for can only be made possible by counter-exposing these forms of hegemony, not forcing them to be either one and the same or unrelated. These narratives provide the initial signs of the possibilities of a performative reading of 'racial' and 'ethnic' relations but cannot on their own cover the ground needed to support such a move.

3

Going for *Shisha*: Doing Ethnicity, Gender and Class

As I enter the cafe Wa'el's hand greets mine and pulls me into a brief embrace, he says '*Marhab abu'l shabab*' ['Welcome lad of lads'] and gives me three firm pats on the shoulder. I don't know him that well but I see Wa'el (Abu Isa) about three times a week since I started my fieldwork. He works behind the counter at 'Downtown cafe' taking food and drink orders and managing the till.

I move on to greet Mohammed Ali, a short and thin Damascene whose job it is to ensure that everyone has a *Shisha* and that it is well fired with fresh coals. Mohammed Ali's is definitely the harder of the two jobs. Both Mohammed and Wa'el work illegally; we never discuss their papers – it would be rude to intrude uninvited on such a matter – but their working conditions seem well designed to exploit the vulnerable. Wa'el has been in London for nearly three years, he is a Palestinian from the dead-end refugee camps of Lebanon where Palestinians are prevented from practising a vast array of vocations and professions for fear that it might make their stay in Lebanon permanent. His father was killed at the age of 26 by Israeli soldiers during their invasion of Lebanon in 1982. He has a catalogue of stories of loss, tribulation, death and discrimination. Yet, despite the tragedy, he always has a smile on his face, especially when he talks about 'Lebnaan' [Lebanon], its *joie de vivre* and his plans to return there on holiday one day.

Mohammed Ali is a sadder character. In his late 30s he is a more recent arrival and seems to find it hard to adapt to his new environment. He speaks no English at all and struggles to pronounce simple greetings and phrases; nonetheless he always asks '*Keif biqulu bilenglezi?*' [How do they say in English?]. Sometimes regular patrons type English words and phrases in phonetic Arabic on his mobile phone where he now has a limited but useful English vocabulary. Wa'el is linguistically the better equipped of the two and therefore deals with the *Ajanib* [foreigners] drawn in by the sweet smell of the *Shisha* smoke drifting onto the street outside or the neon sign above the food counter 'STILL OPEN' late into the night.

Mohammed Ali spends most of his day preparing the tobacco that rests in clay crowns at the top of the *Shisha*. It's a dirty job; the tobacco is sticky and pungent, so much so that it will give you a headache if you breathe it in all day. His fingers are stained a reddish colour as a result of handling the tobacco without gloves. He cleans and refills the glass water vases that form the base of the *Shisha* as well as performing the menial tasks expected of anyone who works in a *Shisha* cafe, cleaning the toilets and the rest of the cafe, stacking shelves and so on. His body looks like it can't take much more, his face taut and wrinkled from the smoke, making him look much older than he is. Part of his job is to inhale intensely to fire up the *Shisha* before passing it onto the customer, meaning that on six nights a week he breathes in copious litres of the thick moist and aromatic smoke both passively and actively. His clothes don't seem to change much from day to day: he is slightly dated wearing black denim from head to toe, his hair in a crew cut with a classic *Ba'athi*-style moustache, wide and bushy, attesting both to his masculinity and recent arrival in the UK.

Mohammed and Wa'el are part of London's informal Arab labour economy which restaurants and cafes exploit unabashedly. They are the first people you encounter when you enter the cafe. Their only reason for working there is misfortune but they play a crucial part in the authenticity of the place and the acting out of social roles and rituals relatively new to London. The cafe stays open, and Mohammed and Wa'el awake, as long as there are customers to serve, there is no such thing as closing time. (Field notes, 17 April 2006, 11:30 p.m.)

I spent a lot of time in a number of cafes across West London, which brought with it a sensitivity towards and awareness of those who work long and underpaid hours for some to socialise, perform and consume and others to profit. In the early 1990s, when these cafes first started to appear in London, they were not regulated beyond normal (food and beverage) licensing laws, operating below the radar of government regulation until the smoking ban in 2007. Boxes of molasses tobacco, which is smoked on the *Shisha*, and the water pipes themselves were regularly bought into Britain in suitcases on flights from Cairo, Beirut and Casablanca. The growing popularity of these cafes and their corresponding viability as businesses caused an explosion in *Shisha* cafes in London, particularly in the years preceding the announcement of the ban on smoking indoors (2007).

The ban was a blow to cafe owners, many of whom have been forced to close down, relocate or serve *Shisha* illicitly. Cafe owners around the country joined the 'Save the *Shisha* campaign', which sought to mobilise and lobby local councils for an exemption to the smoking ban on the grounds that *Shisha* is not only a business but also a cultural right. Those who have been able to have taken the *Shisha* onto the pavements outside their cafes, putting up awnings, installing heaters and paying increased licence fees. The regulation of molasses tobacco and the imposition of import duty, VAT and health warning labelling, has also caused the price of 1 kg of tobacco molasses to increase significantly and naturally a healthy black market in untaxed molasses tobacco has flourished. While the pockets of business and consumers have been hit, and the government has acquired a new source of revenue, it is arguably people like Mohammed Ali and Wa'el Abu Isa, whose wages are little more than £30 a day, who bear the brunt. The drive to keep many *Shisha* cafes open means that, increasingly, it is the exploitation of vulnerable illegal migrants – who are here today and can be deported tomorrow – that keeps a large number of these businesses in profit.

The coffee shop in which I have spent the most time is called Downtown Cafe, an oddly American name for an Arabic *Shisha* cafe in West London (Figure 3.1). It is situated just off Baker Street and Marylebone High Street, a short walk from the London Central Mosque in Regent's Park and the residential areas around Church Street and Harrow Road with their high concentration of Arab migrants. Westminster University, which has a large number of British-born or -raised Arab students, is less than five minutes away and Edgware Road is half a mile to the West. Downtown Cafe is a middle-of-the-range cafe; it is not particularly well decorated but an attempt at recreating some kind of 'Oriental' or Arab aesthetic has been made. Chipboard latticework poses as *Arabesque Mashrabiyah* lining the walls alongside pictures of pre-bellum Beirut in the 1960s. Red upholstered benches line the walls all the way around the space, possibly the best use of the limited space but also reminiscent of the way that a traditional *Majlis* is arranged. A seating area hidden behind the counter is available – ideal for couples or mixed-gender groups who want to stay out of sight of the regular patrons. These areas are common in restaurants in the Arab world and are known as 'family areas'.

There is a food counter where Arabic meze are displayed and fresh juices and hot beverages are prepared. Arabic pop music (mostly chosen

Figure 3.1   Card games and *Shisha*, a scene from Downtown Cafe in 2006
Source: Photo by the author.

by the staff) plays on a cheap stereo that is perched precariously on a makeshift shelf; a flat screen TV hangs on the wall beaming in Arabic satellite channels with titillating video clips from one of the numerous versions of Arabic Music Television or football matches from the Saudi, Egyptian or European leagues. At times of war and crisis this background ambience is replaced by rolling news from Al-Jazeera or Al-Arabiya, depending on the political leanings of the owner and patrons. The cafe front is made almost entirely of glass so that the goings-on are visible to all passers-by and, importantly, so that the outside is visible to those inside. I often watched as curious passers-by peered in, hesitating or exchanging words about the curious-smelling cloud of smoke hanging from the ceiling and drifting out onto the pavement. Outside the cafe you can see anything from a Lamborghini to a BMW, less prestigious cars are typically parked around the corner out of view. Despite the seeming affluence of many of the patrons the cafe itself is shabby, which is confirmed by the state of the toilets, which are tiny and unfailingly grimy. However its shabbiness is part of its *jaww* (appeal and atmosphere). It is an everyday cafe, low on style but affordable, comfortable and informal enough to visit many times a week.

On an average night the *(Q)ahwah* is busy with the sound of card games and backgammon. Groups of men sit four or five to a table playing

Tarneeb, the Arabic equivalent of Bridge. The game is taken extremely seriously by those playing, the banter alternating between laughter and argument; occasionally money is discreetly at stake. Masculinity can be heard and felt in this atmosphere as playing cards are flung down on the tables and backgammon chips crackle as they strike the wooden boards signifying the metaphorical blow-by-blow sparring.

Mango and guava juice sit side by side in the refrigerator with iced tea and the standard Schweppes ensemble. Fairuz and Lazeeza, non-alcoholic malt drinks, with their beer-bottle aesthetic, are also popular signs of the modern, yet religiously informed, lifestyle choice. It is rare to see someone drinking the traditional coffee from which these establishments take their name; they are more likely to be drinking tea with mint or a diet coke. Shani, an overpoweringly sweet cherry fizzy drink, evokes memories and reinforces shared tastes and experiences among some of the patrons. Its dated logo and design stand in contrast to the other canned drinks lined up neatly in the dispenser; even the ring-pull remains preserved in recycle-unfriendly form. Aziz remembers the drink from his childhood growing up in Kuwait, Basil and Ameen from their childhood holidays in Egypt and Syria respectively. The drink was consumed for nostalgia and not only a fondness for its taste; when it is plucked from the fridge, a relatively rare occurrence, it must be followed by a conversation of remembering 'Shani man, old Skool'.

The glass-fronted dispensing refrigerator stands by the door; regulars serve themselves from the refrigerator – what has been consumed is calculated later. The young men that I have been socialising with were just such a group of regulars. They shared the cafe with more recent migrants from Iraq, Lebanon, Palestine and Syria. They had come together partly through meeting at school or university and partly out of chance. They had started hanging out in Downtown Cafe some months before, having moved their custom there with the manager, who had left another cafe in Maida Vale about a mile to the north-west after a dispute with his business partner-wife. Two of the friends lived less than a mile away while the other two lived about 10 miles away. Nonetheless, the cafe was conveniently located, just off the A40 western corridor, so that, with a car, the journey home for Basil, Aziz and I would take about 40 minutes. The group spent a lot of time at the café, usually congregating around 8 p.m. to smoke *Shisha*, play cards and chat. *Shisha* and drinks were always ordered in Arabic, but the conversation between the friends usually continued in English punctuated by Arabic banter or phrases.

'If you're not into pubs, where else can you go?' said Basil, other responses to my questions about why they used *Shisha* cafes included 'to smoke *Shisha*', or, as Ameen put it, 'It's chilled here you can relax catch up with the boys and plan the weekend.' Basil's reference to 'pubs' was a response that I would come to hear quite regularly. For this group of young men and the extended friendship networks of which they were a part, there was a complex evaluation of the class and cultural signification of places they would socialise in and how these reflected upon them. They avoided 'pubs' not because they served alcohol but because they were coded as 'English' 'working-class' spaces. They were, on the other hand, quite happy to spend time in 'bars', which they associated with urbane American culture and in their words 'internationals', a category of people which they saw themselves as being a part of.

The conversations this group of young men had at the *Shisha* cafe were everyday, almost banal, and revolved around organising group holidays, 'girls', marriage, gossip, the previous weekend's exploits, football, work and the associated banter that can be expected among a group of males. They were all in their late 20s and held down jobs with 'good career prospects' in multinationals, banking, architecture and construction. Somewhat conservative, none of them drank alcohol or had a steady girlfriend. Although they had all graduated and started working, they all lived at home with their parents. In my experience the notion of 'moving out' was never a topic of conversation, all of them had lived at home during university and the idea that one would live at home until marriage or migration seemed to be the natural order of things. Despite the seeming harmony of their home and personal life, the group of friends spent time in this and other cafes because there was 'nothing to do at home'. To mainstream society their lifestyle choices may seem odd for a group of seemingly successful young men of their age – no regular girlfriends, no sex, no drinking, no drugs and no overt desire to experience these things through the independence gained by living outside the family home, all standard components of popular notions of adult-making in Britain. Family life at this age seemed more about particular obligations rather than rules. There were expectations in terms of helping with family finances (or at least achieving financial independence), keeping an eye out for a good marriage partner, meeting family and social obligations, making sure that allowances were made for 'family days' (usually a Sunday) where meals would be shared and time spent with parents and siblings.

This period of life seemed to place them on the verge of adulthood, a kind of limbo or waiting area, prior to full manhood, which would be realised upon marriage. A strong network of male friends through which codes of brotherhood, loyalty, solidarity and interdependence are practised, seemed to be an essential vehicle through which this phase was experienced. This in-between-ness is an extension of what Osella and Osella describe as 'college culture': 'In the absence of external structures of validation for their passage towards manhood, the boys turn inwards to the peer group' (1998:191) and the *Shisha* cafe becomes 'a space of male–male relations', a day-to-day arena in which sociability and masculinity outside the home and beyond parental control takes place (see Chopra et al. 2004).

It is important to take into consideration that an array of alternative spaces could be chosen for this day-to-day socialising – someone's flat, a bar, a pub, a normal cafe or bistro. These venues were used sometimes, but none of these other spaces took on the role of home-from-home in the way that the *Shisha* cafe did. People aim at making an impression on others by behaving in a certain fashion, and by adorning themselves and arranging their surroundings in particular ways (see Veblen 2008 [1899]; Goffman 1959; Barthes 1977; Bourdieu 1984; Baudrillard 1996). *Shisha* cafes provide a particular kind of coded social space, not just masculine but 'Arab', nostalgic, authentic, ethnic and distinctive, meanings generated principally through *Shisha* consumption.

Qahwa and its colloquial *Ahwa* mean 'coffee' – the same word is used to describe the drink as well as the place in which it is consumed. When coffee houses emerged in the late fifteenth century they were the subjects of significant religious controversy. Religious literalists and conservatives, who sought to ban the sale of coffee and close down coffee houses, saw the drink as an intoxicant and coffee houses as places of disrepute (see Hattox 1985). Coffee houses became synonymous with late nights, the consumption of drugs, prostitution, street entertainment, music, storytelling and idleness. Unable to stamp them out, the religious establishments in cities like Medina, Cairo, Damascus and Baghdad eventually patronised certain coffee houses providing them with a sense of respectability and legitimacy.

Coffee houses became popular across the social spectrum with different establishments catering for different classes and groups in society. Istanbul, Damascus and Baghdad were famous for their sixteenth-century grand coffee houses frequented by elites and merchants and set amid gardens with water features and tree-shaded areas in the most important parts of town (Hattox 1985: 81). Today, across the region coffee houses have become a feature of working-class urban life, where they act as the principal public space of male sociability. An important feature of this type of sociability is that it isn't 'undertaken with just any men, but rather with social equals' (Almeida, 1996: 91). Therefore, as social space the *(Q)ahwah* is marked by considerations of class, affluence and social status. Equally important, both in the past and present is gender. The coffee house or *(Q)ahwah* is still coded as a male domain, women, married or unmarried, are rarely if ever found passing the time or socialising in traditional coffee houses in the Arab world, and if they are to be found there they usually require legitimation by the presence of a male. Instead, an increasing number of modern up-market *Shisha* cafes cater for mixed-gender groups. Thus the traditional *(Q)ahwah* resembles institutions like the *Kafenio* in Greece and the *Taverna* in Portugal, which have been the principal spaces for male sociability and the nurturing of both emotional and instrumental friendships (see Cowan 1990; Loizos and Papataxiarchis 1991; Almeida 1996).

Shisha: *the Aromas of Gender, Ethnicity and Morality*

Coffee drinking itself has become far less central to the definition of the *(Q)ahwah* where nothing on the menu is as important as the *Shisha*. The *Shisha* has been given some attention by visual anthropology, mainly in reference to nineteenth-century Orientalist art, but has been given little attention in terms of its role in contemporary material culture. Chaouachi argues that western anthropologists and sociologists studying the Middle East and North Africa have been wary of giving the *Shisha* too much attention for fear of being seen as academic 'aristocrats' investigating banal aspects of everyday culture at the expense of research on more existential political and economic matters (Chaouachi, 2006: 179). Within the Arab world *(Q)ahwas* are perceived as a relatively unusual and bold topic for research and one linked to Orientalist scholarship (2006: 179). The *Shisha* cafe has become a global phenomenon described by Chaouachi as '*Shisha*mania', the result of the crossover of tourists, migration and trade (2006: 199). Despite their renewed commercialisation in the region and their spreading beyond the Middle East, *Shisha* cafes have attracted little attention outside medical journals discussing the health effects of smoking molasses tobacco.

The signification of the *Shisha* is analogous to that of the cigar. Callison et al. argue that in American film, cigarette smoking is practised 'as much by the powerless and wretched as by mighty heroes and evil villains' (2002: 1331). In contrast, the meaning associated with cigar smoking seems quite certain: wealth, self-confidence, aggression, hardiness, creativity, power and accomplishment. Like the *Shisha*, cigar smoking is a gendered activity and until recently, few women dared to break into this province of male behaviour. 'Women smoking cigars might well be perceived... as especially daring and power oriented. On the other hand, they also might be deemed unscrupulous, if not reckless, but so with a touch of sophistication' (Callison et al. 2002: 1333).

The thick plumes of aromatic smoke that are blown from the *Shisha*, its design and shape, represent the exotic aesthetic of 'otherness', enticing and intriguing. Among the reasons for its mystique is the often tongue-in-cheek association with the consumption of drugs like opium and hashish. The *Shisha* has transcended the *(Q)ahwah* scene and is (along with belly dancers) one of the most potent visual symbols of 'Arab culture' or Oriental decadence. It has found its way onto the menus of mainstream and ethnic restaurants, it is a must for dinner parties organised by university Arab Societies and, before the smoking ban, could be consumed at exorbitant prices in the VIP sections of trendy nightclubs in London's West End. The *Shisha* has to some extent become fetishised, it is given meaning through its relationship to other objects like the coffee pot, arabesque furniture, carpets, belly dancers and the Oriental aesthetic more broadly.

Following Baudrillard (1996) I argue that the *Shisha* retains functionality and relevance in modernity while at the same time displaying the characteristics of 'antiquity' and 'marginality'. Marginal objects are seen in contrast to those that are purely functional, they 'answer to ... demands such as authenticity, memory, nostalgia and escapism. These objects are experienced as signs and are characterised by their authentic presence and special psychological standing ... serving a purpose at a deeper level' (1996: 75). Baudrillard argues that marginal objects are often part of a 'neo-cultural syndrome', where the quest for *authenticity* represents a quest for an *alibi* (being elsewhere). The *Shisha* has a particular function in the practice of cultural authenticity in the diaspora: it transports people to another place, perhaps the fabled cultural homeland or Oriental reverie, neither of which need be defined too strictly.

For Baudrillard 'man is not "at home" amid pure functionality', marginal objects:

symbolize an inward transcendence, that phantasy [sic] of centre-point which nourishes all mythological consciousness – that phantasy whereby a projected detail comes to stand for the ego, and the rest of the world is organized around it. The phantasy of authenticity is sublime, and it is always located somewhere short of reality (*sub limina*). (2006: 79)

Baudrillard's reading is not only refreshing for its re-articulation of the notion of identity but also the way in which materiality is implicated in the process of making the self and others. Chaouachi argues that the *Shisha* represents a lifestyle: 'The goal is not to smoke to satisfy a dependence or calm anxiety but to take time to talk, listen and share' (2006: 181). While I agree with Chaouachi, a deeper reading of *Shisha* cafes and *Shisha* consumption in London is required so that we might uncover the ideologies behind lifestyles.

Spending time with people at *Shisha* cafes revealed a whole repertoire of meanings, techniques, and know-how related to *Shisha* use among British-born or -raised Arabs. Aficionados discuss and describe its workings with confidence to novices. Then there is the skill of how to adjust the *Shisha* in order to obtain the best results, whether placing ice or rose water in the glass bowl improves flavour, whether to use traditional coals or modern briquettes and even how to place the coals. Which hose you prefer, Egyptian or *Shammi*? How to share and pass the hose without causing offence, what kind of tobacco you choose – modern flavours or traditional? I was shown an astounding array of *Shisha* collections from sports bags packed with *Shisha* components, to aeroplane-luggage style portable *Shishas* with their components carefully nestled between specially crafted foam compartments and electric *Shishas* that can be plugged into a car lighter socket.

Attitudes towards *Shisha* cafes and smoking more broadly have changed significantly in the interplay of meanings and contexts in the diaspora. Many of the young people I spoke to hid the fact that they smoked cigarettes from their parents, however they felt no need to hide their *Shisha* smoking habits in the same way. I asked Shams about whether his parents knew that he spent so much time in *Shisha* cafes?

Shams: Yeah they're used to it, I just say I'm going to *Shayish* [to smoke *Shisha*] or I'm going to the *(Q)ahwah* with the *shabāb* [boys].
Ramy: Do they know you smoke *Shisha*?
Shams: Yeah, yeah.
Ramy: Do you think they mind?
Shams: No not really, my parents have seen me smoke *Shisha* before.
Ramy: Do they know that you smoke cigarettes?

Shams: Well kind of, I never smoke in front of them or in the house out of respect and that. My mum found my cigarettes and of course she lost it … that was a while ago, but still you gotta be careful.

Ramy: So you couldn't say to them 'I'm going out for a cigarette'?

Shams: No man, come on you know how it is!

Ramy: What do you mean man? How come you can tell them that you smoke *Shisha* but you gotta hide your cigarettes?

Shams: It's different, it's *ayb* [shameful] to smoke cigarettes in front of your parents.

Although my fieldwork was principally with young people I did interview some older migrants like Mustapha who was in his late 60s and had come to Britain in the mid 1970s from Cairo. I asked him if he ever spent time in coffee houses as a young man in Alexandria. 'Yes of course,' he replied, 'we used to play backgammon with my friends and smoke *Shisha*, we would pass a lot of time at the *(Q)ahwah*.'

Ramy: And did your father know that you went to these places?

Mustafa: No.

Ramy: Why not? What would happen if he found you sitting at the local *(Q)ahwah*?

Mustafa: He would be very upset and I would be in trouble, it is not a very respectable place to be, not like the *Naadi* [sports club], the *Naadi* is ok, you can say 'I was at the Naadi,' you cannot really say 'I was at the *(Q)ahwah*.'

Ramy: Why's that?

Mustafa: Because *ayb* [it's shameful].

Ramy: And did he know that you smoked cigarettes?

Mustafa: Of course, it was normal in those days for men and women to smoke.

The acceptability of both the *(Q)ahwah* as a social space and different types of smoking have changed over time, place and context. *Ayb* is a notion widely used in order to demarcate what is socially unacceptable to say or do. On a scale of illicitness and shamefulness, smoking *Shisha* and spending time in a coffee house is today far more acceptable than smoking a cigarette in front of your parents for some British-born or -raised Arabs. In fact young men and, to a far lesser extent, young women, seemed not only relaxed about telling their parents that they spent time in *Shisha* cafes but intentionally advertised it as a way of indicating to their parents that they were engaged in an authentic and culturally intelligible 'Arab' activity or pastime. Young people seemed to understand that their parents would accept their choice of frequenting *Shisha* cafes because they saw it as a palatable substitute to the site of everyday British socialisation: the pub. By spending time in *Shisha* cafes young men indicated that they were not just men but Arab men. Young women have a far less certain stake in cultural authenticity through the public consumption of *Shisha*.

Some might assume that the *Shisha* cafe is somehow an Islamically acceptable alternative to British pub culture. However, apart from the obvious absence of alcohol, much of what goes on in a *Shisha* cafe is Islamically dubious, particularly for the emerging ideologues of Islamic reformism. In recent years a number of *Fatwas*[1] have argued that smoking in all its forms is *Haram* (religiously prohibited). These opinions are based on the principle that any activity that damages the human body (and therefore life itself) is forbidden. But it is not only the *Shisha* which attracts the censure of protestant Muslims: passing time (wasting time), chatting (idle talk), playing games and, in the case of orthodox hardliners, listening to music, are all frowned upon as activities that are un-Islamic and unproductive, reviving sixteenth-century critiques of the coffee houses, this time through the logic of 'a nation in decay', whose adherents should be engaged in pro-active projects of renewal and restoration.

I wanted to know how Basil, Aziz, Ameen and Mahir negotiated these nuances. They all prayed regularly and seemed on the surface committed to an Islamic lifestyle. They tended to play down the theological problems with smoking (of all types), instead incorporating smoking into the daily rhythms of being a Muslim. For example, like thousands of other men, they would head to a *Shisha* cafe after the extended evening prayers (*Tarāweeh*) during Ramadan or, more commonly, would agree to meet at the cafe after *Salāt al-Maghrib* (the sunset prayer). Indeed, smoking was not the only exception to a perfect reiteration of an Islamic lifestyle. 'The boys' openly acknowledged that they went clubbing (although they didn't drink), most dated (but abstained from pre-marital sex), and they had no problem socialising in places that served alcohol, all seemingly in contradiction to reformist readings of an 'Islamic lifestyle'. Where drinking was involved, Aziz for example, insisted publicly that he did not drink but confided in me that sometimes he discreetly ordered spirits with mixers that made it appear like a soft drink. His main concern was censure from 'the boys' and fear for his reputation as he felt that drinking publicly would be a sign that one had become 'English'. Thus while they flirted with what are often seen as 'religious' and 'secular' lifestyles, there were limits: alcohol, sex and drugs. While one could privately 'experiment' with these things, discretion was of the utmost importance so that one's public persona, reputation and 'respectability' remained untainted, perhaps following the Islamic notion that one should be discreet about their tribulations with sinfulness.

This type of approach was not shared by all those I encountered. For young people who defined their 'identity' and practices more resolutely through Islam, there were implications for being a Muslim beyond normative attitudes and regular worship, their social world and the physical spaces and activities in which they engaged could not contradict their Islamic ideology. Sulayman and Tamer, for example, had spent a lot of time playing cards at *Shisha* cafes in their late teens but had gradually pulled away from the scene as their lives became increasingly determined by faith and religiously motivated community activism. Tamer had joined or was associated with a global youth movement established by the TV evangelist Amr Khalid called Life Makers (*Sūnā' al-Hayat*). Life Makers has a particular notion of leisure time that argues that, in light of the current state of the *Ummah*, Muslims do not have the luxury of leisure time. Thus young Muslims are encouraged to use their 'spare time' in productive social initiatives. The movement's main objective is 'to encourage our men and women, both young and old, to have effective and beneficial roles in serving our countries. Their roles must be productive, useful and influential.'[2] In the words of its patron, the Life Makers movement seeks to engender 'seriousness' among its followers, 'Flirtatiousness, in other words, shallowness, in other words, triviality. All of those are but symptoms of a hard kind of shackle spreading within many aspects of our daily lives.'[3] A principal goal in the Life Makers project is combating smoking generally and *Shisha* smoking in particular, because, unlike cigarettes, it is imbued with a sense of cultural acceptability and tradition.[4] I would argue therefore that attention should be drawn to the nuanced relationship between 'Arabness' and Islamism by looking at the way that social life is perceived and practised. As Tariq Ramadan has argued: 'Arabic may be the language of Islam but Arab culture is not the culture of Islam' (Ramadan and Nassef 2004). The *Shisha* cafe scene, along with other practices I will turn to in subsequent chapters, are seen as being part of 'Arab culture', which, for protestant Islamic reformers, should be the subject of social prohibition. Within the social circles I participated in and observed the 'Arab scene' was in many senses an alternative to the 'Islamic scene' and, at the very least, there were discernible tensions around the Islamicness of Arab culture.

For those whose notions of sociability are strictly defined by religious conservatism, it is bad enough that young men are wasting their time and health in *Shisha* cafes, and the increasing visibility of women in some *Shisha* cafes seemed tantamount to adding insult to injury. On the one hand some objected to the disruption of traditional notions of (male) public and (female) private spheres. On the other hand others objected to the very fact that young men and women mix in these unsupervised settings. Nonetheless it has become increasingly common to see women, sometimes veiled, socialising and smoking *Shisha* in cafes around London. I argue that this stems in part from a desire by some young Arab and Muslim women in London not just for public space *per se* but for ethnic public spaces. As Almeida and Cowan have noted in relation to the *Kafeteria* in Greece and the *Cafe* in Portugal, the increased presence of women in *Shisha* cafes is not an unproblematic or linear matter of the emancipatory opening of these spaces by women.

The Walk of Shame

> The boys have already arrived and are sitting around a table playing *Tarneeb* (Bridge). I settle in, order a *Shisha* and a mint tea, I notice Basil and Mahir whispering, smiling and giggling … 'What's going on boys?' '*Yabni* [son] look at that table over there, *wooo huneeeeeys*. See that one with the curly hair? I bet she's Egyptian.' Aziz interjects 'Guys shut up! they can hear you! You don't want them to leave do you?' Aziz looks at me, 'These guys are so uncivilised, I think you should go and talk to them, we've got a table at Aura [night club] this weekend,' he says with a cheeky smile. I can't help laughing. The boys are very excited and the flow of a number of card games around the room has been disturbed as the regulars discreetly check out the group of girls. Basil can't help himself, he shouts out to the guy taking care of the coals tonight '*Abu Laban, il gama'a dol shakluhum ayzeen fahhm*' ['Those guys over there look like they need some embers']. We all burst into laughter and high-fives … the girls on the table manage to muster a somewhat reluctant smile … The excitement is over, back to the card game. (Field notes, Tuesday, 7 November 2006)

While it is not uncommon to see women in *Shisha* cafes in London, their presence is still novel and mostly an exception. *Shisha* cafes in London are neither segregated nor gender-neutral spaces. Over a number of months spent at Downtown Cafe I noted how college-aged girls would sometimes come into the cafe in the early evening. According to a group of young men I spent time with at the Red Sea Cafe on Uxbridge Road 'girls' would usually avoid '*the walk of shame*': walking into a cafe unaccompanied. There was of course no physical danger involved in being in the cafe alone, only the gaze and judgement of the men inside. One way of mitigating the rampant gossiping and curiosity created by the presence of women in cafes was for women to be accompanied by a male. Qais and Laila, both British-born Palestinians in their early 20s, had been dating for just over a year and were regulars at Downtown Cafe. I asked Laila how she felt about spending so much time in a *Shisha* cafe. She gave the by now customary response 'Where else are we supposed to go?' The cafe gave her and Qais the opportunity to spend a few nights a week in each other's company in a kind of home-from-home atmosphere for the price of a *Shisha* and cups of tea. Even though Qais was known to some of the male groups who regularly used the cafe he was never drawn into card games or conversations, the couple were usually left to each other's company. There was a sense of respectability that they were choosing to spend time together in the cafe under the watchful eyes of others, in a way proof that they were doing nothing wrong.

While this kind of courtship is acceptable, couples must exercise control over their behaviour in these environments. They may sit together, arms around each other but must observe the boundaries of intimacy and propriety – no public displays of affection. To cross these boundaries would not only have repercussions for the female but also, interestingly, on the establishment itself as a 'respectable' and safe place for women to be seen in. I wondered if Laila felt intimidated by the overwhelmingly male environment?

> No not really, I prefer it. Men are less hassle, I just find girls, especially Arabic girls, really fake. I find it really hard to find a girl who's on the level, I mean everyone has that element of fakeness. I just hate that whole gossiping atmosphere. I can only trust a few of them. I mean I have a lot of Arabic girlfriends but I don't trust them. Maybe cause I'm very similar to them and I actually hate it about myself [she laughed].

Laila's response shows the pervasive appeal of gendered discourses that are disparaging about so-called 'female characteristics'. Female relationships are characterised as problematic, competitive and unreliable; the opposite of male company which is conversely straightforward and revolves around loyalty and solidarity. While she acknowledges the cafe as a male space she plays down the extent to which her feelings of being comfortable stem from her boyfriend's standing among the other regulars, immunising her from their gaze and curiosity. However, being accompanied by a male is not always a guarantee that young women will feel protected from moral scrutiny and curiosity in *Shisha* cafes.

I got to know Suhaila and Tahreer, two young university students of mixed Arab background. One night we arranged to go to the cinema with a group of their friends at the Odeon on Edgware Road. After the film the group debated where we should go to have *Shisha*, Fahd a mutual friend, suggested that we go to al-Dar, quite a well-known cafe right in the middle of the Edgware Road: 'I feel I get treated well there, the service is good,' he offered. Suhaila and Tahreer quickly objected, al-Dar was too public for them and they didn't feel comfortable 'being seen in there', so they suggested another cafe called Fatoush, a Lebanese place at the other end of the Edgware Road which had a seating area downstairs out of sight of the street. 'There's a downstairs and we know some of the guys there, they treat us well and give us *h'alwiyat* [sweets] for free. We could go to Abu Ali but it's a bit *bee'ah*,' said Suhaila. *Bee'ah* is Egyptian slang (literally 'environment') denoting something or somewhere that is down-market, common, crass or vulgar. The more working-class a *Shisha* cafe was, the more likely it would be seen by young women as a place unsuitable to frequent. *Shisha* cafes and their clientele are understood in terms of orientations towards class, taste and notions of conservatism and misogyny. These evaluations also extend to nationality, so that a Lebanese cafe would be seen as more socially liberal and therefore more welcoming of women than an Egyptian cafe.

When we arrived at Fatoush Suhaila and Tahreer were greeted by the waiter who clearly knew them as regulars; there was a group of young males that the girls knew sitting at the far end of the cafe, they waved at each other in acknowledgement. The waiter asked the girls where they would like to sit? '*Taht*' (downstairs) they replied almost in unison, seeming somewhat uncomfortable. The narrow staircase gave way to a reasonably sized space that had a number of booth-like seating areas. Suhaila and Tahreer sat down and looked at each other and then at Fahd and I. 'God they must think we are such slags, we come in here with different guys, it must look bad,' said Suhaila. 'So what!' Tahreer interjected 'I hate hypocrites. These people are normal but they want to appear like angels in front of the community, why do they have to put on such a show?' The two female friends have different reactions to the moral scrutiny of 'the community' Suhaila's response draws our attention to Abu-Lughod's observation that the acknowledgement of the fear of being watched can be seen in and of itself as a claim of virtue (1986:158). Tahreer, in contrast, responds with a rejection of the values of male and female comportment that the 'community' seems to demand. Unlike Laila at Downtown Cafe, Suhaila and Tahreer's social life revolved in different mixed groups. The respect and protection from the gaze and judgement of cafe patrons that Laila enjoyed was based on her attachment to one male, in contrast Suhaila and Tahreer fear the insinuation of promiscuity or of being unattached.

The waiter arrived at the table to take our order, we agreed to share *Shishas* which the girls would choose '*Wahd 'enab w wahd shamam w arba' shay*' ('One grape and one melon and four teas') – very modern choices of flavours, now part of a plethora of tobacco flavours ranging from 'Coca Cola' to Cherry. When the waiter returned with the *Shishas*, he automatically offered them to Fahd and I, but Fahd declined, offering the *Shisha* to Tahreer and saying 'Ladies first'. Getting a *Shisha* going often takes relentless lung power to fire the coals to the point where they begin to make the tobacco smoke, a task usually left to the coal bearer, who removes the plastic tip and inhales deeply straight from the fabric-covered hose, a sign of good service and, among male friends, denoting an intimate knowledge of the *Shisha* and consequently mastery of a certain kind of masculinity. Fahd's gesture shows how codes of etiquette can be mixed, stretched and borrowed for the purpose of context. He forfeits the opportunity to display masculine prowess and knowledge of the *Shisha*, opting instead for a gesture of gentlemanly Victorian politeness. His gesture is neither intelligible in one or the other cultural sphere but only in the sequential and situated imperfect recitation of both.

I asked the girls how they felt about *Shisha* cafes as social space. They both clearly enjoyed smoking *Shisha*. Suhaila told me that she had one at home and that she and her flatmates regularly used it, even if they were just sitting round the TV. But it wasn't the same as going out and socialising in the atmosphere of the different cafes. Their main concerns seemed to revolve not around being seen in public *per se* but around being judged in particular ways. 'My dad knows that I come to these places, he doesn't have a problem with it so why should anyone else?' Suhaila described the considerations that she and her friends took into account when choosing a *Shisha* cafe. They would avoid certain places that were just too male or where they felt like they were being 'perved' over. Another serious consideration was the cleanliness of the toilets. Ideally they chose places where they could sit out of sight of the prying eyes of other Arabs on Edgware Road. 'I don't want to bump into one of my dad's friends or anything like that, that's why we come here because it's out of sight, not right in the middle of it all.'

In the context of London the 'family area' of a cafe is rarely if ever used by families and is instead used mostly by visiting groups of females or couples. The hidden areas of contemporary *Shisha* cafes resemble the spatial contrasts Cowan (1990) noted in relation to the *Kafenio* and the *Kafeteria* in Greece, where the *Kafenio* spills onto the pavement while the *Kafeteria* is hidden away to protect young people from the judgement of the village. *Shisha* cafes in London are still predominantly a male domain into which British-born or -raised women are making inroads but where they remain fundamentally disadvantaged, even though, in many cases, the main clientele are other young British-born or -raised Arab (males). Cowan discusses women's fears of 'being watched' at the *Kafeteria* in similar terms, as an acknowledgement of the 'very real dangers a girl faces to her reputation and to her person, in a patriarchal society' (1990: 76). The notion of urbane liberalism vs. rural conservatism is challenged by the parallels that can be drawn between the gendering practices and discourses in a *Kafeteria* in rural Greece and a *Shisha* cafe in urban London. Similar to the *Kafeteria* in Greece and the *Cafe* in Portugal, the *Shisha* cafe in London has opened up a traditionally masculine space to women, challenging commonly held notions of gender. 'However, the simple opening of masculine space to women may not mean equality in gender ideology' (Almeida 1996: 93).

Shams, who had earlier discussed attitudes towards smoking, described the increasing visibility of women in *Shisha* cafes in London as 'a form of resistance', believing that it was an important part of the project to change attitudes towards women and mixed-gender socialising among Arabs. However, not all attitudes were as progressive, for the friends at Downtown Cafe there was little consensus regarding the increasing visibility of women at *Shisha* cafes as a conversation with Basil and Ameen showed.

Basil: Why shouldn't girls come to the *Shisha* cafe? I mean we bring girls here all the time, they like it and it's a nice place to chill, good music, *Shisha*, food.

Ramy: What about if a girl is wearing hijab and smoking *Shisha*?

Ameen: *La ma biseer* [No, that won't do], if she is wearing hijab she should respect the hijab more. If you are wearing hijab, that's it, you have to behave in a certain way, I don't know, *a'yb yaani* [I mean it's shameful].

Ramy: If your wife didn't wear hijab would you bring her to the *Shisha* cafe?

Ameen: No!

Ramy: Why not? We smoke *Shisha* with women all the time.

Ameen: Because [laughs] no, my wife, it's different. It's a place for me and my friends, what's she going to do here? *Ya'ni* [I mean] there is no need. Ramy, you idiot, just because we live here doesn't mean that we have to do everything like 'the West'.

Basil: I would, why not, it's great if you can socialise with your wife and your friends and if she wants to smoke *Shisha* she can. He's just one of those typical bloody Syrians, extremist, terrorists!

Ameen: Oi you, *masri* [Egyptian] *hū'mar* [donkey], everybody has their way.

The *Shisha* cafe is a site in which Ameen comes to an understanding of his diasporic repertoires of doing 'here and there', 'us and them'. The *Shisha* cafe was not a legitimate public space for Ameen's hypothetical wife to be seen in. This resonates with Cowan's work in Sohos in Greece where the *zaphioplatio* (sweet shop) was seen by men to be a legitimate space in which a husband and wife could socialise in public, but not the *Kafenio*. De Koning (2009) also found sharp distinctions in Cairo in relation to the *Naadi* (sports club), which is coded as family space, lending legitimacy to gender mixing, and contemporary western cafes which were considered by some to be beyond the family domain and related to unsupervised gender mixing. Ameen went on to describe how going out with his wife could involve going to the cinema or a restaurant or even a cafe like Starbucks or Nero but not a *Shisha* café, which for him clearly remained a space for masculine sociability and where ultimately there were no guarantees for his wife's reputation and consequently his honour. For Ameen, at least, this distinction also seemed to place the women that we did socialise with in *Shisha* cafes in one category and marriageable women (for him) in another. 'Arab women', whether veiled or unveiled, have no 'Arab public space' of their own and are seen as visitors from the private familial sphere who enter the domain of male public sociability at their own risk.

With a somewhat fixed notion of the 'East' and 'Arabs' Ameen suggests the transgression of traditional gendered roles, practices and spaces is something that is done by 'the West'. The transgression of norms is here figured as negative, a failure or betrayal of the truth of 'our culture'. We might say, following Bourdieu, that he has acquired a particular kind of habitus with its corresponding dispositions, tastes and prohibitions. But how do we make sense of the scope of that habitus when we consider his socio-economic and contextual proximity to Basil and the divergence in their attitudes towards gendered norms of sociability. The point here is simple, no doubt to Ameen's disappointment, transgression is taking place all around him, both 'here and there' because we cannot control the outcomes of interpolation or assume that norms always work to produce conformity.

As Setha Low and Lawrence-Zúñiga (2003) detail, anthropological interest in the symbolic meanings of space in everyday settings has been particularly focused on the ways these relate to gender (see Bourdieu 1973; Rosaldo 1974; Ardener 1981; Moore 1986). There has been particular concern for the ways in which domestic space materialises and reflects social hierarchies and binaries of public and private, male and female. *Shisha* cafes are 'used strategically to inform identity and produce and reproduce asymmetrical gender relations of power and authority' (Low and Lawrence-Zúñiga 2003: 7). *Shisha* cafes seem to exist on a fault line between the domestic and the public spheres. While being quite firmly understood as settings for public male sociability, these cafes retain characteristics of domestic and private space in the way they are used as alternatives and extensions of the home for both young men and women who share these spaces. While practices of domestication legitimise these spaces, that legitimacy is not experienced equally by young men and women. Sometimes space within the cafes is sequestered or inscribed as private, family space, and thus female space, at other times the legitimacy of women's use of these spaces depends on the attitudes and practices of male peers.

Naturally one thinks of Bourdieu's (1970) work on the division of domestic space in the Kabyle home and the way it reflects a certain cosmological order. Sawalha (2014) argues that early scholarship on the gendering of space in the Middle East tended to veer towards Orientalism by concentrating on settings where there are sharp distinctions and prohibitions in relation to gender. In contrast, settings in the Middle East where men and women share space or where practices of gendering space are less pronounced were under-researched. Sawalha observes, I believe correctly, that recent anthropological accounts of gender and space, such as those of Deeb (2006), Kapchan (2011) and Mahmood (2004), have revealed how women have claimed spaces for themselves outside the private sphere, but that these have focused on religious and underprivileged women, meaning that we know little of the strategies of 'secular, visible, enfranchised' women (Sawalha 2014: 168). Many of the young women I encountered at *Shisha* cafes in West London and those who voiced their concerns about the symbolic inequalities they faced in spaces that they felt they had a right to access, could be described as educated, enfranchised, visible and secular. Sawalha's commentary is set in the context of scholarship on Middle Eastern cities; London of course is not such a setting. However the way in which space and settings in the city are inscribed with diasporic recitations of gender makes us think again about how territoriality can be less consequential to the analysis of life in a global metropolis like London. Here Lefebvre's (1991 [1974]) understanding of space, as being a threefold arrangement of practice, representation and actual spaces seems most helpful. For Lefebvre 'representational spaces' are 'lived' spaces where 'inhabitants' and 'users' create or recite symbolic meanings through their everyday uses and imaginations (1991 [1974]: 33–40). *Shisha* cafes in London are not only spaces where the discursive norms of 'Arab' and 'Muslim' masculinities and femininities are imperfectly reiterated, and a nexus where the traditional division of male public and female private spheres is at once reproduced and undone; equally they are sites where class and ethnicity are central to the way that space is used to assert and reflect commonality and difference.

Our Kind of People, Our Kind of Place

I arrived at the cafe at around 8:30. Phone calls and emails full of humour and banter had been exchanged all day and ended with 'see you at the cafe'. It was a beautiful day and the sun was still shining. It's that time of year where London is at its best. As I pulled up the boys were gathered around Ameen's car chatting. I joined them '*Eh el-nizaam ya shabab*' ['What's up lads?']. The cafe was packed both inside and out; it was full of *Khaleeji* [Gulf] men and Basil was characteristically the most irritated by this. He had gone to speak to one of the staff to empty a table but it was early evening and those tables wouldn't be free for hours. 'It's like an invasion, "dirty Arabs"', he said. '360 degrees of *Khaleeji*-ness,' said Aziz. I suppose they felt that it was their regular and as such they had some kind of right or priority. 'Edgware Road?' I asked, admittedly it was a rhetorical question; I kind of already knew the answer. 'Naa [No] man – Arabs, Somalis and "Pakis" – forget it, let's go to St Christopher's Place,' said Mahir. (Field notes, 17 August 2006)

Basil went to speak to one of the staff to try and get him to reserve a table for us in future, and although he was met with all the right verbal apologies, assurances and compliments it was clearly not going to work. The *Khaleeji* customers stayed for hours and were more forthcoming with their spending. 'The boys' from Downtown Cafe were displaced during the summer months and, I suspect, not wanting to appear to have no standing in the cafe they chose to avoid it altogether for the remainder of the summer. The issue was not only that the cafe was full, on other nights and in other cafes I had noticed how the 'race', class and or nationality of others was seen as an encroachment on a particular kind of space. Negative representations of Gulf Arabs that emanate from 'internal' Arab discourses produce *Khaleejis* as crass, uneducated, backward or 'Bedouin-like' (pejorative) in their behaviour and tastes; they converge with the local (London-based) discourses that associate Gulf Arabs (rightly or wrongly) with undeserved wealth, excessive shopping, being abusive to their staff (drivers, nannies and maids), prostitution and gambling.

The relationship between British-born and -raised Arabs and the *Khaleeji* aesthetic is complex. At times an association is coveted and at other times resisted. Shams told me a story about a friend of his, whose family he described as 'normal and hardworking people'. The young man in question happened to work quite hard in his late teens and managed to save up enough money to buy an impressive car. With the help of his car the young man presented himself as a member of a wealthy *Khaleeji* family to 'white' friends, and particularly to 'white girls', at university, clearly seeking to capitalise on the aura of limitless wealth that is associated with the people of the Gulf. Although anecdotal the implication is that in London, the amorphousness of the term 'Arab' allowed this young man access to the aura of affluence, perhaps even a degree of social mobility albeit one predicated on acting.

For Basil the term 'Arab' was overwhelmingly negative:

> If you say 'Arab' to an English guy you know he is thinking of a guy in a white nightie with a chequered tea towel on his head and an oil barrel under his arm, I don't want people to think that's what I am so I say I'm Egyptian.

Ameen was more nuanced pointing out that among Arabs the term is positive but for the rest of society 'Arab' is negative 'They don't really understand what we mean when we say "Arab"'. In the context of London in the summer 'Arabs' meant *Khaleejis*. It did not refer to other kinds of Arabs or Arabs permanently settled in Britain. Although many young men and women from the *Khaleej* take the opportunity of being in London to remove their national dress and wear western clothes, they remain highly visible – especially so to Arabs settled in London, who seem acutely aware of their presence and areas of activity.

But it was not only *Khaleejis* that some young Arab Londoners seek to dissociate themselves from; other cultures, 'identities' and locales like the Edgware Road, often seen as being at the heart of 'Arab London', were equally to be avoided. Sensitivity towards sharing space with others perceived to be different in terms of class, nationality and /or 'identity' extended to young South Asians and Somalis in particular. As I sat in Kensington Park, just a stone's throw away from the Edgware Road, I asked Hussein, a 23-year-old, how he related to the Edgware Road?

> *Hussein*: I mean we used to hang out on Edgware Road when we were younger but it's really gone downhill. Nowadays you're more likely to find Asians on Edgware Road. Anyway, how much *Shisha* can you smoke!
>
> *Ramy*: So why do you think Asians go to Edgware Road and *Shisha* places these days. Do you think it might be 'cause it's Islamic – no alcohol and so on?
>
> *Hussein*: No man, it's not 'cause they think it's Islamic! They know it's Arab and they love Arab culture and the women! They all want Arabic girlfriends. I've seen it myself at uni they want to learn Arabic lines so that they can get with an Arab girl. They just don't like it [the Arabs]. I mean at uni, I've seen it happen, when a *Shisha* place started filling up with 'Stanis' [pejorative name for Asians] the Arabs just stop going there.
>
> *Ramy*: You're Iranian have you ever experienced anything like that from Arabs?
>
> *Hussein*: No, not really. I mean I grew up with them. I don't speak Arabic but being Iranian is cool, I get respect for it.

There is often a detectable ambivalence between young British South Asians and Arabs in London despite their shared 'Islam'. Many Arabs, even those who are observant Muslims are often disparaging about their South Asian co-religionists, whose lack of Arabic is often taken to mean that they cannot truly understand Islam. This view was expressed to me explicitly by Tamer and Sulayman, both observant Muslims. Despite the inherent doctrinal contradictions, they made a point of not attending mosques or Friday prayers where the congregation was predominantly British South Asian or where the sermon was delivered in Urdu. For his part, Tamer had offered the following in response to my questions about being British and Arab as we sat on his car outside the mosque attached to the Qatari Embassy medical section in Collingham Road: 'Look if there's one thing I could say to them it's that we are not all Pakis.' I took 'them' to refer to the British media or public and the 'we' to refer to not just 'Muslims' but implicitly to 'real Muslims'. The South Asian face of Islamic 'revivalism' in Britain is used as part of a discourse that some Arabs in Britain subscribe to that 'it is the Asians' or 'Pakis', who do not really understand Islam and who are responsible for the current negativity with which Muslims are seen in Britain. This narrative not only excludes the role of 9/11, where it is claimed that all the bombers were Arab, but is also a case of a flagrantly selective repertoire designed to frame British South Asian Muslims as the cause of a deep-seated and complex fear of Islam and Muslims. It also homogenises the religious practices and languages of Pakistani, Indian and Bangladeshi Muslims, which are collapsed upon one another by using a trope from British racist discourse 'Paki'. We may add to this rather distasteful mix that racist attitudes towards South Asians on the part of some Arab Londoners is the result of a borrowed superiority complex based on the attitudes towards South Asian migrant labour prevalent in the Arabian Gulf, where many British-born and -raised Arabs have holidayed or lived.

Conversely, I had spoken with a number of South Asians who were disappointed by the persistent Arab-centric approach to Islam adopted by many of their Arab co-religionists, which in their estimation went against the universalism and anti-racism in Islam. The cultural and leisure practices of (some) Arabs seemed on many occasions to take some British South Asian Muslims by surprise. One young man I met at SOAS who had grown up in the Midlands described being shocked by how 'un-Islamic the Arabs were' when he arrived at university in London. It seems that there is often a presumption that the people (who are assumed) to speak the language in which the Qur'an was revealed will be the most faithful adherents of Islam, and an assumption that 'Arab culture' and 'Islamic culture' are synonymous. Class and race intolerance seemed most prominent in the practices of aspiring bourgeois Arab Londoners, particularly when it came to sharing social space; it was less so in more 'down-market' cafes. Interestingly, religion might have been an important marker of difference in some cases, but equally it often seemed to be disregarded as a point of similarity. The mix of judgements and distastes on the part of young aspiring bourgeois Arab Londoners can be astonishingly intricate. This toxic mix of racism, class and aesthetic intolerance, and notions of a religiously informed superiority, reminded me of an email 'forward' called 'Edgware Road LOL'[5] that had been sent to me in May 2006 by Tamer:

If you're a Muslim and you live in and around London, the likelihood is that you would have had the unfortunate pleasure of visiting the morally bankrupt cesspool of sleaze and corruption that is Edgware road. For the uninitiated, Edgware road (well, part of it anyway) is a place where young hip/cool Muslims hang out, smoke sheesha [sic], chew khat [sic] and eat outrageously priced, sub par chicken *shwarmas*, served by rude arrogant Arab bus-boys who believe that their job title as 'Head Waiter' gives them some sort of intellectual and/or moral authority over you. It started off as a place popular for rich, lonely Arabs from abroad, who would bring their white girlfriends to ridiculously overpriced restaurants and show her off to their fellow pervert friends, while, of course, hitting on any remotely good looking girl who happened to walk in. Causing a scene in the process and eventually being thrown out by an over zealous, pissed off 'Head Waiter'. E-Road (as it's known by regulars) soon became popular with Pakistanis and more recently with P-Diddy clones (aka Somalis). Over time something quite remarkable happened. The non-Arabs had slowly begun (for want of a better word) to metamorphosise into Arabs – This spread of Arab culture amongst non-Arabs was nothing short of astonishing. Pakistanis were using words like 'yalla', 'akhi' and 'habibi' in their regular conversations. The tea towel scarf was now being worn with Shalwar Kameez … the song *'Habibi dah'* was on everyone's play list … men fantasised about one day marrying a fair skinned Arab girl and made plans on how they would take up residence in Dubai once they graduated. The trend continues today and has gotten to the stage where many have deluded themselves into believing that they actually ARE [sic] of Arab extraction, making up some outlandish story about his/her great grandfather was one eighth Syrian or that the 'Ahmed' in their surname somehow proves their Arabian heritage … Morons. You see normally you have to be careful when making gross generalisations about people en masse, but in this case the generalisations are completely justified. Take for example, the now famous E-Road rude boys. They normally hang around in groups of about 300, making an already crowded road an absolute chore to get around. They adorn almost without exception the standard Chavistani (sic) attire. Hoodys, [sic] baseball caps, low riders and Persil white Adiddas [sic] trainers, fake silver chains are also common. Their sole purpose in life is to roam around the Street looking for their female counterparts (Hojabis)[6] who they will invariably greet with the words 'whagwan sister' before proceeding to one of the multitude of classless Arab cafes where they will practise smoking near perfect rings.

These are clearly the views of a young aspiring middle-class Islamic reformist who is gripped with moral, class, race and aesthetic anxiety. Young British Pakistanis and Somalis are characterised as being fundamentally ethnically dissimilar and, perhaps more importantly, as working-class and crass. Equally, 'rich' Arab men are chastised for their salacious and asinine habits. As Bourdieu argues 'a habitus ... amounts to rejecting others as unnatural and therefore vicious. Aesthetic intolerance can be terribly violent. Aversions to different lifestyles constitute perhaps the strongest barriers between classes: class endogamy is evidence of it. The most intolerable thing for those who regard themselves as possessors of legitimate culture is the sacrilegious reuniting of tastes which taste dictates shall be separated. (Bourdieu and Nice 1980: 253–54). Trienekens (2002) argues that the notion of 'cultural capital' as outlined by Bourdieu should not be restricted to the categories of high and low culture, but should include popular and community-based cultural capital. 'Ethnic groups may use one form of cultural capital with a currency in the wider world, while a separate kind of cultural capital establishes status within the group itself' (Hall 1992 in Trienekens 2002).

The practices and discourses of 'othering' to which *Khaleeji* tourists, Somalis and South Asians are subjected suggest that for some British-born or -raised Arabs, *Shisha* smoking and *Shisha* cafes have come to represent their 'ethnic identity' to the extent that sharing them with ethnic and class 'others' is seen to infringe on or alter the signification and distinction this pastime represents. Perhaps these anxieties stem from the fear of being 'confused' with *Khaleejis* (Arab 'others') or British South Asians and Somalis (class, race and religious 'others'), who are all proximate but distinctive. These practices throw into relief the vulnerability of the notion of (Arab/Muslim) 'groups' and 'communities', which might be better understood in terms of subcultures and niche networks that operate often antagonistically under categorical labels of assumed similarity. Fundamentally, they also reveal that the symbolic violence of gender, race and class ascription is constructed. Through these structures of subjection people are made intelligible and a system of meaning is literally mapped upon them at the spatial and discursive levels, and these in turn come to be seen as essential social 'identities'.

So what does this make of the comforting categories of 'Arabs' or 'Muslims'? Groups and subcultures that are sometimes difficult to differentiate solely on the basis of 'race' or class are often more readily distinguished on the basis of leisure preferences (Gottdiener 1995). Leisure practices are gendered, raced and classed, and stringently policed by some. The middle-class boys at Downtown Cafe were just as reluctant to spend an evening in the 'ghetto' surroundings of the Red Sea Cafe on Uxbridge Road, where Yemenis, Somalis, Egyptians, Iraqis and Lebanese men while away the hours chewing *Qat* (*Chat*) leaves and smoking *Shisha* in rather unkempt surroundings, as they would be sharing space with *Khaleeji* tourists or young British South Asians on Edgware Road.

Shisha cafes have gone from being a marginal ethnic form of consumption (among 'Arabs' in London) to one that has drawn in paying consumers from beyond. For some the commercialisation and democratisation of the *Shisha* has added layers of meaning and identification with 'Arab culture' among a larger group of people, while for others its growing popularity is seen as an encroachment and infringement on objects, spaces and practices that are used to reinforce personal and collective 'identities'. The censure of Somalis and Asians on Edgware road is not a reference solely to their perceived class and place in the racial hierarchy of Britain but perhaps equally a reference to a failed 'Arabness' that the 'E-Road' email alludes to. The performance of 'Arabness' by 'non-Arabs' is rejected by (some) on the grounds of race, ethnicity and class. It seems that in contexts where group distinctiveness is a form of symbolic, social and economic capital the desire to *police* the boundaries of these groups is powerful and the exclusion of those who are ethnically, culturally, geographically or religiously proximate can be more vehement than when space is shared with those who constitute the 'other' in more straightforward ways.

I should point out that such desires to police Arabness in London, while common, were not shared by all. Nevertheless these anxieties are perhaps the strongest indications of the emergence of a limited middle-class Arab niche network in London, where one must be from a certain generation, from certain Arab countries (and not others), be upwardly mobile, have the trappings of wealth and display particular dispositions towards taste. The contra-flows of orientation, allegiance, taste and signification in the context of the local and the global suggest that while western-style coffee shops were on the rise in Cairo, Sohos (Greece) and Pardias (Portugal) in the early 1990s, providing a space where female sociability and the consumption of western tastes, styles and sounds was possible, in London the *Shisha* cafe with its 'traditional' Arab aesthetics, sounds, pastimes and codes of behaviour and space, was growing in popularity among the British-born or -raised children of Arab migrants. Choosing between styles reflects a specific stance or orientation where the adoption of local styles represents an allegiance to traditional networks and forms while the adoption of cosmopolitan styles represents a withdrawal from those networks (Ferguson 1999).

For de Koning the choices of 'local' and 'cosmopolitan' coded spaces in Cairo represent 'repertoires that are taken up in personal strategies and performances that signify specific choices, allegiances and modes of belonging in a local context' (2009: 132). What does this say about London? As Wray McDonogh notes: 'the culture of cities is characterised by continual tensions among symbolic processes that imbue social spaces with meaning and social divisions that include and exclude social groups' (2003: 264). Does the choice of social spaces coded as 'Arab' over 'British' suggest a rejection of the 'local' or does it in fact point to a conformity within a particular symbolic system where one is constructed from a very early age as 'ethnic' with corresponding expectations that one will do 'ethnic' things in ethnic spaces? For the young people *doing Arabness* in London, certain practices and culturally coded spaces and objects are arguably part of a project of cultural survival (not preservation) because recognition and social intelligibility within multiculturalism is often achieved by being ethnically and culturally distinctive. This certainly does not apply uncritically to London or to multiculturalism as a whole, but it does reveal some of the insidious consequences of ethnonormativity, heteronormativity and class structures.

What the insights from the *Shisha* cafe, schools, and the other settings I shall turn to tell us is that being gendered, raced and classed through discourses, material conditions, objects, spaces and practices go hand in hand. It is not a question of which process precedes or takes priority over the other or has more import. The time I spent in *Shisha* cafes in West London led me to see them as an easily accessible way of consuming and doing Arabness. By frequenting particular 'classed', 'raced' and 'gendered' social spaces, playing particular games, drinking particular drinks, listening to certain types of music and, importantly, smoking *Shisha*, Arabness is achieved as a notion of 'cultural essence', 'centre-point' and a position within wider society. *Shisha* cafes are also an indication that a sequential reading of the performative effect of being gendered and raced is impoverished if class is not part of the analysis. In this chapter I have referred to habitus, a theoretical scheme with an uncomfortable relationship to performativity. I will have to address the customary philosophical divergence between these two theoretical schemes, in the process of arguing that gender race or class can be read as performative.

4

Dancing Class: Choreographing Arabness in London

There is no doubt that women and politics are the common denominator in any private chat among students … How to strike a strict balance between the subject of women and that of politics has become very difficult indeed. The balance has tilted for the time being, in favour of politics, and thanks anyhow to the U.A.R.[1] it is no wonder then to see most of the lovelies in the Flamingo getting bored. Even the charming smile on Guita's face vanishes from time to time, and it is not really a strange phenomenon to find the Flamingo rather vacant of the sweet sex. (The Flamingo's Ear, *The Arab Review*, March 1958)

The motion was simple, 'Marriage is Necessary for Students'. Mr Baijati a married student of course, spoke first. He tried with all the knowledge at his command, to convince students that there lay their salvation. But, alas, he did not succeed. Issam Ghaidan won. He only had to appeal to their appreciation of beauty, to carry the students with him. Afterwards, everyone left for their various universities, to resume their student lives as bachelors as ever before! (The Spring Festival, The Arab Diary, *The Arab Review*, June 1958)

Al-Ṭayyib Ṣaliḥ's fictional account of Mustapha Sa'eed's time in London in the 1960s in *Season of Migration to the North* (1991 [1966]) is the most recognised literary expression of the potent mix of sexuality and Arab postcoloniality in London in the early 1960s. One of the implicit messages in the novel was that the exploitation of women under colonialism was reversed by the traffic of male students and workers to the former colonial metropolis (Salhi and Netton 2006). Both the extracts from *The Arab Review* and Salih's novel frame the Arab student experience in Britain in the mid-twentieth century from an exclusively male perspective. While men certainly made up the bulk of students from Arab states studying in

Britain at the time, the same cannot be said today. The majority of 'Arab students' at British universities these days are not from the region but are British-born or -raised and, as far as I could discern, included men and women in equal measure.

My search for Arabness in London led me to seek out university Arab Societies at the School of Oriental and African Studies (SOAS), the London School of Economic and Political Sciences, King's College, University College London (UCL), Imperial College, Queen Mary and Westfield (QMW) and Westminster University. I had assumed a great deal about what these societies might be like. Based on the accounts of Arab student activism at British universities from the archive, I assumed I would find long-standing, divided but politicised student societies, preoccupied with the issues of their time: the invasion and occupation of Iraq, the ethnic cleansing of Palestine, region-wide authoritarianism and perhaps even the position of Arabs in Britain in relation to the 'War on Terror'. However, the intemperate modalities of political Arabness both in Britain and beyond seemed to have created an aversion to matters political for university Arab student societies. As Roula, Ghazi and Ahmed signalled in chapter 2, growing up in London created suspicion of national and regional politics generally, as well as informing how people interacted with compatriots and other Arabs in London. The aversion to formal organisational politics that Arab *Mukhabarat*[2] states created among their subjects led to a variety of phrasings of the statement '*Ma lahu b'ilsiyasa*' ('He has no interest in politics') as a standard social anodyne identifying the societally innocuous. With different degrees of political repression across the region, in the most extreme cases like Syria, Iraq and Libya, the avoidance of matters political by the majority of those in the diaspora was an explicit sidestep motivated by survival. Prior to the revolts, rebellions and revolutions that have gripped the region since December 2010 one might go so far as to say that what most Arabs shared, whether in the region or in the diaspora, was a melancholic anti-politics expressed through a narrative of shared subjugation. The continued occupation of Palestine, the American military presence in the region, the destruction of Iraq, political disunity, the exploitation of the region's resources by national elites and 'the West', corruption, authoritarianism, wastefulness, underdevelopment, military defeat, injustice and victimisation are the standard markers of seeing the world through 'Arab' eyes and have become part of what it means *to be* and *to do* Arabness. In retrospect it was no wonder that I could find no politics or activism within Arab student societies at universities in London in 2006 and 2007. I should make clear that I spent time following 'Arab student societies' not national or cause-specific societies like the SOAS Palestine Society, which is renowned for its consistent and tireless activity of raising public awareness and campaigning against the Israeli occupation.

On the whole I feel justified in saying that if, during the twentieth century, London was a stage for Arab student activism, in the twenty-first century it had become emphatically apolitical – partly because British-born and -raised Arabs are not as existentially attached to the 'struggles of the homeland' as their parents and partly because many parents seemed to have avoided exposing their children to the politics of the homeland altogether or had placed strict prohibitions around it. The era when Ba'athists, Nasserites and other Arab nationalists were confronted with each other and interacted at British universities had passed. However, British universities were still an important meeting place for British-born or -raised Arabs, especially for those whose experience of school was characterised by their being 'the only Arab'. Yet meeting other Arabs at university was by no means uncomplicated or reassuring

The tensions of Arab–Arab encounters had shifted from being ideological and political to being about what constituted legitimate diasporic Arabness and, in particular, the implications of ethnic and class endogamy for the process of gendering. As with the ideological encounters of the twentieth century, the collision of different ideas about what doing Arabness involved would bring some together and drive many others away. Although the gender imbalance of the early student and migrant labour population was now a thing of the past, Arab student culture remained resolutely male in its regulatory ideals and involved a pernicious sexual politics with Arab womanhood at its core. The single most consequential factor I encountered within this social scene was endogamy. Even though actually getting married at this stage of life was no more than a distant prospect, university seemed like a place where young people tested and cultivated anxieties, codes and concerns around 'respectability', reputation and marriageability. This was a way of preparing oneself for the aspiring bourgeois Arab 'professional' scene that awaited upon graduation, and finding suitable employment.

The Arab student societies I encountered not only evaded the relentless politics of Arabness, they were busily engaged in a correspondingly apolitical engendering of 'Arab ethnicity' in Britain, which I understand as a project of cultural survival and intelligibility set against the backdrops of ethnicised heteronormativity. In other words being Arab at university was now about 'Arab ethnicity' in Britain and not Arab politics in Britain. In this context I argue that the utterance 'I'm Arab' activates a set of discourses, norms, dispositions towards taste, bodily conventions and prohibitions that together circumscribe social worth and intelligibility.

Emirs *and* Emiras*: Partying with the Stereotype of Arab Wealth*[3]

I spent my first year at SOAS as juxtaposed and polarised as you like, so much so as to make *Black Adder* seem like daily life. It's unbelievable and I spent my first year hanging around with people who not only had been to private schools but had been to the most prestigious educational institutions that one could go to in this country. I spent my first year with a group of students, mainly Arabs who had been to St Paul's School and who had been to Dulwich College and to Reed School and I found that the things that we did have in common were that we were Arab or that we were ethnic or the fact that we both went to university but I felt that the big difference between us wasn't based on our ideas of race, ethnicity or politics, it was based on our economic situation.

We went clubbing a lot. Not from my own pocket because I was mixing with people who were going out to the best clubs in London, who were going out all the time, every night, who were in the habit of spending in one night what I would consider spending in two or three weeks, and it was very interesting and fun but it wasn't life, it wasn't reality for me it was an alien world.

If I'm going to talk about the Arab community at SOAS, I don't think that the important part about the Arab community in SOAS is that they are Arab or the fact that they are Islamic or English or otherwise. For me the important thing about the community at SOAS is the socio-economic background of the students. For me I feel different from Arabs at SOAS not because I am secular, not because I am not Islamic or Christian enough, because a lot of them are like that. I think it's because I haven't had the same material upbringing and the material chances that these people have had. I think I identify more with someone who went to a comprehensive, from an English working-class background, I think that is my major friction at SOAS with Arabs.

Jabir had grown-up and attended school in north-east London, an experience he described to me in mostly negative terms. Apart from his older brother, he was the 'the only Arab' at school. Being Palestinian only added to the bullying he experienced at the hands of students and teachers in what he described as a predominantly 'White working-class and conservative' environment. His peers only seemed able to recognise him as 'Pakistinian' and one teacher in particular seemed to have played a rather venomous role in his development, with thinly veiled insistence that his Arabness meant that he would never amount to anything. I vividly recall the conversation we had one afternoon, over many cups of coffee, when he described these experiences. Each time he recounted an incident of discrimination, his voice would dip to almost a whisper. I was never quite sure if he was so guarded about his experience of discrimination at school because he didn't want anyone to think that he was a victim or that had 'a chip on his shoulder', or because he felt somehow that no one would believe his story or think of it as an excuse for underachieving. He certainly was not an underachiever but those experiences and 'slurs live and thrive in and as the flesh of the addressee' and over time harden, taking on profound meaning as ordering principles that 'count as "reality"' (Butler 1997b: 125).

It seems quite understandable that in his flight from White working-class suburbia to internationalist and cosmopolitan SOAS he would naturally drift towards other Arab students. But whatever primordial bonds we assume to share with others are often quickly undercut by the diacritics of personhood. Jabir articulates this in terms of a contrast in material privilege and class positions, and, despite having a gateway into this lifestyle, the unreality of a life of 'affluence by association' is an artifice he is unable to sustain. The theatricality of *passing for* rich, which Jabir associates quite fittingly with the television series *Black Adder*, also reveals the extent to which class habitus is about a set of material, cultural, social and psychological speech acts. Jabir is not working-class as he tries to suggest; nonetheless he discursively places himself upon a scale of domination laid out by a rather polarised social field of those with money and those without. At that point in his life, or in the context of the narrative that our interaction co-produced, class became a defining feature of similarity and difference. His narrative also alludes to the *amor fati* of working-class habitus. But that *amor fati* is not paradigmatic or fixed and should only be understood in phenomenological terms as part of interpellation and a project of cultural survival. Identification seems to have come full circle for Jabir; from being the ethnic anomaly at school, through the fabled comfort of axiological ethnic similarity as a fresher at university, to the discursive embrace of an English working-class habitus after becoming disillusioned by performing a certain kind of Arabness. The shifting points of identification along the lines of race, nationality, religion, class and politics in Jabir's narrative point to the phantasmic nature of identification, but equally to the propensity and capacity to identify with others so variously and instrumentally. The performative ritual of identification is that process whereby social actors are 'called into social being, inaugurated into sociality by a variety of diffuse and powerful interpellations' (Butler 1999a: 125).

The motivations for and benefits of *passing for* rich are clear enough and are hardly exclusive to Arabs. However, what interests me here is the discursive economy which hails the subject in a specific way, offering some young British-born or -raised Arabs the character of the Arab oil sheikh. The stereotype of *Khaleeji* wealth is one fuelled by actual contact with it in London and the discourses about it – everything from high-profile football sponsorship deals, 'TV Arabs' (Shaheen 1984, 1997, 2008, 2009; see also Semmerling 2006), and the long-standing tradition of 'fake sheikhs' in British newspaper journalism – all of these contribute towards creating the aura of the crass but exotic super-rich and powerful Arab. But there is quite an ambivalent relationship between young Arab Londoners and perennial *Khaleeji* tourists, as Tamara goes on to explain:

> I know we hate that stereotype but when you go into that [night] club you forget that you hate it and you just play on that stereotype ... I see it in these clubs all the time, they don't really have the money, it's just they look like they have money. You can become famous and look glamorous and wealthy like you are someone, in a bigger pond you are no one ... It's just when we all socialise together in a club or anywhere else people can get arrogant and they act like they are all oil barons that rule the world.

Tamara draws our attention to Derrida's assertion that neither the uses to which a sign is put nor the meanings it will reiteratively generate can ever really be forestalled or controlled. However disparaging and vilifying media discourses have been over the last 40 years, this has not deterred some from wanting to bask in the stardust of *Khaleeji* wealth, to experience affluence through prestigious postcodes, mysterious number plates and opulent cars flown in to London for the summer. With 'Arab' being a portmanteau term, the pretence of wealth is easy enough to achieve – with the right props and performance skills and, importantly, the willingness to be seen to spend, almost anyone can *pass for* a *Khaleeji* prince or princess, at least for a night. Tamara continues:

> when the *Emirs* [princes] and the Princesses and all of that lot come over in the summer and they go to the clubs they are not the ones making a

big deal out of themselves, I mean they will drop 30k [thousand] in a night but they are not the ones dancing on the tables or you know like doing all of that stuff.

Thus the indulgences of being *nouveau riche* experienced by the oil boom generation in the Gulf seem to have waned somewhat for subsequent generations of *Khaleejis*, only to be taken up by a new group of people. As one young man put it to me 'the rowdy group of Arab boys from London who are dancing, trying to pick up women … it's just a typical "Arab scene"'. The impulse to maximise one's stake and status within a social milieu means that the temptation to project an image of Arab wealth seems difficult to avoid at times.

Young Arabs in London are not an exception when it comes to the appeal of re-appropriation as a strategy for coping with meanings that are beyond one's control. As Gilroy's (1993) and Hutnyk's (2000) work on the culture industries and the commercialisation of 'ethnic' and 'racial' 'identities' suggests, the fact that Black men can play on the stereotype of physical and sexual prowess, or Asians on the aura of the exotic culture does not signal the demise of the equally profitable and pervasive stereotypes of backwardness and savagery.

No Sex Please We're Arabs

As a social milieu Arab student culture at university in London reflects, incorporates and adapts gender, race and class norms that inform the way in which 'Arab ethnicity' is imagined and enacted in practice. Central to this project is the recreation of the Iraqi, Egyptian, Moroccan or Arab family in the diaspora, a process that relies centrally on endogamy and the regulation of gender norms. These were quite discernible aspects of the university student culture I had come across.

Suad, whom we met in chapter 2, and Ayaat had both played active roles in the Arab Societies at their respective universities. They were among a number of young women I had met who had presided over university Arab student societies. Suad's motivation for joining the Arab Society when she enrolled at UCL at the age of 17 was to meet other Arabs:

> I felt completely isolated [at school] so when I went to uni I was yearning to meet Arabs. I mean that was one of the first things you know, I want to meet up with Arabs … I had a friend with me and we were like 'let's go', we actually wanted to go and check out guys [laughs]

… I mean, we had been in all-girls schools, right? If my dad had his way he would have sent me to an all-girls university too! So we went there and we saw the guys and we were like … 'Really ugly!' Most Arab girls I met didn't want to join because it was like, a lot of them were like 'No we want to get away from it.' The only people who really joined were loads of guys because they wanted to meet Arabic girls, that was their main thing, and football. I wanted to get involved anyway so I ran for president of the society and … I won, [laughs] it was easy. The guys seemed happy to have someone organise things for them, but when it came to organising things though … it was, we tried to, we wanted to, the guys wanted football so we were like, ok we will do that. We wanted to do kind of Arabic nights to do with culture and debates, there was one guy who wanted to help out but the majority overruled us, they just wanted parties and they couldn't be bothered to make the effort so it ended up not really being that active, we ended up having like three parties a year, one each term. It was a typical Arab thing; I mean I used to look at other societies and I used to just think why can't we be like that, because the other societies – they had been there for years and when you are part of a university like UCL, I mean their societies are actually quite reputable, like you have the Jewish Society, the Law Society you know … typical Arabs.

Ayat, a former King's College Arabic Society President continued in a similar vein:

I don't understand it, how can you really be an Arab and not be interested in politics, especially now. Many of them are just not interested in politics, it is also because lots of people have been to demonstrations and lectures and they become disappointed because it doesn't make any difference. They [Arabic Society members] are not willing to take part in venting anger so I said to myself, I have a life to get on with, I don't care any more, I'm not going to argue and fight till I'm blue in the face for like a proper set of society activities that people don't even want. The only thing that people are interested in are parties and dinners. There are so many men and when we organised the parties and dinners they would complain to me that there weren't enough girls at the parties – crazy! It was like they thought it was a dating agency, well it is a dating agency I guess.

Arab Societies may have had female presidents but these seem to have been put to the service of an overwhelmingly male membership who were actively opposed to any society activities beyond football teams, dinners, Arabic parties and belly dancing classes. Perhaps the election of female Arab student society presidents reveals little more than an expectation among male members that a female society president would be more adept at facilitating their interest in meeting Arab girls.

Arab student societies were characterised not only by their lack of engagement in Arab politics but also a complex relationship with Islamic societies. As chapter 3 suggests, the Arab social scene often seemed like an alternative to the Muslim social scene. Mixed-gender parties, the promotion of *Shisha* smoking and belly dancing, the dominant activities of Arabic Societies, were all activities that conflicted considerably with the values of Muslim student societies. According to Suad, relations between her and members of the Islamic society were sometimes complicated by her membership of the Arab Society,

> They would find out that we were having a party and they would get, well quite like disgusted. They would say like 'I thought you were better than this.' They were very quick to judge, you know; there were a couple of Asian girls who I chatted with a few times and, you know, attended some events with them, and when they got to know me they were like 'Oh actually you are quite conservative, you don't drink, you don't go clubbing that much, you are actually very similar to us, your parents are strict, we thought you were a complete "slapper".' Just because I was hanging out with guys! These guys are just friends, they are like my brothers, a lot of them are older than me and they look out for me, we are not doing anything, it's all in public you know, we are having lunch or something.

Gender segregation and the policing of female sexuality are central regulatory ideals for Arab and Muslim womanhood, albeit accorded different degrees of adherence. Suad narrates all the components of an idealised discourse of Arab femininity: the ability to socialise in mixed-gender groups, but at the same time maintain her honour and reputation as a good 'Arab Muslim girl' by not drinking too much or being seen to have too much freedom and importantly seeing the world in terms of kinship ties. Suspicion regarding the nature of her mixed-gender friendships is neutralised by presenting male friends not as potential sexual or romantic partners (which they may or may not be) but as protective brothers (see Joseph 1993, 1994, 1999). Sex and sexuality are central concerns, yet must be consistently renounced. The consequences of being seen to transgress these gendered 'Arab' and 'Islamic' regulatory ideals is the stigma of being seen as sexually available and therefore disreputable and ultimately unfit for marriage.

While the activities promoted by Arab student societies seemed oppositional to Muslim student societies, ultimately both quite comfortably converge to reproduce a version of womanhood that is intimately tied to virtue and virginity. Shams, who was a member of the Arab Society at UCL, offered the following:

> In the Arab Society at UCL you got two types of guys that wanna go to these things [Arabic parties]. Like one girl told me 'It's an Arab speed-dating society' so they're looking for the nice pretty Arab girls – two common minds with two common interests can meet. Then you have another group of Arabs, men who are like – they will not talk to girls although they'd like to, they're quite religious, you know. There was this barbecue event we tried to organise and these religious Arab guys who were also members of the Islamic Society refused to have girls at the event and there was uproar. The girls said 'No we're coming'. I mean, for God's sake, the society president is a girl, are you gonna organise an event where she is not invited? It's so stupid! And then they [religious Arab guys] said ok we'll have a compromise, we'll have two tables one for the guys and one for the girls and we can come over to your table but you can't come over to the boys' table. It was ridiculous! I was disgusted!
>
> Girls are really paranoid about how they are seen and judged, I don't like that, seriously I don't! I don't like the way they are put in that position. I know a lot of girls, I like *Aad'it'hum* [sitting with them/ among them] I like *cotching* with them [hanging out with them]. You need their company sometimes and some of the religious Arab guys didn't like me 'cause I was known as a guy who had a lot of female friends. I didn't really enjoy my time at the Arab Society but I went to the events just to make a statement. It's typical of our political affairs – we just don't always get along. [Pause] In the end of the day the girls want to meet Arab guys. It doesn't matter if she fancies a Black guy or a White guy. 'Cause of family or because of their own personal preferences perhaps, they need Arab men, they need to look for a potential suitor. Where else are they going to find one?

Shams' narrative shows that the regulation of gender segregation is expected as much of men as it is of women. Shams makes connections between religiosity and a set of misogynistic ideals which seek to create passive and pliant Arab Muslim women who are suitable marriage material. While the Arab social scene is the context in which the inscribed norms of reproducing a 'respectable Arab family' are experienced, the failure of that reproduction is articulated in very British terms on the basis of colour. Thus Arabness becomes a contextually meaningful British *ethno-race* in which 'White', 'Black' and 'Asian' are 'others'. The performative effect of multiculturalism as a form of governmentality seems stark here, conforming to multiculturalism involves seeing society through epidermal colour whereby ethnicity, culture, religion, gender, race and class collapse onto each other to provide a map of social possibilities. Indeed, this seems to be a point where the project of multiculturalism on the one hand and diasporic cultural preservationism converge.

The tensions of collective Arabness are as much social as they are about *Realpolitik*. In Shams's account the fault lines run along the themes of secular and religiously informed attitudes towards gender. Peer groups are a moral community, stepping into the shoes of both parental control and state ethnic governmentality by policing what constitutes legitimate and intelligible 'Arab' behaviour. While I maintain that normative injunctions apply to both men and women, it is difficult to overlook the centrality of a particular kind of Arab womanhood to these cultural projects.

Young Arab men make competing and contradictory demands of young Arab women. While men repeatedly stressed that they were looking for an Arabic girl who wasn't 'too Arabic' or 'too English,' they often dismissed many of the 'girls' (perhaps a reference to their presumed virginity and pre-marital status, therefore their pre-womanhood) with whom they socialised at clubs and parties. Many young men openly admitted to me that they would never consider having a serious relationship with an Arabic girl they met at a club or party while others insisted that they would not consider any female they had had sex with as a potential marriage partner. Young Arab women seemed perfectly blameworthy in this scheme, celibacy appeared to represent virtue and frigidity equally, while engaging in pre-marital sex would be tantamount to promiscuity, lead to the loss of reputation and ultimately mean that the woman in question could not be trusted with her sexuality.

Boundaries between 'ethnic' and 'native' others are often centred on the control of female sexuality. In the case of Italian Australians Baldassar notes how 'Australian girls are there to be used while Italian girls are to be respected' and married (1999: 12). But 'respect' in these terms involves framing women within what some have described a 'Mediterranean honour and shame maxim' (Peristiany 1966; Burns et al. 1983), where women are accorded a spiritual and emotional superiority to men which, at the most abstract level, takes the figure of the virgin mother (Mary) as its ideal (Baldassar 1999). Yet simultaneously women are seen to have an innate voracious sexual appetite that requires constant male regulation. Naber finds similar constructs imposed upon Arab American women who are forced to negotiate the terrain between the discursive constructs of 'Arab virgin vs. American(ized) whore' (2006:92). Accordingly for Arab American Christians:

> what distinguished 'us' from 'them' or *al-Arab* from *al-Amerikan* (the Arabs from the Americans) … was a reiterated set of norms that were sexualised, gender specific and performed in utterances such as '*banatna ma bitlaau fil lail*' (our girls don't go out at night). (Naber 2006: 93)

The regulatory ideals around Arab manhood and Arab womanhood are necessarily convergent yet inequitable. While in both cases pre-marital sex is a social and moral 'mistake', for British -born or -raised Arab men such mistakes can be exonerated and even endorsed by peers, whereas for young Arab women a 'mistake' would be considered indefensible and tantamount to a permanent conviction. In many cases young men would actively court Arab girls within these social scenes while planning to marry someone they considered untainted.

The acceptance of and adherence to the particular norms around gender and sexuality constitutes in and of itself one of the principal gateways to the doing of Arab womanhood. Thus the relative dearth of females at Arab Society events and activities suggested by Ayat and Suad might be understood as an evasion of the overbearing regulatory ideals around Arab womanhood as they were interpolated and recited in the context of the Arab social scene at university and beyond. Once again we are confronted with the folly of assuming that diasporic cultures are counter-hegemonic. It is often the case that the culture being mimed is used as a vehicle for the enactment of hegemonic gendered norms (as well as racial and class othering). Cultures are powerful discursive forces through which the body is disciplined, making it intelligible to particular 'moral communities' and within particular ontologies of naturalised effect. Arab womanhood is achieved through a variety of discursive and bodily acts of comportment.

The gestures and codes of this disavowed cult of sexuality are most clearly inscribed in the bodily performance of Middle Eastern dance.

Assuming a Position on Dance

Anya Peterson Royce (1977) provides a detailed historical account of the development of five approaches to dance within anthropology. My engagement with the discourses and practices around dance among young Arab Londoners is concerned with the grammars of improvised *baladi* (folk) dancing and professional belly dancing in London. It falls within the fifth phase, which Royce describes as the 'problem orientated approach' which has been concerned with 'situational analysis' and the ways in which dance reflects or is 'part of social change in the form of modernization, the emergence of new nation-states, urbanization, industrialization and migration' (1977: 27; see also Mitchell 1959 [1956]; Kaeppler 1970). The anthropology of dance has progressively renovated functionalist and structuralist analysis but remains fundamentally informed by these two interpretive schemes which, respectively, look at how dance contributes to social reproduction (functionalist analysis) or read dance as 'grammars' and thus underlying systems of meaning (structuralist analysis) (Peterson Royce 1977:65).

My account of the dance culture of British-born or -raised Arabs is by no means authoritative. As Koutsouba notes: 'once in the field, the first problem I faced was how to decide which dance to examine' (1999: 189). No doubt there are forms of 'Arab' folk dance and dance groups that I have not captured and others that I will over-emphasise. I could and perhaps, some would argue, should have made a more concerted effort to engage with the (few) formal Arab folk dance groups operating in London. Indeed, the 'study of community dance phenomenon is a totally different task from research into the community itself' (1999: 189).

I must admit that I did not initially intend to study dance formally. It was more a case of the serendipity of fieldwork and the process of finding meanings and patterns from the piles of field notes and artefacts I had collected. I was more drawn to popular and improvised forms of dance and how they might inform my attempts to understand the relationship between young Arab men and women in London. Kaeppler (1999) encountered a similar situation during her fieldwork in Tonga in the 1960s, when she was driven more by an interest in aesthetics than she was in dance *per se*. Much anthropological literature on dance is similarly oriented more towards understanding the social, cultural and structural meanings and intentions of dance while folklorists and dance scholars focus on the dance itself as a 'primary unit' (Kaeppler 1999:18–20).

Kaeppler argues that imposing western dance theories upon non-western settings might be inappropriate (2000:121). She qualifies this by saying that the distinction western and non-western is increasingly strained and reflects the broader concern with the 'analytical eye of the ethnographer/ dance studies researcher' (2000: 116), a point which I wholeheartedly support. I understand neither the settings, the people, the normative constructs nor, for that matter, the ethnographer as corresponding to the 'East' and 'West' dichotomy. Instead I see them as synthesising these and other constructs through the imperatives of recitation that, in turn, expose their reiterative possibilities. The account that I present draws upon all the various shades of the anthropology of dance, those that have fallen out of favour and those that continue to be advocated. As such, I draw attention to the grammars and politics of the body in Middle Eastern dance and the connections between dances and dance events and the setting and conditions I am interested in: London, Arabness, heteronormativity and ethnonormativity.

Raqs: *Performance, Comportment and Sexuality*

King's College London Arabic and Iranian Societies
Middle Eastern Cruise II – Celebrating *Sadeh* Festival
Wednesday 15th February 2006
Swan Pier (Blackfriars Bridge) 7:30pm

I board the boat and make my way upstairs to the top deck where most of the activities are taking place. The DJ had set himself up and draped an Iranian flag over the table with the (CD) decks. He is dressed in low-cut jeans with a large chain hanging from his belt loop and a crisp baseball cap, worn 'Street-style' with the tag still attached and the front visor still wide and fresh – no creases. There were no surprises in terms of the music, which is usually a mix of hip-hop and RnB with some Iranian and Arabic [music] thrown in, the staple diet of these events. It makes for a strange mix, Arabic pop music is painfully romantic, kitsch and staggering in the innocence of its themes of unrealised or forbidden love – true love. It teaches a certain type of romance to the younger generation where love takes precedence over lust and sexual desire. Hip-hop and RnB could not be more contrasting in their lyrics and themes, which seem diametrically opposed to the Middle Eastern pop song, yet they are simultaneously enjoyed by these young people who see themselves as connected to them both. '*Habibi bahebak*' ('Darling I love you') hand-in-hand with 'Bling', 'Ice', 'Scrubs' and 'Hos'.

The environment is sexually charged as the music jolts from the serenading movements of Arabic pop to bump and grind of RnB, people rubbing up against each other and getting carried away. Men are openly grabbing women by the waist (including some of the veiled). It seems they feel it's a safe enough setting to enact their sexual desires, definitely not behaving like 'good Muslims' as some might expect. 'That's not what we came here for, we came to dance to Arabic music that's the whole point, and there aren't enough Arabic people. The atmosphere at an Arabic party would have been better,' said Reem. 'Look! They're all over each other, *ya'nni 'ayb b'gad* [I mean it's shameful, seriously]. This like Asian looking guy just tried to grab me by the waist, *eh il araf da!* [How disgusting is that!]'.

Half way through the evening the hip-hop is interrupted by the heavy drums of some traditional *baladi* (Egyptian country/folk) music and one of the party organisers Khalid makes an announcement over the mic in a distinctive Arab London American accent 'We have a beautiful girl who's gonna show us her belly dancing skills, it's Louise from King's, a big round of applause!' Louise, in her early 20s with pale skin and long auburn hair is dressed in a two-piece belly dancing outfit or *badla* [suit] with her midriff, arms, shoulders and legs bare. Her dance rendition is in the sexualised tantric/cabaret belly dance style. Young men are attentively clapping her on, they seem impressed by this version of *baladi*. She is shaking everything, with little left for the imagination. Some of the girls look on, visibly unimpressed and making no effort to hide it. I asked Reem, do you think that an Arabic girl would volunteer to do that. '*Tab'an La!*' ('Of course not!') came the answer abruptly. 'It is definitely not an option for an Arabic girl to dress up as a belly dancer *'ayb awi* [it's utterly shameful], can you imagine what people would say!

The belly dancer is one of the principal symbols of Arabic culture in London; she is the trope for erotic Oriental or Arab sexuality and is used unabashedly for cultural and commercial capital at parties and restaurants around the city. Almost all the belly dancers who perform at Arabic parties and Middle Eastern restaurants in London are non-Arabs. As Dox and others have argued, 'Western women, standing in for the Other, lend authenticity to the dining experience' (2006: 54; see also Erdman 1996; Stavrou 2002; Deagon 2002, 2005; Wilkinson 2002). Ironically, while the belly dancer is the quintessential trope of Oriental female sexuality, young British-born and -raised Arab women have an uneasy relationship with this performance form. The two-piece sequined belly dancing outfit and the cabaret-style belly dancing of contemporary popular culture is something for mostly non-Arab women to indulge in.

Reem's discomfort with the ambience of the boat party is reminiscent of the way in which Archetti (1999) describes the delicate signification of love in the lyrics of tango music. Archetti argues that tango lyrics depict processes of social and cultural change in a historical context that affects traditional family patterns and places the responsibility for love on both men and women. The basic elements in the cultural construction of romantic love within that lyrical tradition are intimacy, companionship (friendship), the existence of mutual empathy and the search for sexual pleasure. The distortion of one of these, such as too much emphasis on sexual pleasure, creates emotional imbalance leading to unhappiness, loneliness and nostalgia (1999: 151). Furthermore, he argues that the:

> Tango clearly illustrates how the behaviour of women is judged to be morally good or bad or indifferent according to the happiness or misery of those involved. What makes men and women unhappy and miserable is the rupture of given moral standards. (1999: 149)

Like tango, the performance of *baladi* within Arabic parties:

> can also be seen as a discourse on human happiness for both men and women. Happiness seems possible only if persons are guided in their behavior by sincere and authentic love. The cabaret, almost by definition, is not a place for the realization of romanticism. (1999: 149)

Reem's reference to 'what people would say' is not only concerned with the solo nature of the dance but the social context and the revealing *badla* (costume), which lies at the heart of this contestation. The traditional village form of *raqs baladi* (folk dance) is a solo improvisation performed to family and friends. In the everyday contexts where dance takes place, it almost never involves the revealing outfit. Instead dancers are fully clothed sometimes with a scarf wrapped around the waist to emphasise the movements of the hips. At weddings everyone does some dancing, clapping is a polite reaction for parents and elders, but often unmarried young women are coaxed or volunteer to dance *baladi* in celebration of the bride and groom, cheered on or joined by both women and men. The women-only henna parties that take place before weddings are renowned for being occasions where women perform less inhibited dances and sometimes wear more revealing costumes. Both these performance contexts are public yet legitimate because they are coded within the familial sphere and the celebration of marriage. The Arab parties I attended seemed to exist on the margin of the formal family sphere too, although there was an element of abandon, peers police the reproduction of gendered norms of virtue and evaluate each other in terms of marriageability, both of which are more compelling for Arab women. Thus for Reem and other young women these parties are settings in which their virtue and comportment are important considerations. In demonstrating their proficiency in Arab womanhood and cultural mores, dancing *baladi* is necessary, it displays 'ethnicity' in a British context and simultaneously exhibits and disavows their sexuality, a project which precludes performances involving the *badla*, however good natured.

I would argue that some distinctions should be drawn between the brand of dancing that contemporary professional dancers perform at university Arabic parties and Middle Eastern restaurants, which I understand as 'belly dancing', and '*baladi*' (folk), which is less sexualised and more improvised. The genealogical relationship between belly dancing and *baladi* somewhat resembles the relationship between ballet as an ethnic dance and 'classical ballet'. Aalten has suggested that if ballet is a form of ethnic dance then classical ballet can indeed be viewed as a reflection of typical nineteenth-century values that are still in effect today (1997: 206). Although folk dances from across the region are central to 'belly dancing' the form owes much to Hollywood, Orientalism and a contemporary international 'belly dancing' industry. The transformation from *baladi* to 'belly dancing' or '*danse de ventre*' took place in the late nineteenth century and was popularised by people like Sol Bloom 'the Music Man' who presented the 'Algerian and Tunisian Village troupe' to the 1893 World's Columbia Exposition in Chicago.

The dancing girls gave performances in a 1,000-seat hall. Their great specialty was the danse de ventre. When the public learned that the literal translation was 'belly dance,' they delightedly concluded that it must be salacious and immoral, and the paying crowds poured in. Bloom states that the danse de ventre, while sensuous and exciting, was a masterpiece of rhythm and beauty. Almost immediately, though, the dance was imitated in amusement parks around the country, and became associated with debasement and vulgarity as a crude, suggestive dance known as the 'Hoochy-Koochy.' (Roth 2000: 4)

Belly dancing soon became a standard-bearer of the 'all-female image of Middle Eastern dance produced by American film corporations' in the early twentieth century (Shay and Sellers-Young 2005: 20). The image of salacious and decadent Oriental *harems* popularised by *A Thousand and One Nights*, Orientalist art and the colonial appeal of Arab women as forbidden fruit, soon produced the two-piece cabaret costume in Hollywood that was motivated as much by the commercialisation of female bodies of all types as it was by Orientalism (see Jarmakani 2008; Nance 2009). In turn, Cairo's cabarets and casinos adopted the genre and its props to cater for the western tastes of Arab elites and curious tourists.

Belly dance reemerged in the West in the 1960s and 1970s out of feminist efforts to claim and express women's sexuality. The growing popularity of belly dance generated a pedagogical taxonomy of movements 'Tunisian hips', 'Turkish backwalk', 'basic Egyptian', 'belly roll', which parsed Middle Eastern dances into individual movements for studio teaching and gave belly dance credibility as a legitimate dance form (Dox 2006: 53). Today 'belly dancing' has become a global phenomenon that somewhat resembles burlesque and is marketed as everything from a form of exercise, a way of cultivating one's sex life or simply a tribute to exotic worldliness.

What was unfailingly consistent at these events was that, even though cabaret and improvised Middle Eastern dance were historically related movement systems, a sharp distinction seemed to be drawn between the type of improvised *baladi* dance that young women attending these parties would engage in on the one hand and the tantric or cabaret forms of belly dancing that were used to *stage* Arab culture as spectacle. These distinctions centre on the both the sexualisation of the choreography and the body. Drawing on the writing of Andrea Deagon, Sellers-Young argues that aggressive displays of female sexuality are often understood as representing the western conventions of belly dancing. Drawing on a number of commentators like McDonough (1995), Kapchan (2011), Hirschmann (1999) and El-Guindi (1999), Dox (2006: 61) finds that choosing not to display the body in public has been interpreted variously as an affirmative gesture that reinforces emotional and psychological autonomy, a strategy for maintaining privacy and preserving family honour, and a form of resistance to sexual permissiveness.

For non-Arab 'belly dancers' like Louise (at the boat party) the *badla* may signify cultural worldliness and an expression of confident female sexuality, but the inherent communicative failure in signification can mean that while she feels a connection and affinity with Arab or Oriental culture through the *badla* and 'belly dancing', it simultaneously casts her as 'female-other', 'moral-other' and sexual object to an Arab audience. The *badla* and the body beneath and between its *texti*le presents us with an antagonism. The bodily cultural politics of the *badla* parodies both Orient and Occident. As Lynne Hanna describes, the *badla* has long been a contentious development because of representational tensions it generates. In 1963 Gamal Abdel Nasser's government (in Egypt) pushed through a new dance code which 'banned the naked midriff to restore respectability … the only proper dance costume was one that covered the chest, stomach, and back and had no opening' (Hanna 1988: 63). Dancers were also prohibited from assuming 'positions or … movements that carry sexual implications'. The restriction did not last for long though and in 1966 the Egyptian government decided to allow dancers to express themselves somewhat more freely, bare their stomachs, and wear skirts slit up the sides (Hanna 1988: 63).

The way in which these tensions are played out in the diaspora setting is interesting as neither the genre nor the people involved are straightfor-wardly eastern or western. Adra (2005) argues that few Arabs will perform belly dance in environments that include foreigners and makes a brief mention of *raqs sharqi* (eastern dance) at Arab parties in the diaspora where he finds that:

> [T]here has been some accommodation to social change and global influences. Currently mixed gender groups of friends and relatives can be seen dancing at the elite nightclubs without loss of respect, at least by their peers. This dance however does not include the same pelvic isolations that would be performed at home among intimates or at gender segregated parties. An adaptation of belly dance that combines small hops and the footwork of traditional local line dances with an elaboration of arm movements, minimising shoulder and pelvic shimmies are performed to Middle Eastern music. This is the variation of dance often performed in mixed gender parties in Arab cities as well as in the diaspora, especially in Europe and the United States. (2005: 38)

I found far less reluctance than Adra; in up-market clubs and bars where young British-born or -raised Arabs share social space with non-Arabs, *raqs baladi* was used by Arab women to enforce and emphasise cultural boundaries and reinforce exotic authenticity, perhaps as a counter to the perceived advantage of sexual availability that non-Arab women are assumed to have. The ability to dance *baladi* or *sharqi* and to display the correct levels of intensity, play and humour; directing flirtatious shimmies and gazes at friends and only evanescently at prospective partners, are ways in which females use their cultural knowledge to show that they can do Arab femininity correctly and that they understand its bodily techniques and aptitudes. However it is important to remember that when improvisation is subject to so many judgements around comportment, composure and movement it comes to resemble formalism. In this sense I am reminded of Paul Spencer's reference to the *minuet*, where he cites the role of the 'critical gaze of the assembled company' that transforms dance into an 'ordeal which epitomized the etiquette and set of values that maintained the distinctiveness of the elite' (1985: 8).

In the context of London, Arab parties are very rarely exclusively Arab but attitudes towards the presence of non-Arabs at these parties are mixed. In a context where there is a premium on ethnic and cultural distinctiveness (or at least an assumption of their possibility as an ideal type) 'others' are vital component of imagining and enacting the individual and collective 'self'.

'Arabic Night' at Pangea: 06/04/06
A text message had gone round a day earlier advertising the night
'DJ Mike from Buddha bar Beirut. Mixing the best in Arabic/R&B/House
10 pm til late @ Pangea, Mayfair.'

Fifteen pounds at the door, exclusive club scene thing going on, drinks at the bar £8. I met Asalah and Amira just after 10 at the door. There were lots of non-Arabs in the queue, Asalah and Amira say '*hwaya Ingleez*' ['lots of English people'] with both surprise and a little disdain. This is the feeling you get at many Arab events, that the expectation is that you are going somewhere to socialise with Arabs and that the mixed crowd of Arab and non-Arab makes it almost dishonest to promote the event as an 'Arabic night'. The usual suspects are there; the kind of 'late 20-something' professional transnational crowd that you see when there is an Arab-related social event in the affluent locales of West London.

The music is mostly western interspersed with Arabic, less pop and more instrumental Arabic music mixed with the electronic beats and the bass of 'house music'. There were large numbers of non-Arab men and women; particularly a large group of English women who were, in comparison, scantily dressed and getting progressively drunk as the evening went on. The Arabic girls balance out their competition by really going for it *baladi*. They know what to do, how to move and many mime the words. This is a serious performance that shows the English girls to be lacking in something … it is a staking-out of cultural territory and also a reaffirmation of their authenticity … not only reaffirming 'identity' but also giving confidence. This creates an interesting effect in terms of the role of Arabic parties as a place for Arab men and women to meet, or at least an opportunity to see and be seen by other Arabs. Men who are more opportunistic may make the most of this themed event, of which they are an authentic Arabic part, to take someone home, probably not an Arabic girl though.

There is an interesting variation in this 'Arabic night', usually these events are symbolised by the image or person of the belly dancer. While a belly dancer did make an appearance just before midnight she was preceded by something different, which I have not seen before. Something for the girls as it were – three Chippendales, naked from the waist upwards wearing *Ghutra* and *Agal* (traditional Bedouin head dress). They were there right from the start of the night and made their way around the club carrying trays of tequila shots, which they tried to sell, mainly to females.

Once again it is a non-Arab body that is used as a medium through which to sexualise or eroticise Arabness. Symbols of Arab sexuality or Orientalist fantasies are needed for all of these events but they are rarely enacted by Arabs themselves … which of these middle-class Arab men would go half-naked and wear a *Ghutra* and *Agal*?

Dana (female) is dancing away; I approach her a few minutes later and we start chatting. She tells me that a guy came up to her and tried to touch her as she was dancing *baladi*. '*Wahid Hindi!* [An Indian guy] '*ya'nni*' [I mean] I didn't come to this place to be touched-up by someone like that … no offence. *Ya'nni wahid zay dah!* [I mean someone like that]. You can look but you can't touch.'

Because he is Asian he is perceived as unsuitable in all ways, on top of this he breaks the codes of behaviour that operate at these parties. Most of the people present are accustomed to socialising with each other; it is very unlikely that anyone would have touched her, even if he was flirting with her, unless she was openly known to be in a relationship with him (or a close male friend). Unlike the younger crowd at the boat party, these young people were much closer to the prospect of marriage and thus there is far more at stake in relation to maintaining a 'virtuous reputation'. As a group they constitute a moral community with codes of behaviour that regulate male/female interactions and flirtation in public. 'Outsiders' may believe this to be just another London club-night, albeit an ethnic one, where the same sexual opportunism that is associated with clubbing can be played out. In so doing they break the conventions of accepted behaviour and, in turn, make some feel that the event is not Arab enough.

I take from this recollected participant-observation two points. The first relates to the propensity for race, gender and classed meanings to sequentially inform and often define social interaction. In separate parties and separate settings, one among university students and the other a group of young 'professional Arabs', females make a point of rejecting the advances of South Asian men who are cast as ethnic and class 'others', regardless of their actual class status (see McClintock 2010). To my mind the censure of British South Asians by some young men within the *Shisha* café scene and here by young women in the party scene is confirmation of the intersection of racist discourses from both British and Arab contexts in relation to British South Asians and South Asians more broadly. The rejection of the advances of South Asian men (British or otherwise) seems to have been a common occurrence. It is not only South Asians who are assigned an inferior class or caste status, equally 'English girls' were subject to similar race, gender and class 'othering'. In its extreme the stereotype of the 'English girl' casts her as White, working-class, without culture, sexually available and unconcerned for her reputation. She is the oppositional 'other' against which being an Arab woman is measured and made intelligible.

As suggested in chapter 3 these different ways of doing womanhood point to a need to disaggregate heteronormativity. As Babayan and Najmabadi (2008: 23) note, heteronormativity functions with particular configurations of desire, subjectivity and marital structures which are various and culturally contingent. Different gendered discourses call into being different ways of being a woman, in this case around notions of sexual availability, reputation, marriageability, class position, culture and ethno-race. 'The adjacent and familiar others' (Barth 1994: 13) of 'diaspora space' make it difficult to represent 'English girls' as indigenous others and 'Arabic girls' as ethnic others (Brah 1996: 209). Yet the shared but distinct configurations of heteronormativity to which these women are *subjected* seem to create divisive strategies of moral othering between them. Interactions in the diaspora space of London often stretch and strain the consistency of constructs like 'eastern' vs 'Euro-American,' or embedded, authentic Orient vs. disembedded and transgressive Occident. Instead I see these interactions as sequential processes of being raced, gendered and classed through diverse cultural processes and meanings all of which produce naturalising and effective forces which play a central role in subjectification.

As Spencer relates, anthropological work has shown an element of competition in dance, and as Bailey suggests each culture has its own idiom of confrontation (in Spencer 1985: 22). In this case ethnic dance is the site of multiple confrontations and competitions: between brands of heteronormativity, with the commercialisation and eroticisation of the female body, with the race and class structures that inform the way that ethnic distinctiveness is achieved and, perhaps most forcefully, the confrontations around marriageability between young middle-class Arab men and women in London.

The second point relates to the long-standing tradition of using the bodies of race and class 'others' as a means of enacting Arab sexuality. In her account of the tango and the political economy of passion, Marta Savigliano (1995) draws attention to the parallels between the tango, the can-can and belly dancing. All three have their social origins in groups that were subordinated on the basis of race and/or class, and all three created what she describes as 'erotic problems'. In the case of the tango and belly dancing, debates in Europe 'immediately amplified' these dances' 'erotic problem' at home (1995: 114). As the ethnographic notes above suggest, the bodies physically adorned to eroticise 'Arabness' at parties in London, be they male or female, are rarely 'Arab'. Far from being a unique cultural adaptation in the diaspora, there is a degree of historical continuity in the use of ethnic and social 'others' to embody, enact and represent the gestures and codes of sexuality in Arab or Middle Eastern dance. Under the Ottoman *Millet* system, non-Muslims or members of 'distinct' ethnic and tribal minorities in the Middle East were associated with or assigned particular roles in the division of labour; and in some cases non-Muslims were exempt from certain laws, norms and restrictions that applied to wider society. Across the Middle East, cultural and ethnic minorities like the Gypsy tribes of the Ghawazi and Bahlawanaat and the Qawlia were renowned as public performers of dance and entertainment. 'Since a Turkish man would not deign to be a public performer' male dancers at the time were often ethnically Greek, Armenian or Jewish (Karayanni 2004: 28). The popular dances of *ouled naïl* of Algeria and the *guedra* of Morocco, belly dancing of the Ghawazi and the Qawlia of Iraq have emerged from marginal, often stigmatised groups to become the basis for contemporary folk dances that represent national 'culture'. These in turn have been eclipsed by the cabaret forms of belly dancing which is now seen by countless Arabs and non-Arabs as a choreographic icon of 'Arab identity'.

I was often left wondering, if Arab-themed parties ('Arabic parties') were contexts in which ethnicity was enacted and 'Arab culture' cited, why didn't young British-born or -raised Arab men and women perform *baladi* or any other folk dances like *debka* at these gathering in a more formal sense? After all the formalisation of national folk dances has been an important component of many Arab states' cultural policies for decades. Was it because, as Ayaat and Suad both mentioned, Arab student society members were simply not pro-active enough for such folk dance ensembles to be formed? Or that hiring a professional dancer provided a simple, ready-made Arabising component for these parties? While both of these are important considerations I would suggest that many young Arabs see cabaret-style belly dancing as traditional and authentic.

The historical *roots* and *routes* of Middle Eastern dance suggest that a set of anxieties around public and private spheres, gender, the body and sexuality have been transported and reiterated over time and space, as have the strategies of using 'social-others' to enact them publicly. Although my discussion so far has focused more on the strategies and performances of women, the dance cultures and conventions of young Arab Londoners was equally revealing of how *baladi* exposes the genealogy of contemporary ideals of Arab masculinity and sexuality.

The Dancing Men: Gender Parody or Ambiguity?

We had agreed to meet at Ayoush, an up-market Egyptian restaurant, bar and cafe on the corner of Wigmore Street and James Street. It was well within the imaginary boundaries of Arab London. Levant, a similarly themed venue, is less than 50 metres away. Round the corner on Baker Street were some Arab financial landmarks like the National Bank of Kuwait, its camel logo signage protruding above the pavement. It is early summer and *Khaleeji* men and women, heavy with shopping bags can be seen emerging from Selfridges and other shops in Oxford Street on their way back to apartments and hotels in the immediate vicinity. James Street, narrow and densely packed with cafes and restaurants is quite unique in that almost all the cafés and restaurants that line it have pavement seating, a rare taste of cafe society in London, perfectly continental or Arab – somewhere where you can see and be seen.

At Ayoush the walls are lined with pictures of Egyptian film stars and singers from the early to mid-20th century, the golden age of Egyptian cinema. It is quite tastefully decorated in a mix of Pharaonic, Moroccan and modern Egyptian themes. Downstairs there is a bar and dining area which has been the venue of a number of birthday parties and get-togethers I have attended. A small dancing area is set among five alcoves where groups sit and eat a variety of Arab cuisines, usually Lebanese, from ornately decorated Moroccan earthenware, a combination typical of London's contemporary Arab foodscape.

Basil was a regular at Ayoush. He had made friends with the staff, Jezel the Brazilian belly dancer and the family that runs the restaurant. As we sat at the bar Basel passed me a *tabla* (goblet drum) and urges me to play as he and some of the boys take to the dance floor singing along with the music, a mixture of *Rai*, Egyptian, Lebanese and *Khaleeji* pop. I can't help notice the gender parody and play in the way 'the boys' are dancing with each other – Basil's rather full-built body goes still apart from his chest, which he shakes from side to side just centimetres from Yaseen, mimicking the way that professional female dancers lean back and forth swaying their shoulders and shaking their breasts. Yaseen bursts into laughter, as does the Egyptian barman, who looks at me and says 'He's such a joker.' Shortly afterwards Basil tells me that the belly dancer would arrive any minute 'She's so fit! She's Brazilian!' The DJ faded the music from Arabic pop to the earthy drum beats of *baladi* (folk/country). Jezel paused at the top of the staircase before making her way down the stairs to the dining area/ dance floor wrapped in a silk shawl and dressed in a revealing sequinned two-piece dancing outfit, a scarf wrapped tightly around her hip bones.

She danced using complex movements of the arms, hips and abdomen typical of contemporary commercial belly dancing and we backed up against the bar surrounding her in a semi-circle, clapping and cheering her on. Jezel made her way around the tight space gracefully, in time to the music as she tried to get male and female guests to join her on the dance floor. The mixed clientele are usually always too intimidated by the dance and the dancer to take part. Although belly dancing comes from an improvised solo dance which, until the mid-twentieth century had no formal style, it has taken on a format which requires physical agility and bodily expertise. Jezel manages to persuade a woman in a party hat (in the middle of her meal) to dance with her. Jezel held her hand as the woman reluctantly got up and shyly moved her hips and made the shape of an 8 using her arms and hands. She quickly turns bright red as Jezel effortlessly moves her hips and shoulders to the beats of the *tabla*. Basil needed no further encouragement, he knew that in order for the show to be successful and fun someone had to accompany Jezel. He joined her on the dance floor returning the flirtatious dance moves she presented, he got up close but never close enough to touch, mimicking shimmies of her shoulders and breasts, his hands raised to shoulder height, his gaze never set straight at her, instead he looked up at the ceiling or at his friends and only fleetingly at her. (Field note, Night out at Ayoush, James Street, 5 July 2006)

Basil stepped in and out of contemporary conventions of masculinity and femininity in contemporary Middle Eastern dance. During other visits to Ayoush I saw Mohammed, a member of staff, and a recent migrant from Egypt in his late 30s, accompany Jezel and other belly dancers in entertaining the customers. For these performances Mohammed would dress in the traditional clothes of a male from the Egyptian countryside. A white scarf wrapped around his head a *Sidiri* (waistcoat) showing through the open buttons of his *Jalabiyah* (traditional gown). His main prop was a thick cane about a metre in length, which he would swing round and balance as he danced. The stick is typically carried by men as a weapon and is sometimes used in a ritualised duel called *Tahteeb* where men posture and cross, swing and joust with their canes. In professional dance duets the cane is sometimes used to lead the female dancer, placed around but not touching the dancers' hips as the couple move around the dance floor, the male dancer leading and controlling, almost taming his female dance partner.

Mohammed's dance is contemporary *raqs sharqi*; because of its formality and the overt masculinity encoded in its gestures, it contrasts sharply with Basil's, which is improvised, informal and cites the gender ambiguity of traditional improvised dance. The strict separation between masculine and feminine forms in folklore and popular dance is largely related to nineteenth-century European gender sensibilities. Anthony Shay argues that, in the post-independence era in Egypt, a re-fashioning of folk dance took place whereby this improvised folk genre was formalised, creating clear distinction between male and female dance forms which sought to provide a level of gendered respectability to the folk genre. This was felt to be necessary as part of the project of nation-building to which 'folklore' plays such a significant part. Egyptian post-independence choreographers like Mahmoud Reda helped to formalise gender-defined roles in folklore dance. Gender definition was in part designed to counter the historical stigma attached to public Middle Eastern folk dance that developed during the European colonial era, and which saw the British for example banning male and female street dancing in Egypt (Shay 2005; see also Shay 2009; Karayanni 2009).

Up until the mid-nineteenth century street dancers were commonly seen in Middle Eastern cities, entertaining people outside taverns and coffee houses, performing a genre rooted in play and humour. In contrast to the Ghawazi (Gypsy public dance performers), the Awalim enjoyed high status, dancing only in all-female gatherings, or, if males were present, silhouetted behind a *mashrabiyah* (Arabesque wooden lattice). Awalim (sing. '*Almah*', literally 'learned') performed almost exclusively for the rich and at court. They were considered to be accomplished artists and were known more for their vocal performances of folk songs and poetry rather than their dancing (Valassopoulos 2007). In contrast the Ghawazi and Khawalāt performed to public audiences for money. They were stigmatised as disreputable, of low status and 'correctly … seen as sexually available' (Shay 2005: 55). Despite their association with prostitution, male and female street performers were popular and took part in public celebrations like *Moulids* (festivals venerating local saints). They were reputed for their athleticism and the humorous sexual references in their displays and performances. Above all they were best known for their dancing, which, in the case of Khawals (who are male) is considered to have been close to 'contemporary belly dancing techniques … What is important to grasp is that the performances of the male and female professional dancers were almost identical' (Shay 2005: 66).

The arrival of European travellers and subsequently European armies was to bring an abrupt end to these popular forms of public entertainment. The *Ghawazi* were banished from Cairo in 1834 by Mohammed Ali Pasha, in an attempt to hide this aspect of local popular culture in his drive to modernise Egypt. Equally, the ban was seen as a way of controlling the cultural judgements of Europeans. As Savigliano suggests in relation to the tango, 'the debates over tango in Europe immediately amplified tango's "erotic problem" at home. Thus scandal and fascination were subject to colonial relationships within a global economy of passion' (1995: 114).

Some Ghawazi tried to remain in Cairo, posing as Awalim, but many were discovered and publicly flogged before being expelled. The expulsion dealt a serious blow to the fortunes of the Ghawazi. They went on to settle in the towns of Upper Egypt, however business in the countryside was not as profitable as in the city (Karayanni 2004). Hanna suggests that, in response to the prohibition against women dancing in public in places like Egypt, Morocco and Turkey, 'young boys … have taken women's place in dance and bed. Older males dressed as women also practiced their arts of allurement, including dance and music. The boys catered to venal pederasty, enticing sexual partners through terpsichorean performance' (1988: 57).

Male street dancers were the subjects of persecution during the British occupation of Egypt (from 1882 onwards). The relentless homophobic censure of the Victorians on the one hand and the adoption of European notions of gender and 'sexuality' by local elites on the other were the main causes of the disappearance of male street performers and dancers.

> Although the Khawal transvestite dancers in Egypt emulated the female Ghawazee [sic] by dancing with castanets self-accompaniment, painting the hands with henna, braiding their hair, plucking facial hair, and affecting the manner of women, the men distinguished themselves from females by a costume that was part male and female. (Hanna 1988: 58)

Karayani (2009) provides a detailed account of the banning of male dancing in the Middle East and North Africa by British and French colonial administrations, as well as an overview of travel writing about male and female dance and their correspondence with the imposition of Europeanising of attitudes towards sexuality in the region (see also Dunne 1996; Menicucci, 1998; Shay and Sellers-Young 2003; Shay, 2005). Today in the modern Egyptian vernacular the word *khawal* is used exclusively as a pejorative description for homosexual males, in particular those who take on the passive role in sex (Karayanni 2004).

During fieldwork I attended numerous Arabic parties and social gatherings where I observed young males perform *baladi* in almost exactly the same way as their female counterparts by taking the diagonal stance, raising their hands above their shoulders and dancing with their waists, chests and hands. Their performances are fun, sometimes skilful and almost always intentionally humorous. In some cases males are celebrated for being able to dance *baladi* with more aptitude and zest than women.

Shay argues that the belief that male dancers are imitating or parodying female dance is mistaken and borne out of tendencies among commentators to apply nineteenth-century Eurocentric approaches to gender and sexuality. While Shay may have a point, it is important to realise that the nineteenth-century European approaches to gender and sexuality remains resolutely consequential today. Indeed, what he describes as Eurocentric approaches to gender and sexuality are not just the basis on which (some) scholars might comment, they are culturally ubiquitous. Parody becomes a possibility as the result of the hardening of gendering ideologies in the first place. There is little disagreement that such processes have become dominant; in fact they are the very basis on which the tensions cited in the literature on the androgynous nature of Middle Eastern dance is based. Karayanni aptly recalls how, as a child, the descriptions of the 'lithe waists and a swaying gait' of Greek men dancing *Chifteteli* caused him and his classmates to giggle and 'sadly confirm[ed] that artistic talent had lost much of its cultural currency and that we were all genuine products of technology and heterosexual virtue' (2009: 255). Thus the now customary anodyne that pre-colonial gendering practices in the Middle East were more fluid must sit side by side with recognition of the sharp gender distinctions in the present and the acknowledgement that Islamic doctrine is just as amenable to those sharp distinctions as Victorian Eurocentrism.

Mason's (1975) account of the ritual context of gender-segregated weddings and wedding dance among the Aguila in Libya uncovers the symbolic and bodily ambivalence, contradiction, and parody that takes place. Mason's account revealed that men danced in the female form to their (all-male) peers with scarf wrapped around their waist while females assumed male roles in their dance to each other. 'This role reversal by members of each sex in their separate ceremonies denote humour and goodwill, and point to the mutual dependency of the sexes as well as to a certain amount of tension between them' (Hanna 1988: 49).

Parody is also a consequence of the practical realities of cultural learning both in the region and in the diaspora. Female *baladi* dance is by far the most prevalent, visually accessible and publicly performed type of Middle Eastern dance; both traditional and contemporary male dance is rarely seen or portrayed and has yet to become as profitable or commercialised. In their account of male dance, Fisher and Shay profile Saleem, a California-based Saudi-born male dancer who says that, 'like most people in the Arab world, as a child and young adult I learned my dancing imitating what I saw on television, where they showed old Egyptian films with great dance stars like Tahia Carioca and Samia Gamal' (2009: 375). As Saleem suggests, the dance itself is neither male nor female, 'it's the audience's perception that determines what is "masculine" and what is "feminine"' (2009: 377).

Despite the attempt to formalise and impose strict gendered dance forms, the informal and playful appeal of folk dance remains strong. However, I am not sure that the dance is radically androgynous as some imply and that is because I believe gender parody to be central to the way men perform improvised *baladi*. It took me some time to come to terms with the idea that there was nothing radically transgressive about seeing a 6ft 2ins male in his early 20s with a pattern shaved in his hair, an intricately shaped goatee and military dog-tags around his neck taking to the dance floor at a party and dancing with his hips, chest and hands. The transgression may have been in seeking to do away with ambiguity through the policing of gender through both legislation and cultural formalism. In the context of heteronormativity, parody, play and mimicking are a visible part of amateur male performances at social occasions and inoculate males against homophobic censure.

Similar patterns of gender parody and ambiguity in Middle Eastern dance can be seen at Iraqi weddings and celebrations where females, and to a lesser extent males, dance *qawlia* to *chobi* (music), characterised by a small drum wrapped around the upper torso. In contrast to the *baladi* style in Egypt, which focuses on the performers' use of the hips, abdomen and chest, the *qawlia* involves the female dancer using her hair to dance by swinging her head in a circular or diagonal (figure of eight) motion. Shimmies of the shoulders and hops are also part of the repertoire. Females sometimes dance facing each other swinging their hair in rapid motions and jolting their bodies forward. Young Iraqis who dance to this music at weddings and events in London exercise a degree of self-censorship, parodying and referring to *qawlia* in their movements as opposed to fully engaging in this vibrant and energetic dance. *Qawlia*, like belly dancing, is coded as female; nonetheless young men cite and enact the moves of *qawlia*, usually with large doses of humour and play. *Qawlia* sits in stark contrast to male dances in Iraq, which are usually formalised line dances that cite tribal ties and masculine fierceness, using props like swords and guns.

The *debka*, a kind of line dance popular in the Greater Syria area and Iraq, has also grown in popularity among British-born or -raised Arabs from those countries. Traditional performances of folk *debka* were spectacular displays of masculinity and strictly gender-segregated, but today they can be mixed. *Debka* is more formalised than the free improvisations of belly dancing; regional variations of steps are plentiful but the basic idea and form are the same. The *debka* has become part of the national folklore of different nation-states and differences in costume, steps and props have been emphasised to fashion particular Palestinian, Iraqi, Syrian and Lebanese *debkas*. The *debka* is less known to Egyptians and North Africans, where other alternatives to *baladi* dancing exist. At parties in London the cultural differences between Arabs can become more obvious when occasions arise where certain kinds of cultural knowledge and practice are required. Commercial Arabic pop is the shared mainstream, the common denominator, while more specific local dances and styles were not known or understood by all.

The anthropology of dance is 'concerned with the tension between cultural norms and human creativity, between socio-historical constraints and human agency' (Grau 1999: 165). I would add that the dance cultures and practices of young Arab Londoners provide insights into the debate about the relationship between performance and performativity. Ethnic dance within the context of the Arab diaspora in multicultural London retains the traces of functionalist and structuralist readings on two levels. First, the grammars of *baladi* dance as performed by young Arab women expose the relationship between 'Arab womanhood' and a specific movement system that is intimately connected to concerns around heterosexual virtue. Within the context of the regulation and prohibitions of pre-martial sex among young Arab men and women in London, Arab themed 'dance events' and *baladi* dancing:

> belong to that group of social institutions which allow sexual play to a moderate and discreet extent, the functions of which are to canalise the forces of sex into socially harmless channels, and by doing so to assist the processes of selection and to protect the institutions of marriage and the family. (Evans-Pritchard 1928: 119–20)

Second, following Mitchell (1959), I would also argue that the way in which *baladi* is used to signify Arabness by young people in London is about the marking of social boundaries between one group and another within the terms of ethnonormativity. In the process of demarcating ethnic boundaries the different demands of heteronormativity are central. In this case they are shown to revolve around the grammars and idioms of Middle Eastern dance. The different heteronormative demands over the female body whereby the erotic and exotic forms of contemporary belly dancing on the one hand and the less brazen, more regulated performance of virtuous Arab womanhood on the other, confront one another. These dance styles are closely related, sometimes seen as synonymous and yet in contestation. Interestingly, they both claim and signify the same object, the sensuous yet virtuous Oriental Arab woman. The dance practices of young men draw us into discussions about the performativity of gender and the way in which, despite the arsenal of regulatory norms, ideals and injunctions, parody and imperfect recitation will always undermine attempts to circumscribe gender and police heteronormativity, even if it is not done in a consciously political way. It is also a reminder, if any were needed, that heteronormativity hails young men as much as young women to regard the body and movement as requiring heterosexual regulation, which in itself sets up the possibility of parody and transgression.

Spencer argues that the structuralist view of dance relies on the idea of 'hidden meanings' that suggest an 'underlying pattern of behavior or belief that is not consciously perceived by the members of the structure [and] may be described as deep structure', arguing that one must 'question any axiomatic assumption that the basic choreographic pattern of every dance must be loaded with an inner subliminal meaning' (1985: 37–38). I am not so certain that a structuralist reading casts meaning as being exclusively hidden or subliminal. The accounts and observations I have presented suggest that there are instances and settings where underlying meanings come forcefully to the surface, so that participants in dance events are well aware of them and take them into consideration in their choices of dance metaphor and style.

John Blacking has argued that:

> it is unnecessary and unacceptable to drag in the unconscious to explain what happens in dance. Not only is the notion of unconscious decisions absurd, it diverts attention from the serious analysis of the process of intuition and unpremeditated decision making, and the structures of non-verbal communication. (1985: 89)

Here too I find a narrow reading of the relevance of the psychological, which is framed as only having relevance in speech. As Royce has pointed out, dance is a 'multi-channel expression' that involves 'the kinesthetic, the visual, the aural the tactile and olfactory' (1977: 197). Blacking's rejection of the relevance of text and discourse in bodily practices speaks of the same scepticism that Geertz (1993) has elaborated.

I understand the psychological in dance as operating at both an individual and a collective level: both may be reified. I find no inconsistency in suggesting that the psychoanalytic scheme of identification, desire, injunctions and mimesis informs the recitation of heteronormativity, ethnonormativity and class within the dance practices of young Arab Londoners. The account I have given here need not be representative or comprehensive because, even in its partiality, it exposes how Arab culture is often assumed and improvised – how what is assumed to be 'quintessentially Arab' is in fact a parody of it, and how the diffusion of belly dancing as a global phenomenon and the recitation of authentic gendered ethnicity in London, reveal processes that are at once the doing and undoing of idealised Arab womanhood and Arab manhood.

It is in these everyday contexts that we may see the relationship between 'performance' and 'performativity' most clearly. Far from being opposing theoretical constructions, I suggest they are intimately related so that, performance is the imperfect recitation of that which is performative: 'Gender', 'Race', 'Sexuality', 'Class', 'Arab' and 'British'. The 'subject effect' that is produced provides us with no resolution to debates on structure and agency, humanism or neo-structuralism, instead it asks us to defer our desires for resolution.

Shay and Sellers-Young (2005) relate how for (some) Arab Americans, the use of belly dancing to represent 'Arabness' has been problematic, because of the way in which it frames the 'Arab world' through phantasmic exotic-otherness. In the following chapter I turn to some of the visual representations and tropes used by young Arab Londoners for self-representation. These visual representations draw them into a process of self-Orientalism. However these ethnic self-portraits I present should be seen not as a false consciousness or a postcolonial slip but as a reflection of the effective and affective forces that lead individuals to fashion themselves as ethnic, authentic, successful, productive and therefore legitimate 'British citizens'.

5

Reclaiming the Orient Through the Diasporic Gaze

I see, I feel, hence I notice, I observe, and I think. (Roland Barthes, *Camera Lucida*, 1982)

In *Camera Lucida* Roland Barthes is concerned with the philosophy and method of visual representation, arriving at the 'curious notion' that a universal approach to the visual might be replaced by 'a new science for each object' (1982: 8). I have chosen two sets of images as the subject of this analysis, they are limited in their number and context and therefore cannot be described as a corpus or a visual movement, instead they are fragmentary objects of expression. The instances where a British Arab imagery was produced or deployed were extremely limited and I mostly came upon these by chance during my fieldwork. The first set of images comprises a selection from the dozens of flyers and posters used to promote Arabic-themed parties and events organised by club promoters and Arab societies at universities around London. The second set is from two photo shoots called 'Folklore Fashion', published in 2005 in the first and third issues of *Sharq* magazine, which at the time was the first magazine produced by British-born or -raised Arabs in the name of 'British Arab culture'.

There are many ways in which the images I present here might be read; they fall between the singular and the universal, their composition points to the inter-textuality of visual cultures and references. What I see in them are the reflections of ethnonormativity within the context of multiculturalism and the commodification of ethnicity, where the device of (visual) Orientalism is key to imagining and composing a legitimate collective self. These images offer an anthropological dimension to the debates on Orientalist art by throwing into relief the project of cultural survival at the heart of semiotic re-appropriation that diasporic youth appoint in their encounter with the hegemonic discourses of their other-ness.

Re-appropriation is often seen as constituting a form of resistance and yet, in this case, the re-apropriated aesthetic is in my opinion grounded on rather apologetic and muted grounds, encrypted with an anxiety which proclaims: 'We are not all extremists', 'We have a worthy civilisation too', 'We are like you', 'We are not ugly, we are beautiful'. These utterances are addressed first and foremost to the (ethnic subject) British Arabs as a form of self-affirmation. Yet that self has within it an encrypted other, namely the Euro-American culture which has vilified and subordinated Arab and Islamic 'cultures' in the process of its own self-realisation.

I begin with Figure 5.1 where a Japanese *Manga* cartoon belly dancer has been copied from the internet and used to adorn a basic 'greyscale' poster for an LSE Arabic Society party. The 'Arabic Mediterranean' party advertised in Figure 5.2 employs the titillating, pearly white odalisque so emblematic of the nineteenth-century European taste for salacious *harem* fantasies. In the final flyer (Figure 5.3) the Arab and Iranian societies at King's University have banded together to celebrate the (mid-winter) Zoroastrian-Persian festival of *Sadeh*, which traditionally involves the lighting of bonfires and yet it is the image of the exotic and erotic cabaret belly dancer, not fire or Persian iconography, which best embodies the desired aesthetics.

Figure 5.1 A *manga*-style belly dancer on a poster advertising an LSE Arabic Society party, January 2006

Source: This illustration is hand-drawn by the author and is based on a photograph.

Figure 5.2   A poster advertising an 'Arabic Mediterranean Party' shows a titillating odalisque revealing pearly white legs from behind a pink *yashmak*, April 2006

Source: This illustration is hand-drawn by the author and is based on a photograph.

The pearly white odalisque which has become the mascot for the Arab party scene in London, and the costumes, repose and props used in the 'Folklore Fashion' photo shoots (which follow) display striking similarities to the stylised iconography of nineteenth- and twentieth-century Orientalist art and photography. At face value, my use of the loaded terms 'Orientalist' and 'Orientalism' implies that young Arabs in London have unwittingly or uncritically embraced the *phantasmic* and objectifying motifs of the colonial panopticon. However, I do not intend to engage in that kind of disenfranchisement. If *Orientalism* is a system of knowing and representing the Orient then these images are a fitting testament to its unrelenting potency. Beyond censuring those who appropriate Orientalism, I argue that we should look at the conditions that motivate these forms of appropriation.

The cabaret belly dancer seems a natural choice of image to promote the 'Arabic party' scene, contrasting sharply with the perception of a masculine and misogynistic Arab world filled with veiled and oppressed Arab and Muslim women. Indeed the exotic Oriental dancer is the discursive opposite: a free, fun and erotic creature, her body acting as the locus of her expression, a perfect antidote to the panic-stricken western imagination. As Dox points out 'westerners' are 'much more likely to identify belly dance with ancient Mesopotamia or Persia than with modern-day Iraq, Iran, or Saudi Arabia, and to link belly dance with

Figure 5.3 A belly dancer is used to advertise a boat party celebrating the Persian festival of *Sadeh* in February 2006. The event was co-organised by the King's College Arabic Society and the King's College Iranian Society

Source: This illustration is hand-drawn by the author and is based on a photograph.

ancient rituals as a way of situating women's sexuality outside of Islam and Christianity, as well as social, economic, and political conditions' (2006: 58). Importantly, these images are not produced by young Arabs specifically for these events, they are readily available online in everything from commercial stock image databases to the various shades of amateur art and photography which are posted online and ubiquitously cannibalised. She is so available because she is part of western popular culture, the result of an accumulation of meanings, references and insinuations that pass through *A Thousand and One Nights*, the imaginations of Gérôme,

Delacroix and Ingres, *The Adventures of Sinbad the Sailor*, colonial postcards, Hollywood, tourism, RnB music videos and everything else in between. Thus, for these young people, the belly dancer is a readymade aesthetic – no embellishment is required.

The use of Orientalist tropes in the diaspora is not limited to London or the early twenty-first century. Arab American musicians in 1950s and 1960s New York and Boston:

> cleverly adapted emblems and symbols of the Orient and popularised a new musical style rooted in their own indigenous traditions. Although the trademarks of Orientalism helped them to achieve unprecedented success, it served to enhance [their] foreignness … placing them in an imaginary world that was exotic even to themselves. (Rasmussen 2005: 172)

Understanding the contexts in which Orientalism is appropriated helps us navigate the possibilities of its reiteration. The alternative reading that I will attempt owes much to an emergent body of literature in art history that has sought to rethink the canon of Orientalism in art (see Celik 1996), advocating its periodisation and the acknowledgement of the heterogeneity in its visual forms (see Lowe 1994; MacKenzie 1995). Orientalist representation has been disaggregated into romantic-realist, phantasmic, impressionist and indigenous shades (see Benjamin et al. 1997; Benjamin and Khemir 1997; Baer 2003; Beaulieu and Roberts 2002; Apostolos-Cappadona 2005). The effect of gender, race and desire, power and political economy are now being written into the interpretation of visual renditions of nineteenth-century popular Orientalism (see Lewis 1995; Weeks 1998; Black 2006). In turn, I attempt to bring ethnographic insight to bear on the way we understand how young people in London have reclaimed the Orient through the diasporic gaze. I believe this move leads us not only to question Orientalism, but also to think about the power of signification and its role in producing intelligible 'ethnic-citizens' within corporatist multiculturalism.

Orientalism in Art: Al-Qanoon[1]

We owe Edward Said's seminal work so much in terms of our understanding of the constellation of meanings and institutions that seek to know, possess and control what the Orient is and what Orientals are. However, Said explicitly excluded art history from his book, instead focusing on the writings of Europeans on the 'Orient'. Nevertheless he provides the cue for a body of literature on Orientalism in art in the following words:

> In the works of Delacroix and literally dozens of other French and British painters the Oriental tableau carried representation into visual expression and a life of its own (which this book unfortunately must scant). Sensuality, promise, terror, sublimity, idyllic pleasure, intense energy: the Orient as a figure in the pre-Romantic, pre-technical Orientalist imagination of late-eighteenth-century Europe was really a chameleonlike quality called (adjectivally) 'Oriental'. (1978: 118–19)

Said's analysis did not take long to find its way into art history, for he had used the unsettling image of *The Snake Charmer* (1880) by the French artist Gérôme as a 'dust jacket for his critical study' (Nochlin, 1989: 35). In 'The Imaginary Orient' (1989) Linda Nochlin takes up some of Said's themes in order to argue against the apolitical and largely celebratory regard in which art historians had held Orientalist art. Up until the mid 1980s curators like Donald Rosenthal insisted that 'The unifying characteristic of nineteenth-century Orientalism was its attempt at documentary realism' (cited in Nochlin 1989: 33; see also Rosenthal 1982), a point which Nochlin contests by uncovering the conventions of the genre. For Nochlin, time always stood still in Orientalist paintings, which typically represented an Oriental world bereft of historical change; the Orient is, in short, picturesque. Picturesque art, including representations of peasant life in France or workers in industrial Britain, was often idyllic, rarely depicting the poverty, hardships and squalid conditions of the urban-proletarian or rural-agrarian life. Picturesque art of this kind was, in a sense, reminiscent of early anthropology, where artists sought to preserve and record 'a form of peculiarly elusive wild-life, requiring increasingly skilful tracking as the delicate prey – an endangered species – disappears farther and farther into the hinterlands, in France as in the Near East' (1989: 36).

Indeed the parallel with 'social science' does not end there, artists like Delacroix and Gérôme were widely believed to be scientific in their representations, with many seeing their renditions to be the works of dispassionate empiricists whose paintings were based on ethnographic exactitude. Their art went on to be labelled as 'realist' by the Academy and salons in recognition of the astonishingly life-like renditions and careful attention to detail in their paintings. Orientalist paintings commonly deployed authenticating objects such as tiling patterns, Quranic inscription, furniture, props and clothes to create an illusion of a pre-existing Oriental reality that the painters simply captured. This technique of proto-realism, argues Nochlin, creates a sense of artlessness where the artists 'make us forget that his art is really art' (1989: 38). The disrepair shown in the architectural detail of many Orientalist paintings refers to the decadence of Arab Islamic societies. In a similar vein 'Oriental' subjects were often depicted in repose, reminding the viewer of the idleness of Oriental peoples. Both Orientalist paintings and their successors, Orientalist photographs, rarely, if ever, showed scenes of work or industry. 'These people – lazy, slothful, and childlike, if colourful – have let their own cultural treasures sink into decay' (cited in Nochlin 1989: 39).

French artists like Delacroix, Ingres and Gérôme showed a deep fascination with female nudity. The fervent accounts of European travel writers like Flaubert, Lane and Renan helped to create an imaginary Orient which became the favoured backdrop against which painters projected their erotic imagination and pushed the boundaries of acceptability in their discipline and societies. Yet Ingres was an 'armchair Orientalist', producing paintings of Oriental odalisques in various states of nudity throughout his career though never having travelled 'any farther south than Rome where his famous *Grand Odalisque* (circa 1814) was painted from European models and Turkish studio props' (Benjamin 1997a: 9).

The penchant for voyeurism soon went beyond *harem* and *hamam*[2] scenes to almost any setting, including public markets, where painters would include naked pearly white women in indulgent poses or powerless submission. These captive women's sole purpose appears to be the satisfaction of the lascivious appetites of cruel Arab Muslim men. 'The inclusion of the white nude in the harem creates a simultaneous identification and opposition between the intended male European audience and the Eastern subjects. European men identified with harem women in their white European-ness' (Black 2006: 19). European masculinity simultaneously revelled in the indulgent poses of the exotic *harem* women, who symbolised the primitive sexuality of the East in contrast with the self-image of the 'corseted' reserve of polite European society.

Here we come almost full circle. In the previous chapter I suggested that at Arab-themed events, venues and parties, non-Arab women tended to take on the role of the authenticating ethnic performance act, 'standing in', as it were, for the estranged referents of belly dancing – Arab women. The Orientalist painters of the nineteenth century seemed to be engaged in a similar pantomime where the white nude set against the Oriental background created a kind of indeterminacy. Both the painted odalisque of the nineteenth century and the belly dancer of the twenty-first century leave us asking – is she Arab? Is she European? What and who does she represent? Either way she is always conveniently the female-other through which fantasies both Oriental and Occidental are realised. Savigliano describes similar dynamics around tango as the 'traffic of the exotic', where the geography of pleasure and the spatial economy of capitalist production and consumption are strongly intertwined (1995: 205; see also Lyotard 2004 [1990]).

Unlike the artists of the nineteenth-century paintings, the producers of images of belly dancers and odalisques used on party flyers today are virtually anonymous. The images selected to promote these parties are quickly collated, compared and selected, a testament to the contemporary appetite for the generic digital image. The amount of thought that goes into these flyers is ephemeral, the parties they advertise come and go without incident or fanfare and yet the meanings that the flyers are encrypted with cannot be silenced or ruled out. The white, exotic and sensual Oriental figure of the belly dancer and odalisque who westernises the East and easternises the West remains as discernible and popular today as she was 200 years ago.

The transformation from Orientalist painting to Orientalist photography took place as early as 1838, the year that photography was invented, when the painter Horace Vernet travelled to photograph Egypt and Palestine (Khemir and Benjamin 1997: 189). Thus it mattered little if 'Orientalistic painting begins to run out of wind or falls into mediocrity. Photography steps in to take up the slack and reactivates the phantasm at its lowest level' (Alloula 1986: 4). Malek Alloula picks up the critique of the visual tools of Orientalism in *The Colonial Harem*, where he focuses on French postcards depicting Algerian women between 1900 and 1930. These postcards took the imaginary of the Orient from *salons* and museums to the masses, making it into:

> the poor man's phantasm ... for a few pennies, displaying racks full of dreams ... It is at once their poetry and their glory captured for the ages; it is also their pseudo-knowledge of the colony. It produces stereotypes in the manner of great seabirds producing guano. It is the fertilizer of the colonial vision. (1986: 4)

French postcard photography of Algeria from the 1880s typically depicted 'Moorish' (*Mauresque*) women in public where they were always veiled from top to bottom in white. This 'obstacle to transparency' frustrated French colonial photographers who, Alloula argues, needed to unveil Algerian women in order to profit from their photography. The photographer's answer to the inaccessibility of Algerian women was to use paid models recruited from the 'margins of society'. The models would be:

> dressed for the occasion in full regalia, down to the jewels that are the indispensable finishing touches of the production, the model will manage, thanks to the art of illusion that is photography, to impersonate, to the point of believability, the unapproachable referent: the *other* Algerian woman, absent in the photo. (Alloula 1986: 17; see also Makhoul 1998)

The use of local models and the deploying of props and tropes like coffee pots, inlaid tables and *hookahs* (*Shisha*) makes these Algerian women 'accessible, credible, and profitable'. Suddenly the pale-skinned female figures of Orientalist painting were replaced by authentic dark-skinned native women who provided a more realistic representation of the fabled Orient.

> The same inlaid table is covered with the same copper platter on which stand the same cups … All this paraphernalia, combined with such poverty of imagination, turns the metaphor into a schema – worse, a stereotype. But that is the expression of a rather banal and yet deadly fate that is very familiar to the postcard. Just like the coffee from which it is inseparable, the hookah, the second symbol of the inner harem, repeats with even greater insistence the stereotypical reference to the Orient. It clumsily completes it. There is no Orient without the hookah. (1986: 17)

The hookah, as Alloula calls it, or the *Shisha* as it is now known, has always been central to all depictions of the East, whether painted or photographed. It is an allegory for so much of what the West thought of the East. The leisurely, aromatic and sometimes illicit practice was the perfect metaphor for idleness and lazy sensuality, diametrically opposed to the industrious Europeans. 'Such idleness was not without its appeal to the civilised inhabitant of the West, who were familiar with complaints voiced in every generation from Rousseau's to beyond Freud, about the way that modern society prevents us from taking time to smell the roses' (Kalmar 2004: 219).

In 1876, over a hundred years before Nochlin and Alloula's critiques of visual Orientalism the influential critic Jules-Antoine Castagnary called on the Academy to 'abandon this movement, and let history be its judge. In a few years' time we will be able to set up a stone and engrave upon it these consoling words: Orientalism was once alive and well in French painting' (in Benjamin 1997a: 18). Although Castagnary's critique of Orientalism was mainly grounded in a technical and philosophical disagreement with 'Romanticism', he also made it clear that he had moral misgivings. Castagnary chided Gérôme for his immorality in almost Said-ean fashion for:

[s]elling off the notes he's made during his voyage to the Orient. His *Almeh* is a note he should have kept in the portfolio. It is of a coldly calculating indecency, and I recoil from describing it. A crabbed technique in any case, mean, unpleasant, boring in the extreme. (in Benjamin 1997a: 17)

Nonetheless, the movement continued and the objects of Oriental material culture and the demeanour of Orientals themselves were visually cast within imperialism's imagination, sustaining the frontier fantasies of discovering, categorising and possessing a world beyond Europe. Orientalism as thought, writing and depiction has consequently been inserted into the counter-narratives and critiques of postcolonial intellectuals who see it as one of Europe's historical crimes. As Marta Savigliano argues, 'perhaps all peoples have practiced exoticism of one kind or another, but western exoticism accompanied by world imperialism has had the power to establish Eurocentric exoticism as a universally applicable paradigm' (1995: 169). Yet the artistic conventions of visual Orientalism have survived and been appropriated by, among others, young British-born or -raised Arabs who have accepted and adopted its props and technical conventions while intending it to stand for something other than their historical subordination to Europe. However, their appropriation cannot silence or control past meanings.

An Orient in My Likeness

In January 2005 a group of self-styled 'British-Arabs' launched *Sharq* (*East*) magazine. Some kind of 'Arab community' publication was long awaited and *Sharq* was the first publication to be produced by young British Arabs. While the magazine adopted the broad and inclusive label 'British-Arab' it was largely centred on middle-class Arab life in West London and quickly turned into a glossy lifestyle magazine showcasing the beautiful and successful people of the middle-class Arab scene. The magazine was sold in a handful of newsstands and five star hotels in the West End and ultimately failed to secure a large enough readership to sustain itself, with publication ceasing less than a year after it began. Like so many previous attempts at launching a local Arab community publication (*Arab Star, Hahoona, Local Arabia*), *Sharq* was unable to fashion itself as a platform of expression. Although it was short-lived, *Sharq* was an important indicator of the developments taking place among British-born and -raised Arabs, especially in relation to the hyphened identities logic. Like the first Arab publications and associations which emerged in Britain in the 1930s, negative perceptions and representation of 'the Arabs' remained a central theme in *Sharq*'s editorial vision:

> The *Sharq* vision is simple. With more people emigrating to the 'West' and continued negative publicity surrounding the regimes and people of the 'East', *Sharq* [magazine] aims to support integration whilst encouraging people to embrace, take pride in and promote the uniqueness of their heritage and culture ... We are hybrids – united by our language, our parents, our loss, our heritage, our distant cousins, our summer holidays. We are not a race and therefore not easily identified. We must therefore identify ourselves. We need to let go of our history to embrace our future. They can co-exist if we let them. If we let go of our guilt.

These opening statements reflect so many of the themes under consideration in this exploration of the reach of gender performativity into ethnicity and race; from the celebration of a paradigmatic hybridity advocated by corporatist multiculturalism to the way in which race frames social recognition and intelligibility in Britain through to the burdens of Arab otherness, the 'guilt' of being vassals, occupied, destitute and divided that structure identification and desire. What the editor of *Sharq* describes as 'guilt' I would describe in a performative sense as 'failure'; the failure of contemporary Arabness both as a collective narrative and as a socio-political phenomenon to recite the ideals of the Arab Islamic past.

The project of helping people feel more comfortable in their 'British-Arab skin' which *Sharq* set out to achieve relied on nurturing a kind of redemptive gaze, a point which came across in the first and third issues of the (monthly) magazine. *Sharq* ran two photo shoots called 'Folklore Fashion'. The first was simply introduced as 'Young British-Arabs model the finest traditional costumes from the Arab world'. The second, two months later had more to say: 'Folklore Fashion II – These young Arab professionals, who hold careers in fields ranging from finance to production, in prestigious international companies, seem far removed from the lifestyles these outfits represent. Yet, they model traditional costumes from various Arabic countries with pride.' I have reproduced these photographs in sketches to protect the identities of the people who appear in them while maintaining their composition as accurately as possible (Figures 5.4, 5.5 and 5.6).

Figure 5.4 'Folklore Fashion I' (illustration 1). This illustration is hand-drawn by the author and the names of people appearing in the original photographs have been changed. The original caption reads: 'Ahmed wears Moroccan dress, Yaseen wears Lebanese dress'. Each person in the photo shoot is asked to describe what drives him or her. Ahmed (top left) says 'My desire is to be my own boss and run a successful business' – Ahmed Hassan 27, Service Advisor – Mercedes Benz, West London

Source: Based on a photo from *Sharq Magazine* 2005, issue 1.

Figure 5.5   'Folklore Fashion II' (illustration 2). This illustration is hand-drawn by the author and the name of the person appearing in the original photographs has been changed. The caption reads: 'Yusef wears traditional dress from the Gulf, Najlaa wears Palestinian dress.' Yusef's mantra reads 'Seeking justice for those denied it' Yusef Halabi, Journalist. Najlaa's mantra reads 'The pursuit of a happy and fulfilled life' – Najlaa Maqdisi, 25, Medical Sales Representative, Merk Harp & Dome Ltd.

Source: Based on a photograph from *Sharq Magazine* 2005, issue 1.

The extent to which these compositions share the '*stadium*' (Barthes 1982: 35) of ocular Orientalism critiqued by Nochlin (1989) and Alloula (1986) is striking. Although the photographs have been taken in London, no trace of London is to be found. Only feet away, the modern city has been excluded for the sake of nostalgia and the picturesque, so that the pre-modernity of these Orientals is not broken by the present-day modernity of the bustling city around them. In line with the most insidious

Figure 5.6 'Folklore Fashion II' (illustration 3). This illustration is hand-drawn by the author and the name of the person appearing in the original photographs has been changed. The caption reads: 'Lu'ay wears a Palestinian housecoat over a cotton galabiya.' Lu'ay al-Bustani – Producer, Arab Satellite Network. 'What motivates you?' 'Smiles.'

Orientalist art, characters are shown in repose, there are no scenes of work, and the subjects appear leisurely. The punctum on which this idleness is contested is the 'success' of these individuals and their assiduousness on behalf of 'prestigious international companies'. Inlaid tables, copper platters, *Mashrabiyah*, *Shisha*, cigarettes, soft lights and furnishings, all of which Alloula finds so troubling, are used as the authenticating backdrop for these ethnic self-portraits.

These images contain the 'raw materials of ethnological knowledge' (Barthes 1982: 28) that symbolise romantic Oriental otherness. In many ways these contemporary photographs go further than 'time standing still', they go back in time, a testament to the 'exaggerated medievalisation' of the contemporary Arab self-image, which has invested so much in 'the quasi-magical identification with the great period of classical Arabian culture' (Aloaui 1974: 156, in Benjamin 1997b: 33). This self-image not only constitutes a mythical vision of the past but, importantly, it defines the future, a state best described by Sabiha Khemir as 'waiting in the future for the past to come' (1994). Through photographic illusion the scattered fragments of history are brought together as a coherent object known as 'Arab civilisation' – resources for the economies of the imagination. The world or 'lifestyle' that these renditions refer to, are, as Barthes' introspective reflections on photography suggest, *habitable*:

> An old house, a shadowy porch, tiles, a crumbling Arab decoration, a man sitting against the wall, a deserted street, a Mediterranean tree (Charles Clifford's *Alhambra*): this old photograph (1854) touches me: It is quite simply *there* that I should like to live. This desire affects me at a depth and according to roots I do not know: warmth of climate? Mediterranean myth? Apollonism? Defection? Withdrawal? Anonymity? Nobility? (Barthes 1982: 38)

Thus these British-born or -raised Arabs are engaged in the quintessential middle-class pursuit of 'restoration' (Baudrillard 1996). Rosenthal insists that 'Orientalist art should not be confused with Oriental art: it (Orientalist art) represents the European artist's view of an unfamiliar culture, rather than a view of that culture from within' (1982: 8). These ethnic self-portraits problematise Rosenthal's binary. The people depicted in the photographs and the team behind the photo shoot, have no claim to being either entirely European or entirely Arab, they are inconveniently both. Is their gaze that of well-informed Europeans or the authentic and thus legitimate Oriental eye from within?

'It's just too glossy … It's fake, come on, since when would that lot wear any of that stuff, they wouldn't be seen dead wearing that stuff in real life – nobody wears that stuff any more' said one young man at a regular salon in north London for young Middle East politicos, where heads shook with disapproval 'It's so Orientalist.' Yet to stop there seems all too simplistic. As with sociability around *Shisha* cafes in chapter 2, fashions and aesthetic orientation in the Arab world and the Arab diaspora seem to flow in opposite directions. While middle-class Arab lifestyle magazines in the Middle East abound with images of Arabs in the latest western fashions and interiors as testament to their inclusion in (a European) modernity. Arabs in London draw on the folkloric Arab past to make the same kind of self-validating visual statements about themselves within the context of multicultural London. So we are left with the question, why use images of a somewhat distant and *phantasmic* past to validate a place in the present and perhaps the future of London? As suggested earlier, understanding the context of production is vital to understanding the extent to which these images adhere to a Said-ean Orientalist system of knowledge. I interviewed Fadwa, the editor of the magazine, who described herself as the 'creative director' of the 'Folklore Fashion' photo shoots.

Fadwa: If it was just photos of people wearing national dress it wouldn't have a meaning, what it has is the age, name and company that they work at. Sadly a lot of people took that as us trying to date-match people, which we had no intention of doing, it wasn't our purpose. What we were trying to say was, look at this girl who works for Lehman Brothers and look at her take pride in her national dress. She is an Arab, she is so proud of being an Arab that she is wearing her national dress and it wasn't Orientalist in the belly dancing kind of way, this is national dress that they genuinely wear and ... on a fashion level it looked good, on a visual level and then the whole point of the magazine – introducing Arab society to each other in Britain. Not because people want to date each other but for me, let's say for one of our male readers to be able to say 'Look at that girl, she might have my mentality, she might have my thought' I mean not just about male–female. Maybe a British Arab girl who thinks 'God I'm too British' has a bit of confusion with her identity, who may look at the photos and think 'God, she works for Lehman Brothers and she is 25 and she is wearing an Arab outfit' and so she can feel proud of that identity.

Ramy: What is the Arab outfit meant to symbolise, what is it meant to do?

Fadwa: Acceptance and pride in our heritage. I have no problems with wearing jeans and a t-shirt. Here I don't expect to wear national dress in this society because it is not the done thing. But it symbolises and is representative of our entire identity. That is the idea. That visually what we can do is have this outfit that symbolises our heritage our background, and we didn't just do it with the outfits we did it with the location and the props.

Ramy: Tell me more about that.

Fadwa: Momos' [restaurant], it was established and is currently owned and run by a successful Arab who brought Arab cuisine to the UK, well North African cuisine to the UK and everybody loved it. Just as the Asians were very successful in bringing the curries, he did the same with North African cuisine and people love Momos' and when they talk about Momos' they don't talk about 'that Arab place', they just talk about the food. It's just very positive and even if we would have a fashion show with these clothes, westerners would say how beautiful they are.

So the idea was that it visually represents our culture – but so does this rap artist in Denmark, 'Majid', who is Arab and he actually raps about Arab political issues which is partly why I adore his music. But ultimately he also represents our culture and our music. He doesn't have the, his music isn't culturally Arab or historically Arab because he uses western beats, but ultimately he is an Arab but visually he doesn't look it so we would write a profile about him, but here we are saying look she is not oppressed, let's say one of the girls in the photo shoot, she's not oppressed, she is not wearing a veil, she is not wearing a skimpy outfit she is not either-or, she is not extreme 'West' and she is not extreme 'East' but she is proud enough of her culture to wear this outfit and she works for Lehman Brothers, so she is a success and she is comfortable, it's almost like a skin, an Arab skin, and visually straight away you see that it represents something, this is her showing her Arab skin, which is great, it's all about what we are doing, promoting pride.

Ramy: Tell me about the props.

Fadwa: They are props that you would find in Arab cafes in Arab countries. So again just visually, when I go to Syria and go to a cafe it would look like that scene. Perhaps not as glamorous but it would look like that scene. So it's sort of supposed to be comforting and also remembering that some of our readership was not Arab, a nice visual. It's particularly popular with English people, they [the Arabesque backdrop/props] are old, they are beautiful, so some people, just like I was referring to before, some people will look at these photos and think – 'Beautiful'. I want people to look and think 'Beautiful'.

Ramy: Why do you feel the urge to do that?

Fadwa: Because everybody should take pride in their history and culture and not feel the need to hide it.

Ramy: Do you feel that people have had to hide it?

Fadwa: Yeah, I think they have. Particularly the wealthy Arabs in London, they have no interest. Those who became wealthy, there is a feeling that they left that primitive stuff behind. They see it as primitive and now that they are wealthy all they want to do is go out on shopping sprees on Bond Street and that is 'class'. Well no, it might be class in this culture, but class in the Arab world exists – but it exists in a different cultural format. So a wealthy guy, although nowadays a lot of the Arab countries have adopted the western cultural class system. But back in the day, say, the wealthy Egyptian wouldn't say I want a Savile Row shirt and belt to show that I have succeeded. They would just get a silk *Jalabiyah* [traditional gown], so that is the idea. It doesn't mean if you want to raise yourself that you adopt a western approach which … I have no problem with western culture, but I don't want people to look down upon eastern culture, and not to see the East as primitive and the West as progressive. Every society has their progressive and their primitive and it has got to the point where, actually, when we talk about progression and modernisation we only talk about the West, and the East is primitive.

Ramy: Who was the photographer?

Fadwa: Anne Houghton.

Ramy: What role did she have in the way that the photo shoot was designed or executed?

Fadwa: She was the photographer, not the creative director, so she is a great photographer and she took care of lighting but …

Ramy: Who was the creative director?

Fadwa: Me and mum actually. Mum because she is the fashion expert and me because I was the editor. In fact I really did the creative directing for most of our photo shoots … if you do go to the old town in Syria or Egypt or wherever, that is what it looks like, we do have inlaid tables and we do have *Shisha* and the soft furnishings and it's beautiful just like when you go to a bar, like a hip bar in London, great sleek architecture that is what defines them – what defines us culturally, now in terms of interiors, is this look and it's lovely and it's beautiful to the extent that many western interiors are now copying them … It's art and our art is different to art here and it's not something that shows us to be primitive. The sad thing is that when the Arabs see – now we are way past the Orientalism of the nineteenth and twentieth centuries and the westerners actually appreciate our art now, and they are adopting it in their homes and restaurants and bars. Now that the Arabs see that, they are taking pride in it and liking it. But they had to get the acceptance of the westerners.

Fadwa's account places the photography firmly within the rubric of multiculturalism. Her narrative is structured by a crisis of 'identity' which requires that one fashion a positive image of 'British-Arabs' to help them be proud of their Arabness and therefore themselves, showing that Arabs in Britain, like Asians in Britain are cultured, beautiful, tasteful and successful. Although Fadwa insists that she wants to show that Arab culture is not primitive she is ironically led by a particular mode of multicultural validation to rely on the mystical imagery of romantic pre-modern Orientalism to capture that message. Perhaps we should not worry too much that postcolonial intellectuals like Alloula (1986), Kabbani et al. (2008), Djebar (1999) or Salhi and Netton (2006) would be disturbed to find that the romantic Orientalism of the nineteenth and twentieth centuries has been re-appropriated by young Arabs in London in the twenty-first century to achieve civil emancipation.

Fadwa insists that the material features of these compositions, the clothes, the inlaid tables, soft furnishings and *Shisha*, are a genuine part of the Arab aesthetic and representative of 'our entire identity', even describing it as an 'Arab skin'. Should Arabs be estranged from their own material culture because of the way some Europeans have used it to subordinate the Orient? John MacKenzie, who is a vociferous opponent of Edward Said's thesis on *Orientalism*, seems more in tune with Fadwa's ability to see 'Orientalism of the nineteenth and twentieth century' as the past. For MacKenzie the relationship between European representations of the Orient and the European colonial project is tenuous. He argues that in many cases in Orientalist paintings 'tiles and wooden latticework (*Mashrabiyah*), are lovingly portrayed, not only because they presented technical problems of pattern, texture and light, but also because they represented architectural adornment that could be and were adopted in the West' (1995: 65). He sees a genuine admiration, fascination and interest on the part of European artists who:

> expressed both sublime fear and a sense of liberating themselves and their art; both admiration for the outward forms of an alien religion and anxiety about its inner meanings; both fright at cultural difference and an admiring fascination with characteristics their own societies had repressed. Above all they held out a programme for renewal to their own highly urbanised, excessively industrialised and overripe societies. (1995: 65; see also Kabbani et al. 2008)

Fadwa's account shows us that her 'western' photographer played only a small part in the way the images and subjects were composed, essentially filling the role of a technician. It was in fact Fadwa, in her role as diasporic 'Oriental' who chose how her 'Arab' subjects were to be represented. This is very similar to assertions made by Celik (1996) and Weeks (1998), who both provide accounts of 'Orientals' actively engaged in the production of portraiture, sometimes at the expense of the desires and imagination of the western painters and photographers employed to execute the image. 'Zeinab … stamped her foot and said … that the portrait must be done according to her wishes, or –"not at all" – I could not risk the "not at all"' (Mary Adelaide Walker, 1886, cited in Beaulieu and Roberts 2002: 1). Zeinab, an Ottoman noblewoman, insisted that she be painted wearing the latest fashions from Paris and not, as Mary Adelaide had hoped, in traditional Ottoman costume. As Beaulieu and Roberts note, the fact that we are surprised that the 'Oriental' subject does not correspond to western notions of the 'compliant odalisque' reveals the extent to which the idea of a passive and predictable 'Oriental' has 'saturated our understanding of this period, even in those postcolonial accounts critical of this western mythology' (2002: 2).

Emily Weeks (1998) demonstrates how David Wilkie's portrait of Mohammed Ali Pasha saw the Viceroy use the technical ability of a European artist to fashion his own propaganda and serve his political ends and strategic designs much in the same way that Fadwa describes the photo shoot to have specific political messages about the Arab self-image and to counter what she calls 'negative publicity'. The use of European artistic techniques to formulate corrective visual messages is a well-established counter-movement within the genre of Orientalist art. The (late) nineteenth-century Ottoman painter Osman Hamdi Bey trained in France under the technical supervision of Jean-Leon Gérôme. Hamdi Bey was among a number of 'indigenous artists' who used European techniques of oil on canvas and followed similar themes and subjects, which made his art easily identifiable as part of the 'Orientalist' school; however, the underlying purpose of his work was to critique 'the major themes of Orientalist painters from his critical stance as an insider on the outside' (Celik 2002: 23).

In contrast to Gérôme's series of paintings on Islamic worship, which rather single-mindedly conveyed fanaticism, exoticism and even violence, Hamdi Bey presented Islam as a religion that 'encouraged intellectual curiosity, discussion, debate, even doubt'. The subjects in his paintings are commonly seen in discussion, holding books, listening attentively and, importantly, they are shown upright 'as an expression of their human dignity' (Celik 2002). His painting *From the Harem* is one of a number of compositions of the life of Ottoman women where he depicts the reserve of these women and the mundane aspects of *harem* life. There are no *hookahs*, mysterious black slaves or nudity, instead washing hangs overhead, the women are covered and they sit on woven straw flooring, hardly exotic. Other paintings by Hamdi Bey show women reading, walking freely in the street, all in an effort to undermine the cliché of the Oriental woman as a captive sex object. It was not only people like Hamdi Bey, Azouza Mammeri and Mohammed Racim who were producing paintings that challenged the *phantasmic* notions of mainstream Orientalist artists and art buyers in Europe. Reina Lewis revisits Henrietta Browne painting *A Visit* (1860), in which she depicted a reserved and family oriented *harem* which fell far short of the imaginative fantasies of buyers in London and Paris (1996; see also Layal Ftouni's detailed discussion of the appropriation of visual Orientalism by contemporary Arab artists [n.d.]).

The Folklore Fashion shoots also seeks to convey a corrective message yet they diverge considerably from the efforts of painters who sought to undermine phantasmic Orientalism. It is difficult, even somewhat unfair, to compare the work by Mammeri, Hamdi Bey, Racim and Browne to the Folklore Fashion shoot. These artists were consciously and professionally engaged in an attempt to undermine romantic and phantasmic Orientalism in European art and the ideology of subordination that it helped to reinforce. In contrast, the Folklore Fashion shoot is concerned with a kind of collective redemption within multiculturalism in which 'origin' and 'authenticity' are vital mechanisms.

British-born or -raised Arabs are not the only people who have a taste for romantic Orientalist art. Since the mid 1970s the market for Orientalist art has been driven by buyers from the Middle East. Orientalist art appeals to Arab buyers because it satisfies their 'pan-Arab impulses' and yet 'for students of Orientalism raised in the tradition of Edward Said, the Arab taste for Orientalist art seems paradoxical' (Benjamin 1997b: 32). The aesthetic favoured by buyers and used in the Folklore Fashion photo shoots is the hyper-realist finish popularised by Gérôme, the arch-Orientalist. As Brahim ben Hossain Aloaui, Curator of Contemporary Art at the Institute du Monde Arabe describes:

That image of the Orient which set the Occident dreaming in the nineteenth century returns something to those Orientals [sic] who also seek an image of their past. They find in these paintings a world on its way to disappearing: this Orient that is highly coloured, shimmering, this Orient of Arabesques, of costumes and the richness of forms is in the process of being eclipsed by a much more modern world. The image that was fixed by the Occident in the nineteenth century – the Orientals are now attempting to recover it. (Aloaui in Benjamin 1997b: 33)

Nostalgic communication provides a means of symbolically escaping a present cultural condition that does not correspond to an individual or a collective's sense of 'true self'. For many people the representations of the Orient from the nineteenth century give them a glimpse of a perceived pre-capitalist, pre-colonialist Arab and Islamic world. 'Back in the day', as Fadwa describes it, represents the indigenous, autonomous and sovereign collective self. This is of course a gross oversimplification of Middle Eastern history but, nevertheless, as nostalgia it serves the purpose of giving substance to an Arab civilisation that is lost and mourned. According to the popular discourses of civilisation among Arabs, Arab innovation, science, literature and episteme laid the foundations for what became known as 'western civilisation'. Although they see themselves as having played a vital role in the ongoing story of human progress, the western narrative of how modernity and the present came to be casts Arab and Islamic culture as inimical to 'progress' and incompatible with modernity. Thus, Arab civilisation becomes a fable, something that is lost and not yet recovered, but alive and well in people's imaginations as a redemptive moment.

> They told me the
> Arabs named the stars
> algol, sirius, aldebaran …
> My mother's olive shaped eyes
> sandaled feet
> led me into centuries
> of vast empires
> forgotten treasures
> Now, only ruins remain
>
> This was the summer
> I bathed in olive oil
> and sat on the sidewalks
> of Jerusalem eating
> pistachio ice-cream
> with the old man
> whose ancient face tried
> to explain to me that we fought

with our hearts and
not our heads – therefore
we would never win.

I am dead to my tribe
I will never learn all
its salty secrets
So tonight I want to sleep
With vega, deneb, altair…
Because they will disappear
In the morning sun,
And only ruins remain

('Pistachio Ice Cream',
by Annemarie Jacir, in Handal 2001)

The Arab nostalgia for a fabled past 'combines bitterness and sweetness, the lost and found, the far and near, the past which is over and gone, from which we have been or are being removed … renewed … more enchanting and more lovely' than the present (Ralph Harper 1966, in Wilson 2005: 23). During numerous conversations with young Arabs born or raised in London I was reminded that 'While we were discovering science, anatomy and astrology these Europeans were still living in caves.' Europe is at once the principal vector, yet one that is erased and disavowed. The demand for recognition itself becomes a 'symptom of the pathology of colonisation … the former slave wants to make himself recognised' (Fanon 1967a: 217). It is not an exaggeration to say that what the Arab world continues to covet more than anything else is acceptance from Europe and recognition that Arab and Islamic cultures are worthy of emulation, that they have something to offer humanity.

Although the innovative, scientific and culturally rich 'Arab civilisation' (singular) of the past is preserved in books and buildings it is nowhere more visually accessible than in the brush-strokes and camera lenses of European artists, fantasy-driven or otherwise. Thus the Arab nostalgia for a past self is realised through the European gaze, placing the western 'other' at the very heart of Arab collective self-identification. While the relationship between the Arab world and Europe is dissected and analysed in formal analysis and academic debates, the visual self-representations of British-born or -raised Arabs reveal the ways in which the Occident is encrypted but always under erasure in the self-image of 'the Arabs'. Vicky Bell argues that the notion of 'encryption', which Butler borrows from

Freud in order to illustrate the way in which homosexuality is encrypted and always under erasure in the psychic structures of heterosexuality is absent from ethnic relations arguing, I think too hastily, that 'in the case of ethnicity, it is more difficult to assert that there is an encrypted other, a comparable knowledge that, accurate or inaccurate or distorted, faithful or unfaithful, for the identification to take place' (Bell 1999b: 154). Yet the images used by British-born or -raised Arabs to represent themselves are replete with these encrypted others and framed by melancholia.

The Encrypted Others of Melancholia

For at least 200 years European values and models of social organisation and government have been emanated and advocated as a way for Arabs to take their place among 'the civilised nations'. Taha Hussayn, dubbed 'the Dean of Arabic literature', argued that: 'We must follow the path of Europeans so as to be their equals and partners in civilisation, in its good and evil, its sweetness and bitterness, what can be loved or hated, what can be praised or blamed' (Hourani 1962: 330). Preceding Hussayn, Rifaa' al-Tahtawi believed that European states (particularly France) were the standards to which Arabs could aspire, so that in order to be modern one had somehow to become European. Makdisi argues 'the goal of the process of modernisation as it was formulated by al-Tahtawi is therefore impossible; it means becoming the other' (1995: 183, see also Makdisi 1992, 1998). A reified Europe, romanticised, often simplified, sometimes vilified, is deeply embedded within the collective Arab psyche, encrypted in the very structures of what it means to be Arab and to see the world through Arab eyes. The Arab world suffers from a collective melancholia. That melancholia is often articulated as an Arab Islamic civilisational malaise which, in Du Bois' terms we might see as a 'double consciousness' (2007 [1903]).

One of the central points of contestation between pan-Arabism and pan-Islamism has been the debate about an autonomous (characterised as Islamic) versus a mimetic (characterised as a Europeanising) vision of modernity; as if mimesis does not always implicate both. Indeed that double consciousness has once again come to the fore in the wake of the revolts, revolutions and uprisings that have gripped parts of the Arab world (see Aksikas 2009). It is as yet unresolved but is a testament to collective Arab melancholia. Apart from the obvious sources of that melancholia, which are evident in everything from occupation and state failure to the appalling state of human development; collective Arab melancholia is about the Arab failure to resist Europe or offer an alternative to it. It is also fundamentally about a failure to be European, which remains synonymous with being 'modern'. For many Arabs, that failure is all the more painful in light of what many see as a glorious Arab Islamic civilisational past (see Nehme 2009).

In Freud's essay 'Mourning and Melancholia' the ego copes with the experience of losing another human being that it has loved by incorporating the lost other in the very structure of the ego by 'taking on attributes of the other and sustaining' the other through magical acts of imitation (Freud 1922). The loss of the other, whom one desires and loves, is overcome through the specific act of identification that seeks to harbour that other within the very structure of the self. In *Gender Trouble* (1990) Judith Butler claims that Freud only alludes to gender and melancholia in his work in passing. It was not until the late 1980s that readings of melancholia began to be elaborated in relation to gender in the work of Butler (1990, 1993), Silverman (1988) and Schiesari (1992). There have also been attempts to think about melancholia as a culturally instituted condition that, in part, dictates 'desire' and informs our understanding of what will and what will not be a loveable object.

Cheng suggests that 'melancholia alludes not to loss *per se* but to the … multiple layers of denial and exclusion that the melancholic must exercise in order to maintain [an] elaborate structure of loss-but-not-loss' (2001: 8–9). Melancholia is an entangled relationship with loss and, she argues:

> [it is constitutive of] an American ideological dilemma and its constitutional practice … America is most shamefaced and traumatised by its betrayal of its own democratic ideology (the genocide of the Native Americans, slavery, segregation, immigration discrimination), nonetheless it most virulently – and melancholically – espouses human value and brotherhood'. (2001: 11)

In other words there has been a constant and inherent contradiction in the American self-image and the realities of the American condition.

Gilroy argues that Britain suffers from a postcolonial melancholia where the fantasy of imperial omnipotence coupled with an 'island race notion of self' are constructed as lost, but not yet mourned. In this postcolonial malaise 'incoming strangers [who] are trapped inside our perverse logic of race, nation and ethnic absolutism not only represent vanished empire but also refer consciousness to the unacknowledged pain of its loss and the unsettling shame of its bloody management' (2006: 110). Collective melancholia may be based on abstraction and reification, but no more so than that involved in the making of the pathological ego itself. Cheng and Gilroy's readings place ethno-race at the centre of collective American and British melancholia. It is the infrahuman political body of 'indigenous' and 'ethnic' others that comes to represent all the discomforting ambiguities of painful and shameful, but apparently exhilarating histories.

Within these nation-state settings the logic of ethnonormativity prevails so that an ethnic or racial identification comes second only to the very 'fact' of being a man or a woman. Thus social actors are subject to injunctions that seek to institute their 'ethnic otherness', in this case their *Arabness*. Yet there is nothing but negativity attributed to that identification which conflates Arab and Muslim and assigns to both a catalogue of by now well-known pejoratives. This gives way to a number of mimetic options which are reminiscent of the nineteenth-century *Nahda* in the Middle East: (1) the project of Europeanisation, where one abandons the Arab 'identity' altogether, which is what Fadwa suggests that 'wealthy Arabs' do in London; (2) to renounce European modernity altogether, which is perceived by many as the retreat into or the resurgence of Islam; or (3) as Fadwa does in the photo shoot and the discourses that she employs, to seek an accommodation, in this case through intelligibility within multiculturalism – through the parading of colourful foods, clothes and sounds. In a sense young Arabs in London are *subject to* and the *subject of* both the melancholia of postcolonial Britain and the yearning for the quasi-magical Arab golden age, each of which relies on the encrypted other as its nemesis and ultimate cause of its undoing.

Validation also requires that one prove that immigrants and the minorities they spawn make a vital contribution to the British economy and welfare state. 'The ethnic entrepreneur is the assimilationist hero' (Keith 1993: 44), an assertion which has now become a crucial part of the evidence marshalled to convince the British public that immigration has not ruined *this sceptred isle*. What Fadwa seeks to say through the adornment of 'ethnic-chic' (see Tarlo 1996, 2010) is: 'We are here, we are not bearded or veiled, this is our likeness, we are authentic yet modern, we are colourful, beautiful, exotic and mysterious, yet we are productive and successful citizens.' Fadwa's project seeks to legitimise and assert the ideals of secular, middle-class British Arabness, a way of being which must be made distinct from the amorphous and frightening apparition of 'British Muslims'. Katherine Brown offers an analysis of some of the instances in which the 'securitized caricature' of Muslims propagated in parts of the media has been resisted through the promotion of alternative representations through publications like the Muslim lifestyle magazine *Emel* (*Hope*). These can involve initiatives like the 'Muslim Women Power List' and the showcasing of Muslim 'success stories' like the businessman/celebrity James Khan (2010: 178). However, Brown concludes, in my opinion correctly, that the terms upon which such 'positive' and successful representations are formulated 'remain the socially validated ones of hard work and conspicuous consumption' (2010: 180).

Before we can resort to the comfort of 'cosmopolitan hybridity' we must interrogate the very real political and economic processes that so skilfully silence the political grounds on which these ethnic self-portraits are founded. The shifting strategies of the mode of production, benefits from the reification of homeland, the framing of hybrid forms in terms of marginality and centre (Gilroy 2000b) and the development of identity-specific forms of marketing (Hall 1997).

> Is the aestheticisation of cultural 'quirks' according to capitalist rationality (that all differences can be equated at the market) something that can be fought and won at the level of 'cultural struggle'? Surely all that is fought for at this level is authenticity – and not material redress and transformation. (Hutnyk 2000: 121)

Identity politics as governmentality is divisive, it entices and calls ethnicities into being. Legitimate otherness provides recognition within a hierarchical multicultural system of signification but skirts around the deeply embedded and most complex aspect of subaltern belonging in this ostensibly 'postcolonial' world – the slavery and genocide upon which the 'First World' was built, and the war, occupation and neocolonialism on which it continues to be sustained.

Objects like the *Shisha*, the inlaid table, ethnic costumes and fabrics provide easily accessible worn worlds and interiors that cite ethnicity and belonging. Adorning oneself and one's surroundings with the material objects of ethnicity is a far easier basis on which to stake a claim to Arabness than one based on literature, poetry, experience or politics. For British-born or -raised Arabs, Arabness can become an identification that is donned and doffed, that is purchased on holiday and arranged in a living room, a material ensemble but one that ultimately cannot escape the meta-narratives of the Orient and the Occident and one that reflects how ethnicity should be normatively experienced in a multicultural setting.

The spectacle is not a collection of images; it is a social relation between people that is mediated by images … [it] cannot be understood as a mere visual deception produced by mass media technologies. It is a view of the world that has actually been materialised, a view of the world that has become objective. Understood in its totality, the spectacle is both the result and the goal of the dominant mode of production. It is not mere decoration added to the real world. It is the very heart of this real society's unreality. (Debord 2013: 4)

Can the use of the belly dancer as a trope for the Arab party scene or the re-appropriation of romantic Orientalism by young Arabs in London be seen as stemming from a radically free or paradigmatic hybridity or as the result of free choice or agency? These visual exchanges should be seen in relation to the structures of subjection and the power of discourse, the belly dancer and romantic Orientalism are in fact the result of no choice at all. 'In dealing with each other those identified as exotics refer to the very categorisations that keep them bound and struggle to expand their identities through exotic reappropriations. Exotics negotiate their status as passionate objects so as to gain agency over their passionateness' (Savigliano 1995: 169). These images are attempts to visually enunciate 'Arab ethnicity' within the context of multicultural praxis in London. I cannot overlook the extent to which these appropriations are adopted under a melancholic duress, where nostalgia and a phantasmic past offer the only avenues for positive self-identification, the ultimate testament to the continued, albeit, reconfigured prominence of Orientalism as an affliction of both 'East' and 'West'. These fragments of meaning are barely resistance; instead they are the affirmation of the de-politicisation of struggle at the altar of the market and the logic of corporatist multi-culturalism. Does the flight into nostalgia represent a loss of faith in the future, the characteristic postmodern condition (Jameson 1984)? Do these pastiche, retro images used by British-born or -raised Arabs show them as incapable of producing serious images and texts that give people meaning and direction (McRobbie 1989)? If perhaps Fadwa had not inscribed or described these photo as representing so much essence, I might not have been able to see them as anything more or less than the fad for period drama costumes, medieval re-enactment troupes, retro or *Trekkie* conventions. However both Fadwa and I seem, in our own ways, to see these photographs as saying much more.

The performative matrix in which 'being ethnic' and doing Arabness in London is, as Butler describes, 'a project of survival'; it is not confirmation of the reality of 'ethnicity' or the paradigmatic nature of hybridity's third spaces (Bhabha 1994: 36), but something that shows ethnicities in all their colours and colourlessness as parodies of each other. Yet the tension persists unabated; while the imagery I present here is undoubtedly Orientalist in terms of its visual conventions and composition, we cannot simply read it as a collective affliction or postcolonial *faux pas* if we take the uncontrollability or *différance* of meaning *seriously*. If, as Derrida argues, the *iterability* of signs reactivates all meanings past, present and unforeseen then meanings are diachronic and thus never original or fixed.

6

Performativity and the Undoing of Identity

I began with a simple motivation, to understand how one might become an 'Arab' or do Arabness in London. To be able to take on questions of how Arabness is achieved through everyday settings, discourses and practices in contemporary London, I have had to address basic questions (of a normative nature) like the causes and waves of migration, the scale and extent of Arab migration to Britain, and how Arabs have been represented in the British public imagination. That level of examination has provided me with the ability to contextualise this ethnography in relation to local, regional and global systems (Marcus 1995). My reading of Arab migration to Britain suggests three interrelated factors: these are (1) Britain's colonial past and neocolonial present in the Middle East; (2) the ebbs, flows and failings of pan-Arabism as a postcolonial movement and a regional state system; and (3) the British state's long relationship with 'race', once at arm's length out in the colonies, now a feature of its towns and cities.

In their quest for geo-political control of the Middle East and North Africa in the nineteenth and twentieth centuries, Britain and France created nascent nation-states in the Middle East, destroyed others (Palestine) and installed or sustained local elites to further their interests and aspirations. Despite Britain's central role in the emergence of the Arab state system and the legacy of its colonial exploitation, migration from Arab states to Britain has been a trickle in comparison to the movement of people within the Middle East and migration from Arab states to North and South America, France, Spain, Italy and Australia.

Like migrants and settlers from the Caribbean, South Asia and Africa, 'Arabs' came to Britain (admittedly in far fewer numbers) as students and labour migrants. However, unlike other migrations to Britain, Arab migration is an example of non-Commonwealth migration that has been shaped not only by the colonial past but, more forcefully, by Britain's neocolonial present. 'The immigrant is now here because Britain, Europe was once out there; that basic fact of global history is not usually deniable' (Gilroy 1993: 115). The story of Arab migration to Britain prompts the reconsideration of the idea that Britain is *after Empire*. Britain is still 'out there', nowhere more than in the Middle East. Indeed, the tens of thousands of Iraqi refugees who came to Britain in the wake of the 1991 and 2003 Gulf Wars, in which Britain was a principal belligerent, are a testament to that fact and an unambiguous expression of the postcolonial melancholia that Gilroy (2000b) speaks of.

Equally, many Arab migrants to Britain were and are driven to leave their countries because of the socio-economic failures and brutality of 'Arab regimes'. The arrival of the majority of Arab migrants in Britain since the mid 1990s corresponded with an era when state failure, civil war, poverty and repression were at an all-time high. That remains a central theme in the story of Arab migration today, as tens of thousands of Syrians have fled their homes in the direction of Europe, many of them hoping to find refuge in Britain. However, as it stands at the moment, Arab migration to Britain is in large measure an Iraqi story (see Figure 6.1). Migrants and refugees from Iraq are the single largest group of Arab migrants, refugees and asylum seekers. It is important to remember that among them are a considerable number of Iraqi Kurds who do not necessarily identify themselves as Arabs. Furthermore Iraqi Arabs in Britain are afflicted with Shia and Sunni sectarianism that reflects the policies during the Saddam era as well as the more recent sectarian politics and violence since 2003. Quite understandably they have had little time for the luxury of pan-Arab identification and political action and maintain a difficult relationship with the country that has been a principal cause of their misery and a refuge at the same time. National, sub-national and denominational identification have been more prominent levels of solidarity and organisation in their struggles to settle and survive after often violent and forced displacement.

Iraqis are not alone in this sense; relations and organisation among say, Egyptians in Britain also reflect the class, ethnic, ideological and sectarian fractures within Egypt, so that, for example, Christian Egyptians and Nubian Egyptians organise separately. More recently a new and poisonous fracture has opened within the 'Egyptian community' on the basis of whether one is pro-military or pro-Muslim Brotherhood. This of course does not make these reified communities any different from any other migrant group, but it does make it difficult to think of them as coherent 'communities' in Britain. While accepting that, on some level, we may speak of 'Arab migrants', 'Arab Londoners' or 'British Arabs' as a reified

Figure 6.1 The remains of an Iraqi election poster on a wall on Bell Street NW1 in 2006

Source: Photo by the author.

category of strategic essentialism, it is clear to me that, in a political and organisational sense, that reification is extremely precarious.

In some settings like the United States, Arabs have organised and institutionalised themselves as a minority, but in Britain Arab migrants seem by and large disengaged from local and national politics. For some the disengagement was based on 'myths of return' (Anwar 1979), others were captivated more by the struggles of their respective homelands than they were by either their collective Arabness in Britain or the struggle for rights, equality and anti-racism in Britain. The centrality of the race relations paradigm in Britain meant that Arabs, a racially and geographically diverse identification, were on the whole 'hidden' and unintelligible to the state and society. They seem to have been understood almost exclusively in relation to the spectacles of petro-dollar tourism and investment on the one hand and a long catalogue of acts of political violence perpetrated by Arab regimes and political movements on the other.

It is reasonable to conclude that there have been few incentives for migrants from Arab states to recite the political norms of 'pan-Arab communitarianism' within the context of British 'multiculturalism'. This performative failure to create an instituted collective Arabness is a matter that some lament; others, like myself, may be relieved by the failure to pander to the normative and often divisive ideals of Arab political ideologies or British identity and bio politics. Despite the performative failure of Arab communitarianism, 'Arabness' (along with other ethnic and religious identifications) in Britain has been subject to racialisation so that saying 'I am Arab' is often less about 'Arab culture' and more about not being 'Black', 'Asian' or 'White' as these are understood in Britain. That process has culminated in the incorporation of 'Arab' into checkbox multiculturalism where recognition and inclusion are extended on the basis of contemporary modes of colonial counting and the neoliberal commodification of 'Britishness' and ethnic difference (see Appadurai 1993; see also Smith 1985; Cohn 1987; Benson 1996; Hesse 2000; Cole 2003; Comaroff and Comaroff 2009; Kappor 2013).

Gilroy suggests that 'there is more at stake in the current interest in identity than we often appreciate' (2000b: 98). The circulation of the term 'identity', particularly within policy circles, and global commerce and marketing, has added considerably to the term's fragmentation and manipulation as a catch-all interpretive device. 'We are constantly informed', he writes, 'that to share an identity is to be bonded on the most fundamental levels: national, "racial", ethnic, regional and local. Identity is always bounded and particular', noting that sadly nobody speaks of a human identity (2000: 155). 'The idea of collective identity has emerged as an object of political thinking even if its appearance signals the sorry state of affairs in which distinctive rules that define modern political culture are consciously set aside' (2000: 155).

When I began my research it seemed in a common-sense way to sit within what has come to be known in Britain as 'ethnic and racial studies', 'migration studies' or the study of multiculturalism which, Vertovec (2007) argues has been given uneven attention by anthropologists in comparison to say 'transnationalism' or perhaps even the study of British Muslims an area of research which has become a veritable academic industry funded in large part by post-911 and 7/7 apprehensions. Although this ethnography has been concerned with trying to account for the structural dynamics of pan-Arabism, British 'multiculturalism' and Arab migration, I now realise that what has driven me throughout this process is how these might be read as recitations and reiterations of far more deeply embedded normative structures: heteronormativity, ethnonormativity and class. While I could simply restate this as gender, race and class, I find that by emphasising *normativity* I am constantly reminded of the need to question their ontological status and the processes that install and disrupt them.

My central assertion in this ethnography is that far from simply being born 'Arab' or possessing a common-sense Arab 'identity', or embodying a voluntary British Arabness the stories, experiences and practices of young people in this ethnography reveal discursive and material injunctions that hail and draw individuals into a process of *subjectification* through which one becomes a gendered, raced and classed subject. The very essence of what Butler sets out to do by theorising 'performativity' is to postulate it as a 'vehicle through which ontological effects are established and installed (Butler 1996:111–12, see also 1993:12, 234). What I describe as ethnonormativity is a deeply embedded set of beliefs about essential sameness and difference that naturalise the notion of 'ethnicity' and provide it with the status of a proper (ontological) object with which the expansive potential of self and human relationships are predicated. Ethnonormativity is relentlessly enduring; in its history it has manifested itself as that which is incommensurable about 'race', 'ethnicity', 'religion', 'nation' and 'culture'. Today 'Identity' has become both a synonym and suffix of these forms of incommensurability.

What I hope this ethnography might demonstrate is the constant need for a twofold move in relation to the study of ethnicity. The first is the recognition that ethnonormative thinking still structures people's sense of self (identity) and socio-political praxis (ethnic identity politics and racial governmentality). What I understand as the persistence of ethnonormativity seems to go very much against the assertions that post-ethnic, voluntary ethnicity can resolve the problems of multiculturalism (see Hollinger 1995). Equally I would argue that ethnonormativity is a persistent undercurrent in the way race, culture and ethnic 'hybridity' are understood. The second move draws me into an analysis that cannot think about the structuring power of ethnonormativity without also thinking about how it is inflected by heteronormativity and class. It is not a question of which process precedes, takes priority over or has more import than the other – it is their interdependence that is most critical for sequential readings of the processes that mark interpolation and subject making.

The position that I take – that 'one is not born but becomes Arab' – is not a constructivist one. Constructivist approaches to 'identity' have resolutely failed to help in overcoming the grotesque consequences of ethnonormative thinking. Practices around identity (as race, ethnicity, religion and culture) have been confused with the ontological status of 'identity'. Indeed the relationship between social constructivism and identity politics has been characterised by Gergen (2001) as a kind of cathartic 'love affair' where anti-essentialism 'within different identity-based political positions' has the result of strengthening foundationalist identity politics (Gupta 2007: 30). For Cooper and Brubaker the constructivist approach to identity in contemporary anthropological and sociological research is at best a 'clichéd constructivism' where soft conceptions of identity are 'routinely packaged with standard qualifiers ... which have become so familiar – indeed obligatory – in recent years that one reads (and writes) them virtually automatically': 'multiple', 'contingent', 'unstable', 'in flux', 'fragmented', 'constructed', 'negotiated' (2000: 38).

The effort to think of identity in terms of plurality has led to a rather superficial supplanting of the singular form 'identity' with the plural 'identities'. The hyphenated identities of multiracial and multicultural systems where one is Black-British or African-American are a testament to race logic, for what are these labels if not binaries with the enigmatic hyphen attesting to their dissolution. These binaries hide a violent and racialised hierarchy: 'One of the two terms governs the other or has the upper hand' (Derrida 1981: 41). Radhakrishnan (2003a) makes the point that ethnic labelling in the United States has privileged ethnicity over American identity in a horizontal classification convention (e.g. African-American, Native-American and Italian-American). In the British context people can be Black British, British Asian or in our case British Arab. What are the implications of these labels and how are they formulated? Is it simply how the label rolls of the tongue that determines its formulation or are there underlying implications? Is it acceptable to be assertively Black but not so if you are Asian, Arab or Muslim? Or does blackness incontrovertibly come first? If so to what extent are the historical and semiotic structures of racism a part of this condition? 'Indeed these constructions embody a logic that valorises the first term while subordinating the second. And this is not simply a matter of semantics because such classificatory practices carry material consequence' (Miron and Inda 2000: 97).

'Identity' carries with it the expectation of cultural specificity and, increasingly, 'identity and specificity work interchangeably' so that the 'subject position' becomes self-referential, leading to a kind of 'closed circuitry' or 'cultural solipsism' (Butler 2000b: 441). Through this type of identity politics we are encouraged to think of marking our position as the ultimate act of political emancipation, responsibility and accountability. 'The unmediated first person voice is offered as the final phenomenological legitimation for a political claim' stemming from a continued emphasis on the language of *positions* that reflect an individual's place in a social hierarchy and from where they speak' (2000b: 440).

And when politics is reduced to political moralism of this sort, the self-referential declarations of *possessing* an 'identity' is elevated to the status of an ethical imperative, restricting the field of public discourse to individualist declarations or to claims first grounded in such declarations. (2000b: 442, emphasis added)

In research and activism taking account of one's 'race' [read as 'identity'] is thus equated with ethical responsibility, so that I end up wanting to mark myself out as, for example, an 'Arab anthropologist', unwittingly reducing myself and the object of research to 'ethnonormativity', so that what begins as reflexivity can often fall far short of progress. Butler suggests that 'if "identity" becomes the unit that is multiplied, then the principle of identity is repeated – and reconfirmed without ever yielding to another set of terms' (2000b: 439). Often what we mean by identity is recognis-ability, representation, culture, agency, meaning, historical formation and contextualisation (2000b:440), biology, affinities, affiliations, belongings, commonalities and connectedness, self-understanding and self-identifica-tion. All the meanings and consequences that these categories carry are distilled into the notion of 'identity' or 'identities' (Brubaker 2006).

I would argue that, to some extent, there is a slippage between the desire to assert distinctive individualism (and thus humanist agency) and the notion of 'identity'. Amit, for example, argues that 'any notion of community, of society or culture that posits such collectivities as prior to or superseding the individual is fundamentally illusory' (Amit and Rapport 2002). I choose to throw caution to the wind and say that attempts to theorise ethnicity, community and society by positioning individualism prior to those constructs are equally flawed and illusionary. The partial truths in ethnography are least effective and sincere when they are used as the basis for the resolution of an irresolvable entanglement. I feel I can move beyond the limitations of constructivism, humanism and structuralism by saying that we should try and rethink and reformulate these questions in a way that does not elicit theoretical finality and conclusiveness. One way of doing that is to think of this ethnographic account as one that reveals the interplays between *performance* and *performativity*.

I would argue that to picture, to compose, to speak, to dance and move, to regulate, to consume, is to recite imperfectly or perform that which is performative. Rather than continuing to see *performance* and *performativity* as sitting at opposite ends of a theoretical scale, I choose to subvert that tension and suggest that neither humanistic readings of *performance* nor anti-materialist readings of *performativity* can lay any claims to resolving the questions that we pose about agency, individualism, structure and collectivity on their own. As Morris (1995: 571) argues, much of the appeal of performativity lies in its potential to address the crisis of structuralism by offering something between an anti-structuralist and a neo-structuralist rubric. For me this ethnography is all about the entangled and ongoing relationship between *how people do* hetero-, ethno- and class normativity – performance; and *why they do these things* in particular ways – performativity.

A Performative Reading of Becoming Arab in London

'The Arab(s) in/and/of London' is a problematic within the terms of ethnonormativity. A problematic is, in an Althusserian sense, 'a defined theoretical structure or conceptual framework which determines the forms of posing of all problems and what is seen as relevant to the problem' (Glucksmann 1974: 3). That problematic is fortified by discursive practices and representations that are key to understanding how one is hailed as an 'Arab in London'. These are various so that, on the one hand political ideologies cast 'Arabism' (a political project) as a 'collective identity' of essential concord. That 'identity' is simultaneously underwritten by a collective melancholia that has modernity, occupation, defeat, failure, poverty, authoritarianism, suspicion and discord at its core. On the other hand, mediated representations of Arabs in Britain build upon a long-standing tradition of Orientalism that casts Arabs as having a primitive, violent and misogynistic culture (singular) and thus essence (see Steet 2000; Khattak 2008). The fetishisation of 'the Arabs' means that 'Arab' becomes synonymous with terrorist and petro-dollar 'exotics'. Political projects, acts of violence and conspicuous consumption are divorced from the people behind them to become distilled into a knowable discursive object 'the Arabs'. It has been the burden of Arabs in London, from Dr Zada in 1933 to Dr Mehdi in the 1970s all the way through to those raised and living in London in the early twenty-first century like Fadwa, to object to that representation and to try and 'correct it'.

Discourses are pervasive, powerful and uncontrollable; they hail subjects into reciting them imperfectly (see Hall 1997; hooks 1999). In the process of growing up in London, some try to evade the injunction *to be* 'Arab' through attempts to redefine *identification* and *desire* and through acts of mimesis. In this ethnography Suad's miming of middle-class Englishness was motivated by her search for commonality with her 'English' peers. For both Suad and Ahmed the failure to pass for White or 'English' seems to have thrust them into the embrace of their Arabness and, on some level, shifts their notions of identification and desire once more, this time in the direction of their ethnic Arabness which, through its interpolation comes to provide them with a semblance of social intelligibility and the prospect of cultural survival. Roula, Suad and others revealed how the experience of being 'the only Arab at school' was in part due to the recognition by some of the harm that might follow from being identified as 'Arab', which in turn led them to adopt strategies of *hiding* and *passing*. *Hiding* and *passing* are clear confirmations of the psychological and physical consequences of the discourse 'the Arabs' upon those that are its subjects. The references to *Arabs in hiding* at school suggest the appropriation of whiteness or passing for White is as much about a practical project of survival within a system of signification where Arabness remains inherently negative and stigmatised, and not solely the result of an instituted desire for whiteness. The ways in which this happens are complex; for Ahmed it led to a forced identification with the despot who was the cause of his family's dislocation and the destruction of his country. Ahmed and others came to make use of the discourses of their ethnic otherness by embodying it, and inscribing their recitations of masculinity and femininity with it. As 'other Arabs' appear in the narratives of school, gendered Arabness becomes a basis on which personal and psychological safety, solidarity and resistance are fashioned. The chameleon-like nature of the discourse of 'the Arabs' also leads to the appropriation of the very meanings that are used to subordinate and circumscribe, so that some proudly declare 'We're all terrorists' while others covet the aura of wealth, power and prestige by playing the parts of *Khaleeji Emirs* and *Emiras* in London's nightclubs.

The media is not the only institution that acts to circulate the problematic 'Arab in/and/of London'. The ethnonormative concerns of wider society are reflected in institutions like schools, where there is a tendency to see these young people primarily as 'ethnic subjects'. Hailing is not only something that the reified bureaucracy is capable of. The utterances of peers at school have a lasting effect upon those who have been *subject to* them. Thus the sound of a falling bomb, being told that 'you are not English' or taunts like 'you dirty Arab' not only perfectly reflect the discourse of 'the Arabs' in Britain and ethnonormativity more broadly, they also suggest that young people are acutely aware of the meanings that inform belonging in their society, as well as those that convey symbolic violence.

Parents have a part to play in reproducing heteronormativity and ethnonormativity when they seek to reproduce idealised forms of ethnic womanhood and manhood in their children through an array of disciplines, discourses, bodily regulations and injunctions. Zainab and

Suad's narratives in particular reveal the competing demands of 'Arab' and 'western' brands of heteronormativity that are equally insistent on claiming them through the regulation of their bodies and sexuality. For Zainab the intersections of heteronormativity, ethnonormativity and class produced competing and complementary demands that led her to fashion a fictitious Arab social life that she hoped would make her intelligible to all. She also explicitly states that not everyone is able to recite these injunctions, and that there are personal and social consequences to that failure. I feel justified in adding more layers to the way I understand heteronormativity, which requires a degree of periodisation and disaggregation. This ethnography has shown that the raced, gendered and classed projects of survival and social intelligibility can involve reciting different types of ethnicised and classed gender. Together heteronormativity, ethnonormativity and class regulation can produce a divisive sexual politics between Arab and English women that revolves around class, virtue, female sexuality and anxieties around the reproduction of the diasporic Arab family and thus the ethnic subject.

The narratives of growing up in London and learning to be Arab reveal competing structures of subjection and suggest that, for some, becoming an Arab man or an Arab woman is first and foremost an involuntary act, one that is motivated primarily by the project of cultural survival and social intelligibility. Ahmed and Suad explicitly suggest that their respective recitations of 'Arab' masculinity and femininity were someone else's doing – parents, peers, war and politics. The performative injunctions to be an 'Arab in/and/of London' are produced by a schema of (collective, individual and institutional) ethnonormative, heteronormative and class-based discourses, and practices that result in forced recitations. These always fall short of resolving the foundational problematic 'Arab in/and/ of London'. For young people alienation and disenfranchisement is not simply about the struggles for rights in the countries in which they were born or raised, it is to a large extent about acceptance of their versions of subjecthood in situ. Lisa Lowe (1996) cites Maxine Hong Kingston who suggests that one of the more important stories of the Asian American experience is about the process of receiving and re-articulating cultural traditions in the face of a dominant national discourse that 'exoticises' and 'orientalises' Asians, a point which resonates with Arabs in Britain. She asks Chinese Americans:

When you try to understand what things in you are Chinese, how do you separate what is peculiar to childhood, to poverty, to insanities, one's family, your mother who marked your growing with stories, from what is Chinese? What is Chinese tradition and what is 'the movies'? (Lowe 1996: 137)

Performativity and iterability can answer Hong Kingston's question by pointing to the parody and indeterminacy through which all things idiosyncratic, phantasmic, (in)authentic and all the other possible meanings of being 'Chinese' or 'Arab' are included within what it is *to do*. Their recitations are unintelligible only to those who police the ethnonormative, hetronormative and class matrix. If there is an 'identity crisis' in this scheme it is not one that belongs to young people but to those most committed to the reproduction of certain kinds of gendered, raced and classed subjects.

Ethnonormativity does not entail a single, universal configuration of *identification* and *desire* as some have suggested (see Rottenberg 2004a, 2004b, 2004c). As psychic schemes, identification and desire contain the possibility of maintaining points of continuity with structures of 'whiteness' while at the same time adapting to new manifestations of race-thinking like ethnic assertiveness or racial governmentality. We cannot assume that the configuration of racialised identifications and desires are fixed, or that we have completely understood their nuances, instead we might do well to think of identification, desire and mimesis as maintaining complex connections with each other. Indeed contemporary accounts of *passing* in American literature suggest that blackness has been cast as the ideal desired identity, reversing the racial dynamic of more traditional passing narratives (Harrison-Kahan 2005). Similarly Elam finds that mono-racial complacency has been replaced by an ironic 'mestizo imperative' in post-passing narratives (2007: 765).

The way in which some young people have experienced growing up in London and Britain suggests that within the context of a *multiculturalism* of 'groups' and 'communities' in competition over their ethnic distinctiveness, there are affective and material imperatives and incentives for people to behave, feel and desire their ethnicity – in other words to conform to the racial and cultural division of society into 'ethnic groups'. Ethnonormativity institutes the 'reality' and the desirability of arboreal 'ethnic identity' and its fundamental difference from other ethnicities. This was as much the case with Suad's peers who discounted the possibility of her being 'English' because she was not 'Anglo Saxon' as it was in the email about Edgware Road where an Arab Londoner censured British Muslim

South Asians for 'deluding themselves into believing that they actually ARE [sic] of Arab extraction'.

A performative reading does not have to force the modalities of gender, race and class to be one and the same or schematically unrelated. Thus, insightful though it is, Rottenberg's (2004a, 2004b) rejection of the move from performative gender to performative race runs the risk of casting identification and desire in a fixed configuration instead of seeing it as an adaptive or dynamic structure that is always in the process of being reinstalled imperfectly. Rottenberg (2004c) also rules out a performative reading of class because its interpolation does not speak to the same configuration of identification, desire, mimesis, encryption, melancholia and cultural survival that we find in Butler's theorising of performative gender. Her assertion relies upon a particular reading of class in the United States which leaves me concerned that she relies on a kind of structural monism where gender, class and race relations are manifest in fundamentally different, knowable and unchanging configurations. Ultimately this reproduces the dualism of *subjective* and *objective* 'effects' in Bourdieu where habitus is temporal and historically located but the *social field* is timeless and unresponsive. I would second the caution that we must be wary of modes of analysis 'or versions of multiculturalism that try to keep processes of gendering and racing radically distinct' (Bell, 1999d: 168) and we must equally take care not to obscure the possibility of a performative reading of social class.

While accepting her limited understanding of economics, Butler has advocated experimentation with performativity in relation to economics as an analytical strategy uncovering effects as causes and questioning the ontological status of proper objects like 'the market'. What performative economics offers is an approach to 'market economics' which uncovers the 'processes that work to fortify that very assumption, but also to call into question its pre-given ontological status as well as the supposition that it operates by causal necessity' (Butler 2010: 158; see also Callon 2006).

Butler's scheme of gender performativity is a beginning and not an end; it opens up avenues for analysis and those should not be closed down on the basis of intellectual devoteeism or paradigmatic sanctity. This is well demonstrated by Jeremy Lane's (2012) analysis of Didier Eribon's autobiography *Retour á Reims* (2010), which demonstrates the way in which an unbending approach to epistemological schemes can constrain phenomenological analyses, even autobiographical ones. Contrary to the Bourdieusian scheme he is so attached to, Eribon 'speculates that it may have been his rejection of heterosexual identity that proved the catalyst and motor for his miraculous academic success and for his flight from his working-class origins' (Lane 2012: 133). Furthermore, Eribon's account of his family's relationship to their working-class 'identity' seems to paint a far more complex picture than the assumed *amor fati* (love of [one's own] class fate) suggested by Bourdieu. He is also unable to adhere to Bourdieu when articulating *affect* and the transformative, creative and emancipatory potential of (homo)sexual shame.

I would argue that more concerted efforts should be made to interrelate the analysis of social class to ethno- and hetero- normativity. Although I have not been able to theorise performative class sufficiently, class and consumption are central to the process of becoming socially intelligible. The processes of becoming are not simply about being made into a British Arab man or woman; the acquisition of particular dispositions towards taste, class and consumption are also expected. In this ethnography that has included the parading of 'successful' bourgeois careerism in the ethnic self-portraits of the first British Arab magazine; the frequenting or avoiding of particular spaces and places that signify certain race gender and class subjecthood; the theatrical appropriating of the character of the Arab oil Sheikh, or the opposite experience, of rejecting the true-lie of Arab affluence and coming to identify more with English working-classness, even if some, like Jabir, have been unceremoniously excluded from it in their past.

The ways in which young people interpolate injunctions *to be* British Arab men and women involves the synchronisation and synthesis of structures of subjection on a daily basis. They do not experience being raced, gendered and classed one at a time but simultaneously; nor do these result in coherent social identities. What the young people I interacted with meant by 'Arabness' and how they achieved it was far from straight-forward. Ethnographic insight reveals the nuances of interpolation and uncovers the contingency of the categories that we assume to exist or to be reproduced on the one hand, and the outcomes we expect to flow from processes on the other. The accounts of young men and women unsettle the notion of a coherent 'Arab community' or 'Arab culture' in London. In reciting raced, gendered and classed subjecthood people populate the world around them with race gender and class 'others' in complex ways. The group of young men who so religiously frequented *Shisha* cafes in order to assert their bourgeois, masculine 'Arabness' were so concerned with achieving 'distinction' that they would abandon their regular haunt to avoid being associated with *Khaleeji* tourists, and would equally steer clear of cafes and locales frequented by working-class Arabs because they were too 'ghetto'. They seem to have actually been more comfortable sharing social space with those who constitute 'otherness' in more straightforward ways, as those have the potential to enhance their exoticism and distinctiveness. Furthermore, Noura and Jabir show us that there are different and contesting ways of being Arab that revolve around religious and secular repertoires. Jamal's narrative showed that the feminisation of *Khaleeji* 'others' played an important role in how he recited the norms of 'Arab' masculinity at school.

Equally the ethnographic account that I offer here asks searching questions about the assumed affinities of Muslims in Britain. Regrettably, many of the young middle-class British-born or -raised Arabs that I interacted with would blend British and Arab anti-South Asian racist discourses. Time and again Arab women would openly reject the advances of British South Asian men, in large measure because of their assumed position within the racial and class hierarchy, or the social, cultural and identitarian consequences of rejecting endogamy. Observant middle-class Arab Muslim men seemed to care little for the theological contradictions of distancing themselves from their South Asian co-religionists on the basis that they did not have a sufficient command of the sacred language of Arabic and so would never be as authentically Muslim as they were (see Bashear 1997).

Over the past two decades, European Muslims have increasingly come to be understood *qua* Muslims, with this aspect of their 'identity' viewed as trumping others. This has involved the ascription of *Islamism* upon all Muslims. Indeed this phenomenon is not restricted to Britain; it is now well documented in France (see Gessier 2010) The United States (Gotanda 2011) and Germany (Ramm 2010). It is now common to impute Muslimness based on the 'ethnic community' which a person is presumed to be a part of, the country of migration from which they or their parents have come, or simply their name. Consequently people with Muslim 'heritage' are assumed to see the world through Muslim eyes, to have Muslim concerns and sensibilities regardless of their actual relationship to Islam and other Muslims.

I would argue that many young people whose parents come from Muslim majority countries or who were raised as Muslims but whose lives and practices cannot be reduced to a 'religious identity' are at the mercy of two curiously proximate constituencies busily advocating their opposed yet complementary projects of Islamic racialisation. On the one hand, those who propagate anti-Muslim prejudice and depict a monolithic, incommensurable and irreconcilable *Islamism* at the core of every Muslim living in 'the West' and, on the other hand, Islamists who, Sayyid argues, attempt to transform Islam from a 'nodal point in a variety of discourses into a master signifier' (2003: 47; see also Halliday 1996). Beyond the constituency of people whose lives are visibly and practically defined entirely by Islam, it seems of little interest that there are others from the 'Islamic world' or 'Muslim communities' of Britain who may be non-practising, secular, agnostic, atheist or simply nominally Muslim, yet in an everyday sense less interested in Islamic orthodoxy than they are in capitalism, consumerism, accumulation and class. In the process of reiterating the injunctions to be Arab or Muslim, young people are drawn into imperfect recitation where they conform to and transgress, resist and submit, reproduce and undermine these norms and categories. Those processes are attributable to the reiterative possibilities afforded by the norms in a given context as much as they might be attributed to political choice, resistance or agency.

The context in this case is London. Niedermüller argues that, in cities marked by global and local processes of late modernity, there is a necessity for:

> ethnic groups ... to construct and reconstruct their roots ... because they understand the political and social potential inherent in this search. They recognise that their 'original' culture can be turned into symbolic capital, and this is the only capital they have in the social arena of late modern societies. (2000:53)

Cities like London 'are the symbolic and social stage of contemporary societies on which different actors within the ethnoscape face each other. It is here that symbolic negotiations about ethnicity and ethnic identities are performed' (2000: 47–48). I agree with Niedermüller but would add that the way in which young middle-class Arab Londoners inscribed London (as space and place) often undermines the idea of coherent ethnoscapes like 'Arab London' or even 'Iraqi London'.

In Figure 6.2 the red brick walls of Hammersmith and West London College have been festooned with postcodes that claim parts of London as 'Baghdad Zones'. This not only cites the fad for postcode gangs and wars in London, it implicitly refers to the sectarian and security zoning of Baghdad itself after the British and American invasion of 2003. This and other acts of demarcation, regulation and inscription that produce the effect of 'self' and 'other' in this ethnography, call for the disaggregation of Arabness and Muslim-ness in London. Space and place are not simply inscribed by ethnicity; heteronormativity and class; other forms of normative structures like religion are equally consequential.

Figure 6.2   London postcodes SE5, SW8, SW9 and SW10 are claimed as 'Baghdad Zonez' on a college wall in West London, 2008

Source: Photo by the author.

The grammars of ethnic dance and portraiture point to the arbitrary relationship between signifiers and that which is signified. Both improvised and professional Middle Eastern dance signify 'Arab culture', 'Arab womanhood' and 'Arab manhood'. While these proximate but contesting movement repertoires claim the same object, they signify them in distinct ways and, in the process, reveal the antagonisms around male and female bodies and sexuality. British-born or -raised Arab women may recognise themselves in some way as being the objects of cabaret belly dancing, yet they are alienated from it by the regulatory demands of Arab womanhood itself. Similarly, young men's recitation of ethnic dance is designed to assert their cultural knowledge as young 'Arab men', yet many are not conscious that by dancing what has come to be understood as the female form of *baladi*, they transgress and unsettle the colonial and postcolonial ideologies of sex and gender that have sought to erase the gender ambiguity in Middle Eastern dance. This prompts a reconsideration of how we understand the relationships between hidden meanings and surface meanings. I would argue that within the context of dance the conventions of regulatory Arab womanhood are very apparent to those who participate in public dances; indeed, to a large extent, those regulations determine the movement idioms and repertoires that are adopted. The gender ambiguity in Middle Eastern dance is, in contrast, an example of what I would understand as being hidden meaning; but the extent to which male dances involve parody should draw our attention to how visible and apparent those meanings can be sometimes. What is thought to be authentic at first sight quickly reveals itself as farce and parody as the bodies that enact Arab sexuality are those of 'ethnic others', the gendered conventions imposed upon dance are both Arab and European, and those thought to be most authentically signified by Middle Eastern dance appear to be those whose relationship with it is most orchestrated and regulated. The broaching and breaching of Arab masculinity and femininity in this way is structured by the cultural and discursive conditions that mark out the possibilities of reiteration. These may continue to demand that Arabness be recited in certain ways, but will always fail to foreclose how it will be interpolated cited and grafted and can never completely silence past meanings.

The composition of the ethnic portraits in chapter 5 supports the notions that meanings can never be controlled and authorial intention is always subject to communicative failure. Thinking about the way in which *affect* might be structured through representational systems helps to explain the folklore fashion shoots and the use of the *Odalisque* as a trope for Arabness. These instances of appropriation and recitation must be put in context; they are attempts to redeem Arabness through the appropriation of Orientalist aesthetics and representational conventions. That appropriation is set against the backdrop of both Arab and British melancholic formations. The aesthetics of a pre-colonial Arab world and material culture, rendered so vividly, composed so carefully and fanned by Orientalist fantasy now provide the ethnological knowledge for those in the diaspora who make new meanings out of it but can never silence the reverberations of past meanings. The intended meanings are – 'This is our origin, we are unveiled, we are relaxed, we are beautiful, exotic, colourful and decadent. We are successful and productive just like other ethnic subjects in Britain.'

I can't help feeling that something links the nineteenth-century ethnographic showcase to the twenty-first-century ethnic self-portrait. However much I try to erase that idea from my mind it impresses itself upon me more persuasively. 'Our new fellow countrymen' reads the caption of the Cabinet photograph depicting the *Schautruppe* from Samoa performing in the Berliner Tiergarten in 1901. German, Dutch and Irish villages, among others, with native people in traditional clothing were also (re)presented at the world fairs as part of the national exhibits, staged in this case, however, by the exhibited peoples themselves, not their colonisers (Corbey 1993: 343–44). Beth Conklin's (1997:711) account of the way in which native Amazonians proclaim cultural distinctiveness through the adornment of head-dresses, body paint, beads and feathers suggests that while this has been interpreted by some anthropologists as political assertiveness and pride in being Indian, it is as much about learning to use western visual codes, aesthetics, and expectations about native people to position themselves politically. The use of exotic appearances as markers of indigenous authenticity has been used to great effect by native Amazonians in their project to resist encroachment upon their landscape and gain recognition and rights within the states in which they live. However, as Conklin points out, insisting that native Amazonian activists embody 'authenticity', may force them to act 'inauthentically' (1997: 728–29). Cohen's account of *Masquerade Politics* shows how the Notting Hill Carnival became entangled in what he calls 'the aestheticisation of politics' so that it was slowly wrenched away from its relationship to social struggle and transformed into a tourist attraction (1993:155). I would argue that the images used by young people speak to the same processes whereby collective Arabness in Britain has been diverted from the most pressing issues that underlie a progressive politics of equality and historical reconciliation to the parading of 'arboreal origins' (Gilroy, 1993, 1995), traditions and exoticism within the context of neoliberal multicultural London.

What the discourses and practices in this ethnography suggest is that the relationship between Arabness and Britishness as narrated and lived do not make sense without also thinking about heteronormativity and class, the local and the global, the instances in people's lives when conscious subversion is possible and others when injunctions *to be* overpower them and produce involuntary, imperfect recitations.

Eriksen argues that 'no amount of benevolent intentions will be able to change people's structures of relevance overnight, and so rather than try and think them away, we must understand and come to terms with their enduring power' (2000: 203). I could not agree more that we must continue to try and understand the enduring power of what he describes as 'structures of relevance' and what I understand in this ethnography to be the interplay between as hetero-, ethno- and class normativity. However, I strongly disagree that we should show any resignation towards the project of putting these structures in their rightful place. As Banton (1983) and Smith (2002) argue, we cannot be content to argue that voluntary ethnicity is the ideal of race relations or that ascription is inevitable.

We should not be left with a false choice, to think of race, ethnicity, culture and identity as illusions or to succumb to their role in the incontrovertible permanence of existing social hierarchies. The challenge that any kind of progressive politics faces is how to understand the processes behind ethnonormativity and to do so without giving intellectual cover for the projects of common-sense or over-zealous 'othering' which are at the heart of ethnic distinctiveness. As Gilroy argues, 'the first task on which we must risk the gains secured on the back of identity politics is that the call to the demise of race is not something that should be feared' (2000b: 12). As a performative reading of ethnonormativity might have it, the collectivities which Modood (2005: 51) argues exist *a priori* to racism and other false beliefs, are not forms of '*being*' as he suggests, but forms of *doing* (see also Modood et al. 2002; Smith 2002).

As an anthropologist, the words of Nancy Scheper-Hughes and Paul Gilroy ring in my ears as I ponder the comfort of submitting to 'the reality' of hetero-, ethno- and class normativity. Scheper-Hughes asks 'what anthropology might become if it existed on two fronts: as a field of knowledge (as a "discipline") and as a field of action ... or a site of struggle' (1995: 419–20). Paul Gilroy reminds us that 'the human sensorium has had to be educated to the appreciation of racial differences' (2000b: 42). In the context of late modern urban societies we cannot treat ethnicity and ethnic identity as 'natural' (Niedermüller 2000: 49) or provide it with legitimacy as counter-hegemonic diasporic redemption, nor give refuge to the nation-states' need for a controllable monoculture or commodifiable multiculture. It is incumbent upon us to assert, time and again, that the results of symbolic, cultural and political processes of 'othering' are often hideously divisive and harmful. This is not a call for a theory of colour, gender or class 'blindness' but for the continued relevance of the project of undermining the ontological status of race, gender and class as proper objects and organising principles. That overtly political and intellectual move sits comfortably with a performative reading of these structures of subjectification which asserts that, through their reiteration and recitation through different times, places and mediums of expression, they carry within them the constant possibility of miscommunication, of their own failure, and for that we should be thankful.

I began this research with ideological and emotional convictions regarding the notion of 'being Arab' that have been exposed to intense scrutiny through the narratives, practices and texts of others. It has been through the everyday lives, experiences and practices of British-born or -raised people who identify as Arabs (among other things) that the idea of '*everyday Arabness*' has been most clearly articulated to me. I argue that, when trying to understand Arabness as a diasporic experience, one must try to recognise the nuances and to draw distinctions between 'Arabism' as a political project and 'everyday Arabness', a cultural identification experienced in everyday setting, discourses and practices and with different intensities and significance over a life course. *Everyday Arabness* among the British-born or -raised people I engaged with seemed to be experienced at school and in the playground, at university, through the discourses of 'the Arabs', news headlines of war and violence, while socialising in a cafe and consuming *Shisha*, at an Arabic party, while dancing at a social event, or playing in an 'Arab' football team, and through sexual politics, endogamy, consumption practices, tastes, aspirations, bodily regulation and self-representations. I would argue that these practices make far more sense as attempts to interpolate and placate ethno-, hetero- and class normativity; as projects of social intelligibility and cultural survival, rather than Arab identity or identities.

I feel that I have asked and addressed questions I had not anticipated and have engaged with theoretical approaches and perspectives I would have instinctively avoided. My motivation for understanding 'what it means to be Arab in London' was the result of sorrowfulness within my own family not scientific curiosity *per se*. Yet in the process I feel that a certain kind of 'science' has been undone. I have some relief from that sorrowfulness; different kinds of questions now impose themselves.

Notes

Introduction

1. ONS, *Ethnic Group, National Identity, Religion and Language Consultation*, Summary report on responses to the 2011 Census stakeholders consultation 2006/07, p. 20.
2. While the ONS recognised the need to amend the ethnic group question, logistical and financial constraints meant that only two new ethnic groups could be introduced in the 2011 census. Along with an 'Equality Impact Assessment' the 'Prioritisation Tool' was used to evaluate evidence for a large number of proposed ethnic groups.
3. *Can the Office of National Statistics be Trusted with the 2011 Census?*, report commissioned by the Sikh Federation UK, January 2010.
4. Following Heidegger, Derrida argues that concepts can only be considered and used *sous rature* or 'under erasure' whereby the inherent paradox of language and the possibilities of meaning (aleph-null) resembles a (permanent) state of erasure of a word on a page whereby the word concept exists but has been suppressed by deletion which acts only to reinforce its ambivalence.
5. This phrase derives from Deleuze and Guattari (1987) and was developed by Gilroy (1993, 1995), criticising the way in which people are thought to have roots, like a tree. It is thus a critique of territoriality, embeddedness and fixity. See also Hall (1996), Clifford (1994) and Gilroy (2000b).
6. With the exception of Halliday (1992) and Lawless (1995), all works cited on Arabs in Britain appear in peer-reviewed journals or as chapters or sections in edited volumes.
7. 'Arabism' refers to the ideologies and movements that advocate political and economic unification/unity among Arabic-speaking peoples in the Middle East and North Africa.

1 Critical Junctures in the Making of Arab London

1. 'The London "plot"'. *The Near East*, 1 January 1925.
2. 'Arabic Cultural Association'. *The Arabic World*, 30 June 1933. The first meeting was held at the Royal Egyptian Club at 71 Baker Street, and Moroccans, Somalis, Egyptians, Saudis and Palestinians are reported to have been in attendance.

3. 'The Arabic World, Its Extent, Its Unity and Its Aspirations'. *The Arabic World*, 16 June 1933.

4. *To-day's Cinema*, August 1933.

5. 'Oxford Anglo-Arab Union'. *Great Britain and the East*, 13 July 1939.

6. Letters to the Editor, 'Education in the Middle East', from C.T. Barber, *The Times*, 5 April 1958, p. 7.

7. Letters to the Editor, 'Arab Students', from Mr E.L. Spears, *The Times*, 8 April 1958, p. 9.

8. 'Oxford Undergraduates Lobby "Wavering" MPs: More Protests against Suez Policy'. *Manchester Guardian*, 6 November 1956, p. 3.

9. 'Fights at Universities during Anti-war Demonstrations: Staff and Students Sign Protest'. *Manchester Guardian*, 3 November 1956.

10. 'Arab Students to Boycott Lectures: Demonstration at Iraqi Embassy'. *The Times*, 6 November 1956, p. 7.

11. *The Arab Review*, March 1958, p. 14.

12. 'New Threat to Jewish Targets in London'. *The Times*, 30 August 1969.

13. The emergence of Palestinian guerrilla movements and their oscillation between different sponsors and territories came to a climax in September 1970 when the extent of Palestinian guerrilla activity in Jordan caused the near collapse of the state. In an attempt to salvage its authority the Jordanian government began a military campaign against the armed Palestinian groups operating throughout the country but mostly on the eastern bank of the river Jordan and in Amman. The Syrian regime threw its weight behind the Palestinian factions and launched a short-lived invasion of Jordan, reaching the city of Irbid. These events are known as 'Black September'. Later that year the Black September organisation was formed. The group is infamous for the 1972 Munich Olympics incident in which 11 Israeli athletes were killed.

14. 'London March in Support of Palestinians'. *The Times*, 27 September 1970.

15. 'Guerrillas Admit Murder Attempt on Jordan Envoy in Kensington'. *The Times*, 16 December 1971.

16. 'Women Head Procession of Arabs in London'. *The Times*, 2 October 1970.

17. The first disturbance took place on the evening of 8 March at the Cooperative Hall in Westminster, and a further incident took place on 19 March at Marylebone's Central London Polytechnic, where a brawl broke out in the meeting room ('The Times Diary'. *The Times*, 21 March 1975).

18. 'London Cool on Arab Investment Reports'. *The Times*, 28 August 1974.

19. 'London: Drops from Ocean of Arab Cash'. *The Times*, 4 March 1975; 'Bonn: Ideal Climate for Investment'. *The Times*, 4 March 1975; 'Paris: No Petrodollars Yet'. *The Times*, 4 March 1975.

20. 'Polishing the Arab Image'. *The Times*, 27 August 1976.

21. 'Why High-Rollers Are Switching Their Bets'. *The Times*, 4 December 1979.

22. Letters to the Editor: 'Arabs at Universities', from Mr Antony Sherwood, Head of Africa and Middle East Division at the British Council, *The Times*,

21 March 1977. See also: 'Foreign Students in Britain, Lucrative University Summer Schools: Attentive Response to Literature and Culture'. *The Times*, 27 August 1977. And see: Letters to the Editor: 'Arabs at Universities'. *The Times*, 16 March 1977, 22 March 1977; 'Foreign Students in Britain 2: Lucrative University Summer Schools: Attentive Response to Literature and Culture'. *The Times*, 23 August 1977.

23. 'Former Yemeni Prime Minister and Wife Die in Triple Shooting'. *The Times*, 11 April 11 1977.

24. 'Witnesses to Bombed Car Sought'. *The Times*, 3 January 1978.

25. 'Gunman Assassinates PLO Leader in London: PLO Holds Britain Responsible'. *The Times*, 5 January 1978.

26. 'London New Arena for Arab State Rivalries'. *The Times*, 29 July 1978, p. 3. See also 'Owen Warning after Grenade Attack on Iraqi Ambassador'. *The Times*, 29 July 1978.

27. 'Security Against Terrorism'. *The Times*, 22 August 1978, p. 13.

28. Letters to the Editor: 'An Arab's View of London'. *The Times*, 19 May 1980.

29. Marwan al-Banna, Hussain Ahmed Ghassan Said and Nayaf Rosan, all members of the Palestinian Abu Nidal Organisation were convicted and sentenced to between 30 and 35 years' imprisonment each. The invasion of Lebanon did nothing to stop attacks on Israeli targets in London and elsewhere. On 31 August 1983 a bomb exploded outside the Israeli owned Bank Leumi near Oxford Circus. On the same day a bomb exploded in the doorway of a diamond merchant in Holborn and outside an American construction executive's house in Knightsbridge. Responsibility was claimed by the Abu Nidal Organisation. On Christmas Day 1983 a 1–3 lb bomb exploded in a waste bin in Orchard Street, between Marks and Spencer and Selfridges. Tunisian Habib Maamar (25) was arrested in Paris in May 1986 and allegedly confessed to the bombing in London and other European cities which he said were organised by the Abu Ibrahim group.

30. 'Britain Puts Libya under Pressure'. *The Times*, 12 March 1984.

31. 'Key Libyan Targets get Armed Guard after Wave of Bomb Attacks'. *The Times*, 12 March 1984. 'Libyans Quizzed in Hit Squad Hunt'. *The Evening Standard*, 13 March 1984. See also: 'Street Terror'. *The Evening Standard*, 12 March 1984; '8 Libyans being Held over Bombs'. *The Evening Standard*, 13 March 1984.

32. I would like to thank Mr Ellison for getting in touch with me and clarifying some of the circumstances around Mr Giahour's plight.

33. 'Libyan Children Searched'. *The Evening Standard*, 18 April 1984.

34. 'Arab Held in Bomb Hunt / British Police Arrest Suspect Hindawi Over Plot to Place Explosives on El Al Jet at Heathrow'. *The Guardian* (London), 19 April 1986.

35. 'Racist Suit against Sun Blocked / Attorney General Blocks Arab League Bid to Prosecute Tabloid Newspaper'. *The Guardian* (London), 4 September 1986.

36. In data extractions from the census for London, the 'Middle East' covers migrants from Iraq, Syria, Lebanon, Israel, the Occupied Territories, Jordan and the Gulf states.

37. In the first round of the 1991 Algerian elections the Front Islamique du Salut (الجبهة الإسلامية للإنقاذ) secured almost 200 out of the 429 parliamentary seats, leaving the ruling party with only 15 seats. This led to the military effectively seizing control of the country and nullifying the election results. Between November 1991 and April 1997 the majority of the civilian population had managed to avoid the spiralling political violence.

38. While the average number of Algerians acquiring British citizenship during the 1990s was 114 persons per annum, between 2002 and 2007 that figure rose to an average of 1,234 per annum. Further analysis of the Algerian-born community from the 2001 census shows that only 29 per cent of those born in Algeria and granted British citizenship were female, suggesting a large proportion of marriages between Algerian men and (non-Algerian) British citizens. During this latter period (2002–07) the proportion of Algerians gaining British citizenship based on marriage to a British citizen fell from 49 per cent (1990–2001) to 23 per cent (2002–07), while the proportion of those obtaining citizenship through residence or relevant employment rose from 36 per cent (1990–2001) to 56 per cent (2002–07).

39. The civil war in Sudan and the breakdown of the state system in Somali, as well as the post-civil war economic decline in Lebanon and the increasing use of South and East Asian labour in the Gulf States, are also contributing factors in the increase in the scale of migration from Arab states to Britain.

40. Excluding migration from Somalia.

41. Jim White, 'Five Thousand Guys Named Mo'. *The Independent*, 11 September 1992.

2   *Learning to Be Arab: Growing Up in London*

1. 'Club Siege "Linked to Iraqi Invasion"'. *The Independent*, 14 May 1991; 'Motive for Dummy Bomb Raid on Club "a Mystery"'. *The Independent*. 8 May 1991; 'Man Jailed Over Siege at Nightclub'. *The Independent*, 1 June 1991.

2. 'Crisis in the Gulf: Expulsion of Arabs Could Backfire'. *The Independent*, 5 January 1991; 'Crisis in the Gulf: Court Refuses to Help Detainees'. *The Independent*, 2 February 1991; 'Arabs Faced "McCarthyite Questioning"'. *The Guardian*, 8 March 1991. The security round-up in London led to similar crackdowns in France and Germany. Diplomats began referring to a Europe-wide 'Arab witch hunt' as 200,000 police, wearing bullet-proof vests and toting machineguns, were deployed in France under the 'Vigipirate plan' which, it was claimed, was intended to prevent terrorism, keep the peace within the Arab immigrant communities and prevent racist violence. In Germany 100 Iraqis, Jordanians and North Africans were detained.

3. On 15 September 1991 23 Iraqi students and businessmen living in Britain were expelled. The following week, on 21 September, the British government announced a ban on new Iraqi students coming to the UK. Two days later, on 23 September, more than 100 Iraqis, including students and members of the diplomatic mission, were expelled. On Sunday 11 November two Iraqi directors of a Coventry-based engineering firm, Adnan Amiri and Hana Jon were ordered out of Britain for breaching the trade embargo. On Sunday 13 January Britain ordered the expulsion of 28 Iraqi embassy staff. On Wednesday 16 January the 28 were detained on the grounds of national security. Home Office says no plans to intern Iraqis if war breaks out. On Thursday 17 January the Home Office announces a further 35 Iraqis are to be deported on the grounds of national security (see: *Gulf Crisis Chronology*, compiled by the BBC World Service, London: Longman, 1991; see also 'Crisis in the Gulf: Expulsion of Arabs Could Backfire'. *The Independent*, 5 January 1991).

4. 'Crisis in the Gulf: War Brings Out the Racist Streak'. *The Independent*, 26 January 1991.

5. '*Sham*' is the Arabic word used to describe both the Greater Syria area (Syria, Lebanon and Palestine) and also the city of Damascus.

3 *Going for* Shisha: *Doing Ethnicity, Gender and Class*

1. A *Fatwa* is a non-binding legal opinion. It does not, as is often thought, automatically denote criticism or censure. A *Fatwa* can also authorise and legitimise activities and approaches. Typically there are a number of *Fatwa*s for a given issue, often they are contradictory (some legitimising while other forbid). Muslims can choose which opinion to follow or reject at their discretion, although many do not appreciate the notion of choice of opinion or the non-binding nature of a *Fatwa*, instead seeing their preferred or adopted *Fatwa* as a authoritative and obligatory for all.

2. See: http://amrkhaled.net/articles/articles62.html

3. See: http://amrkhaled.net/articles/articles69.html

4. See: http://amrkhaled.net/articles/articles70.html

5. LOL is an email or SMS expression used to abbreviate the words 'laugh out loud'.

6. *Hojabi* is a pejorative combining 'Ho' (West coast American slang for 'Whore') and hijab, and is often used in reference to young teenage females who are veiled but are seen to behave in 'contradiction' to the bodily ideals of Islamic hijab.

4 *Dancing Class: Choreographing Arabness in London*

1. The United Arab Republic was the official name of the brief union between Egypt and Syria between 1958 and 1961.

2. Police State reliant on institutional and societal espionage.
3. *Emir* (prince), *emira* (princess).

5   *Reclaiming the Orient Through the Diasporic Gaze*

1. The canon.
2. Baths.

Bibliography

Aalten, A. (1997) 'Performing the Body, Creating Culture', *European Journal of Women's Studies*, Vol. 4 No. 2, pp. 197–215.

Abraham, N. and Shryock, A. (2000) *Arab Detroit: From Margin to Mainstream* (Detroit: Wayne State University Press).

Abu-Lughod, L. (1988) *Veiled Sentiments: Honor and Poetry in a Bedouin Society* (Berkeley: University of California Press).

—— (1991) 'Writing against Culture', in R.G. Fox (ed.) *Recapturing Anthropology: Working in the Present* (Santa Fe, NM: SAR Press).

Adelson, R. (1995) *London and the Invention of the Middle East: Money, Power, and War, 1902–1922* (New Haven, CT: Yale University Press).

Adra, N. (2005) 'Belly Dance: An Urban Folk Genre', in A. Shay and B. Sellers-Young (eds) *Belly Dance: Orientalism, Transnationalism, and Harem Fantasy* (Costa Mesa, CA: Mazda Publisher).

Ahmed, S. (2006) 'Chicken Tikka Massala', in N. Ali, V.S. Kalra and S. Sayyid (eds) *A Postcolonial People: South Asians in Britain* (Grand Rapids, MI: Wm. B. Eerdmans).

Ajami, F. (1978) 'The End of Pan-Arabism', *Foreign Affairs*, Vol. 57 No. 2, pp. 355–373.

—— (1999) *The Dream Palace of the Arabs: A Generation's Odyssey* (New York: Vintage Books).

Aksikas, J. (2009) *Arab Modernities: Islamism, Nationalism, and Liberalism in the Post-Colonial Arab World* (New York: Peter Lang).

Al-Ali, N. (2007) *Iraqi Women: Untold Stories From 1948 to the Present* (London: Zed Books).

Al-Enazy, A.H. (2009) *The Creation of Saudi Arabia: Ibn Saud and British Imperial Policy, 1914–1927* (London: Routledge).

Alexander, B.K. (2004) 'Passing, Cultural Performance, and Individual Agency: Performative Reflections on Black Masculine Identity', *Cultural Studies* ↔ *Critical Methodologies*, Vol. 4 No. 3, pp. 377–404.

Alexander, C. (2002) 'Beyond Black: Rethinking the Colour/Culture Divide', *Ethnic and Racial Studies*, Vol. 25 No. 4, pp. 552–571.

—— (2005) 'Rethinking Mixed Race', *Ethnic and Racial Studies*, Vol. 25 No. 4, pp. 698–699.

—— (2006a) 'Introduction: Mapping the Issues', *Ethnic and Racial Studies*, Vol. 29 No. 3, pp. 397–410.

—— (2006b). *Writing Race: Ethnography and Difference* (London: Routledge).

Alexander, C. (2006c) 'Imagining the Politics of BrAsian Youth', in N. Ali, V.S. Kalra and S. Sayyid (eds) *A Postcolonial People: South Asians in Britain* (Grand Rapids, MI: Wm. B. Eerdmans).

Alexander, C. and Knowles, C. (2005) *Making Race Matter: Bodies, Space, and Identity* (New York: Palgrave Macmillan).

Alloula, M. (1986) *The Colonial Harem* (Minneapolis: University of Minnesota Press).

Almeida, M.V.D. (1996) *The Hegemonic Male: Masculinity in a Portuguese Town* (London: Berghahn Books).

Al-Rasheed, M. (1991) 'Invisible and Divided Communities', in R. El-Rayyes (ed.) *Arab Communities in London* (London: Riad El-Rayyes Books).

—— (1992) 'Political Migration and Downward Socio-Economic Mobility: The Iraqi Community in London', *New Community*, Vol. 18 No. 4, pp. 537–549.

—— (1993) 'The Meaning of Marriage and Status in Exile: The Experience of Iraqi Women', *Journal of Refugee Studies*, Vol. 6 No. 2, pp. 89–104.

—— (1994). 'The Myth of Return: Iraqi Arabs and Assyrian Refugees in London', *Journal of Refugee Studies*, Vol. 7 No. 2, pp. 219–236.

—— (1995a) 'In Search of Ethnic Visibility: Iraqi Assyrian Christians in London', in G. Baumann and T. Sunier (eds) *Post-Migration Ethnicity* (The Hague: Martinus Nijhoff International), pp. 10–35.

—— (1995b) 'Iraqi Assyrians in London: Beyond the Immigrant–Refugee Divide', *Journal of the Anthropological Society of Oxford*, Vol. 26 No. 3, pp. 241–255.

——(1996) 'The Other-Other Population in the 1991 Census of Great Britain', in C. Peach (ed.) *Ethnic Minorities in Britain* (HMSO, OPCS), pp. 206–220.

—— (1998) *Iraqi Assyrian Christians in London: The Construction of Ethnicity* (London: Edwin Mellen Press).

—— (2002) *A History of Saudi Arabia* (Cambridge: Cambridge University Press).

—— (2005) *Transnational Connections and the Arab Gulf* (London: Routledge).

Amit, V. and Rapport, N. (2002) *The Trouble with Community: Anthropological Reflections on Movement, Identity and Collectivity* (London: Pluto Press).

Anderson, E. (1992) *Streetwise: Race, Class and Change in an Urban Community* (Chicago: University of Chicago Press).

Anon. (2004) 'An Interview with Tariq Ramadan', available at: http://www.theamericanmuslim.org/tam.php/features/articles/interview_with_tariq_ramadan/ (accessed August 2010).

Anthias, F. (1998) *Sociological Debates: Thinking about Social Divisions* (London: Greenwich University Press).

—— (2002) 'Beyond Feminism and Multiculturalism: Locating Difference and the Politics of Location', *Women's Studies International Forum*, Vol. 25 No. 3, pp. 275–286.

Anthias, F., Yuval-Davis, N. and Cain, H. (1993) *Racialized Boundaries: Race, Nation, Gender, Colour and Class and the Anti-racist Struggle* (London: Routledge).

Anwar, M. (1976) 'Young Asians Between Two Cultures', *New Society*, Vol. 38 No. 16, pp. 563–565.

—— (1979) *The Myth of Return: Pakistanis in Britain* (London: Heinemann).

—— (2002) *Between Cultures: Continuity and Change in the Lives of Young Asians*. (London: Routledge).

Apostolos-Cappadona, D. (2005) Discerning the Hand of Fatima: An Iconological Investigation of the Role of Gender in Religious Art', in A. El-Azhary Sonbol (ed.) *Beyond the Exotic: Women's Histories in Islamic Societies* (Syracuse, NY: Syracuse University Press).

Appadurai, A. (1993) 'Number in the Colonial Imagination', in C. Appadurai Breckenridge and P. van der Veer (eds) *Orientalism and the Postcolonial Predicament: Perspectives on South Asia* (Philadelphia, PA: University of Pennsylvania Press).

Archetti, E.P. (1999) *Masculinities: Football, Polo and the Tango in Argentina* (Oxford: Berg).

Ardener, S. (1981) *Women and Space: Ground Rules and Social Maps* (London: Croom Helm).

Aull-Davies, C. (1999) *Reflexive Ethnography: A Guide to Researching Selves and Others* (London: Routledge).

Austin, J. (1962) *How to Do Things with Words* (Wotton-under-Edge: Clarendon Press).

Ayubi, N. (1995) *Over-stating the Arab State: Politics and Society in the Middle East* (London: I.B. Tauris).

Axel, B. (2002a) 'National Interruption: Diaspora Theory and Multiculturalism in the UK', *Cultural Dynamics*, Vol. 14 No. 3, pp. 235–256.

—— (2002b) 'The Diasporic Imaginary', *Public Culture*, Vol. 14 No. 2, pp. 411–428.

Babayan, K. and A. Najmabadi (2008) *Islamicate Sexualities: Translations across Temporal Geographies of Desire* (Harvard: CMES).

Back, L. (1996) *New Ethnicities and Urban Culture: Racisms and Multiculture in Young Lives* (London: Routledge).

Baer, E. (2003) *The Human Figure in Islamic Art: Inheritances and Islamic Transformations* (Costa Mesa, CA: Mazda Publisher).

Bakhtin, M. (1981) *The Dialogic Imagination: Four Essays* (Austin: University of Texas Press).

Baldassar, L. (1999) 'Marias and Marriage: Ethnicity, Gender and Sexuality among Italo-Australian Youth in Perth', *Journal of Sociology*, Vol. 35 No. 1, pp. 1–22.

Balibar, É. and Wallerstein, I.M. (1991) *Race, Nation, Class: Ambiguous Identities* (New York: Verso).

Ballard, R. (1979) 'Comparing Performance in Multi-Racial Schools: South Asian Pupils at 16+', *New Community*, Vol. 7 No. 2, pp. 143–153.

Ballard, R. and Banks, M. (1994) *Desh Pardesh: The South Asian Presence in Britain* (London: C. Hurst & Co.).

Banks, M. (1996) *Ethnicity: Anthropological Constructions* (London: Routledge).

Banton, M. (1977) *The Idea of Race* (Sydney: Law Book Co. of Australasia).

—— 1983. *Racial and Ethnic Competition* (Cambridge: Cambridge University Press).

Banton, M. and Whitaker, B. (1983) *Teaching about Prejudice* (London: Minority Rights Group).

Barth, F. (1994) 'Enduring and Emerging Issues in the Analysis of Ethnicity', in H. Vermeulen and C. Govers (eds) *The Anthropology of Ethnicity: Beyond 'Ethnic Groups and Boundaries'* (Amsterdam: Het Spinhuis).

Barthes, R. (1977) *Elements of Semiology* (New York: Hill & Wang).

—— (1982) *Camera Lucida: Reflections on Photography* (New York: Hill & Wang).

Bashear, S. (1997) *Arabs and Others in Early Islam* (Princeton, NJ: Darwin Press).

Basit, T.N. (1997a) '"I want more freedom, but not too much": British Muslim Girls and the Dynamism of Family Values', *Gender and Education*, Vol. 9 No. 4, pp. 425–440.

Basit, T.N. (1997b) *Eastern Values, Western Milieu: Identities and Aspirations of Adolescent British Muslim Girls* (Aldershot: Ashgate).

Baudrillard, J. (1996) *The System of Objects* (New York: Verso).

Baumann, G. (1999) *The Multicultural Riddle: Rethinking National, Ethnic and Religious Identities* (London: Routledge).

Baumann, G. and Sunier, T. (1995) *Post-migration Ethnicity: De-essentializing Cohesion, Commitments, and Comparison* (Amsterdam: Het Spinhuis).

Bearn, G. (1995a) 'Derrida Dry: Iterating Iterability Analytically', *Diacritics*, Vol. 25 No. 3, pp. 3–25.

—— (1995b) 'The Possibility of Puns: A Defence of Derrida', *Philosophy and Literature*, Vol. 19 No. 2, pp. 330–335.

—— (2000) 'Differentiating Derrida and Deleuze', *Continental Philosophy Review*, Vol. 33 No. 4, pp. 441–465.

Beaulieu, J. and Roberts, M. (2002) *Orientalism's Interlocutors: Painting, Architecture, Photography* (Durham, NC: Duke University Press).

Beauvoir, S. de (1997 [1949]) *The Second Sex* (London: Vintage).

Bell, D., Binnie J., Cream J. and Valentine G. (1994) 'All Hyped Up and No Place To Go', *Gender, Place & Culture: A Journal of Feminist Geography*, Vol. 1 No. 1, pp. 31–47.

Bell, V. (1999a) 'Historical Memory, Global Movements and Violence', *Theory, Culture & Society*, Vol. 16 No. 2, pp. 21–40.

—— (1999b) 'Mimesis as Cultural Survival', *Theory, Culture & Society*, Vol. 16 No. 2, pp. 133–161.

—— (1999c) 'Performativity and Belonging', *Theory, Culture & Society*, Vol. 16 No. 2, pp. 1–10.

—— (1999d) 'On Speech, Race and Melancholia: An Interview with Judith Butler', *Theory, Culture & Society*, Vol. 16 No. 2, pp. 163–174.

Belluscio, S. (2006) *To Be Suddenly White: Literary Realism and Racial Passing* (Columbia, MO: University of Missouri Press).

Benhabib, S., Butler, J., Cornell, D. and Fraser, N. (eds) (1995) *Feminist Contentions: A Philosophical Exchange* (New York: Routledge).

Benjamin, R. (1997a) 'The Oriental Mirage', in R. Benjamin, M. Khemir, U. Prunster and L. Thornton (eds) *Orientalism: Delacroix to Klee* (Australia: Art Gallery of New South Wales).

Benjamin, R. (1997b) 'Post-Colonial Taste: Non-Western Markets for Orientalist Art', in R. Benjamin et al. (eds) *Orientalism: Delacroix to Klee* (Australia: Art Gallery of New South Wales).

Benjamin, R. and Khemir, M. (1997) *Orientalist Aesthetics: Art, Colonialism, and French North Africa, 1880–1930* (Berkeley: University of California Press).

Benjamin, R., Khemir, M., Prunster, U. and Thornton, L. (1997) *Orientalism: Delacroix to Klee* (Australia: Art Gallery of New South Wales).

Benson, S. (1996) 'Asians Have Culture, West Indians Have Problems: Discourses of Race and Ethnicity In and Out of Anthropology', in T. Ranger, Y. Samad and O. Stuart (eds) *Culture, Identity and Politics: Ethnic Minorities in Britain* (Aldershot: Avebury).

Benthall, J. (1991) 'The Middle East: Fantasies and Realities', *Anthropology Today*, Vol. 7 No. 3, pp. 16–18.

Berry, K. and Henderson, M. (2002) *Geographical Identities of Ethnic America: Race, Space, and Place* (Reno, NV: University of Nevada Press).

Bhabha, H. (1989) 'Of Mimicry and Man: The Ambivalence of Colonial Discourse', in P. Michelson (ed.) *October: The First Decade* (Cambridge, MA: MIT Press).

—— (1990) 'Interrogating Identity: The Postcolonial Prerogative', in D.T. Goldberg (ed.) *The Anatomy of Racism* (Minneapolis: University of Minnesota Press), pp. 183–209.

—— (1994) *The Location of Culture* (London: Routledge).

—— (2003 [1990]) 'The Third Space: Interview with Homi Bhabha', in J. Rutherford (ed.) *Identity: Community, Culture, Difference*, London: Lawrence & Wishart), pp. 207–221.

Bhatt, A. (2003) 'Asian Indians and the Model Minority Narrative: A Neocolonial System', in E. Kramer (ed.) *The Emerging Monoculture: Assimilation and the 'Model Minority'* (Westport, CT: Praeger).

Black, J. (2006) 'Re-visioning White Nudes: Race and Sexual Discourse in Ottoman Harems 1700–1900', *Hilltop Review*, Vol. 2 No. 16, pp. 16–26.

Blacking, J. (1985) 'Movement, Dance, Music and Venda Girls' Initiation'. In P. Spencer (ed.) *Society and the Dance: The Social Anthropology of Process and Performance* (Cambridge: Cambridge University Press).

Blandford, L. (1977) *Oil Sheikhs* (London: W.H. Allen).

Bloch, M. (1992) *From Blessing to Violence: History and Ideology in the Circumcision Ritual of the Merina* (Cambridge: Cambridge University Press).

Boelstroff, T. (2007) 'Queer Studies in the House of Anthropology', *Annual Review of Anthropology*, Vol. 36, pp. 17–35.

Bourdieu, P. (1970) 'The Berber House or the World Reversed', *Social Science Information* 9(2): 151–170.

—— (1987) *Distinction: A Social Critique of the Judgement of Taste* (Cambridge, MA: Harvard University Press).

—— (1990) *The Logic of Practice* (Stanford, CA: Stanford University Press).

Bourdieu, P. and Nice, R. (1980) 'The Aristocracy of Culture', *Media, Culture & Society*, Vol. 2, pp. 225–254.

Bourdieu, P. and Wacquant, L. (1992) *An Invitation to Reflexive Sociology* (Chicago: University of Chicago Press).

Bowie, F. (2005) *The Anthropology of Religion: An Introduction* (Malden, MA: Wiley-Blackwell).

Boyarin, D. and Boyarin, J. (1993) 'Diaspora: Generation and the Ground of Jewish Identity', *Critical Inquiry*, Vol. 19 No. 4, pp. 693–725.

Boyarin, J. (1996) *Thinking in Jewish* (Chicago: University of Chicago Press).

Brah, A. (1996) *Cartographies of Diaspora: Contesting Identities* (London: Routledge).

Brah, A. (2006) 'The Asians in Britain', in N. Ali, V.S. Kalra and S. Sayyid (eds) *A Postcolonial People: South Asians in Britain* (Grand Rapids, MI: Wm. B. Eerdmans).

Brah, A. and Phoenix, A. (2004) 'Ain't I a Woman? Revisiting Intersectionality', *Journal of International Women's Studies*, Vol. 5 No. 3, pp. 75–86.

Brandes, S. (1982) 'Ethnographic Autobiographies in American Anthropology', in E.A. Hoebel, R.L. Currier and S. Kaiser (eds) *Crisis in Anthropology: View from Spring Hill, 1980* (New York: Garland Publishing).

Breunlin, R. and Regis, H. (2006) *Putting the Ninth Ward on the Map: Race, Place, and Transformation in Desire, New Orleans* (Emmitsburg, MD: National Emergency Training Center).

Brickell, C. (2003) 'Performativity or Performance? Clarifications in the Sociology of Gender', *New Zealand Sociology*, Vol. 18 No. 2, pp. 158–178.

—— (2005) 'Masculinities, Performativity, and Subversion: A Sociological Reappraisal', *Men and Masculinities*, Vol. 8 No. 1, pp. 24–43.

Brodkin, K. (2009) 'How Did Jews Become White Folks?', in T. Ore (ed.) *The Social Construction of Difference and Inequality: Race, Class, Gender and Sexuality* (Boston, MA: McGraw-Hill Higher Education).

Brooke, N. and Samura, M. (2011) 'Social Geographies of Race: Connecting Race and Space', *Ethnic and Racial Studies*, Vol. 34 No. 11, pp. 1933–1952.

Brown, K.E. (2010) 'Contesting the Securitization of British Muslims: Citizenship and Resistance', *Interventions*, Vol. 12 No. 2, pp. 171–182.

Brubaker, R. (2003) 'Neither Individualism nor "Groupism"', *Ethnicities*, Vol. 3 No. 4, pp. 553–557.

—— (2005) 'The "Diaspora" Diaspora', *Ethnic and Racial Studies*, Vol. 28 No. 1, pp. 1–19.

—— (2006) *Ethnicity without Groups* (Cambridge, MA: Harvard University Press).

Brubaker, R. and Cooper, F. (2000) 'Beyond "Identity"', *Theory and Society*, Vol. 29 No. 1, pp. 1–47.

Buckland, T. (1999) *Dance in the Field* (New York: Palgrave Macmillan).

Burns, A., Bottomley, G. and Jools, P. (1983) *The Family in the Modern World: Australian Perspectives* (Crows Nest, Australia: Allen & Unwin).

Busby, C. (2000) *The Performance of Gender: An Anthropology of Everyday Life in a South Indian Fishing Village* (London: Berg).

Butler, J. (1988) 'Performative Acts and Gender Constitution: An Essay in Phenomenology and Feminist Theory', *Theatre Journal*, Vol. 40 No. 4, pp. 519–538.

—— (1990) *Gender Trouble: Feminism and the Subversion of Identity* (London: Routledge).

—— (1993) *Bodies that Matter: On the Discursive Limits of Sex* (London: Routledge).

—— (1994) 'Against Proper Objects', *Differences: A Journal of Feminist Cultural Studies*, Vol. 6 Nos 2–3, pp. 1–25.

—— (1996) 'Gender as Performance', in P. Osborne (ed.) *A Critical Sense: Interviews with Intellectuals* (London: Routledge).

—— (1997a) *The Psychic Life of Power: Theories in Subjection* (Stanford, CA: Stanford University Press).

—— (1997b) *Excitable Speech: A Politics of the Performative* (London: Routledge).

—— (1998) 'Subjects of Sex/Gender/Desire', in A. Phillips (ed.) *Feminsim and Politics* (Oxford: Oxford University Press).

—— (1999a) 'Performativity's Social Magic', in R. Shusterman (ed.) *Bourdieu: A Critical Reader* (New York: Wiley-Blackwell).

—— (1999b) 'Revisiting Bodies and Pleasures', *Theory, Culture & Society*, Vol. 16 No. 2, pp. 11–20.

—— (1999c) *Subjects of Desire* (New York: Columbia University Press).

—— (1999d) *Gender Trouble: Tenth Anniversary Edition* (London: Taylor & Francis).

—— (2000a) 'Critically Queer', in D.P. du Gay, J. Evans and P. Redman (eds) *Identity: A Reader*. London: Sage.

—— (2000b) 'Agencies of Style for a Liminal Subject', in P. Gilroy, L. Grossberg and A. McRobbie (eds) *Without Guarantees: In Honour of Stuart Hall* (London: Verso).

—— (2004) *Undoing Gender* (London: Routledge).

—— (2005) *Giving an Account of Oneself* (New York: Fordham University Press).

—— (2006) *Precarious Life: The Powers of Mourning and Violence* (London: Verso).

—— (2010) 'Performative Agency', *Journal of Cultural Economy*, Vol. 3 No. 2, pp. 147–161.

Butler, J. and Spivak, G.C. (2007) *Who Sings the Nation-State? Language, Politics, Belonging* (Kolkata: Seagull Books).

Butler, J., Osborne, P. and Segal, L. (1994) 'Gender as Performance: An Interview with Judith Butler', *Radical Philosophy*, Vol. 67 (Summer), pp. 32–39.Callison, C., Karrh, J.A. and Zillmann, D. (2002) 'The Aura of Tobacco Smoke: Cigars and Cigarettes as Image Makers', *Journal of Applied Social Psychology*, Vol. 32 No. 7, pp. 1329–1343.

Callon, M. (2006) 'What Does It Mean to Say that Economics Is Performative?', Centre de Sociologie de l'innovation, Ecole des Mines de Paris, Working Paper Series No. 5.

Caputo, J. (1996) *Deconstruction in a Nutshell: Conversation with Jacques Derrida* (New York: Fordham University Press).

Celik, Z. (1996) 'Colonialism, Orientalism, and the Canon', *Art Bulletin*, Vol. 78 No. 2, pp. 198–217.

Celik, Z. (2002) 'Speaking Back to Orientalist Discourse', in J. Beaulieu and M. Roberts (eds) *Orientalism's Interlocutors: Painting, Architecture, Photography* (Durham, NC: Duke University Press).

Celik, Z., Camille, M., Onians, J. and Steiner, C.B. (1996) 'Rethinking the Canon', *Art Bulletin*, Vol. 78 No. 2, pp. 198–217.

Cesarani, D. and Fulbrook, M. (1996) *Citizenship, Nationality and Migration in Europe* (London: Routledge).

Certeau, M. de (1988) *The Practice of Everyday Life* (Berkeley: University of California Press).

Césaire, A. (2001 [1973]) *Discourse on Colonialism* (New York: Monthly Review Press).

Chang, H. (2008) *Autoethnography as Method* (Walnut Creek, CA: Left Coast Press).

Chaouachi, K. (2006) 'Culture Matérielle et Orientalisme: L'exemple d'une Recherche Socio-anthropologique sur le Narguilé', *Arabica*, Vol. 53 No. 2, pp. 177–209.

Cheng, A. (2001) *The Melancholy of Race* (Oxford: Oxford University Press).

Chopra, R., Osella, C. and Osella, F. (2004) *South Asian Masculinities: Context of Change, Sites of Continuity* (Delhi: Women Unlimited an associate of Kali for Women).

Choueiri, Y.M. (1989) *Arab History and the Nation State: A Study in Modern Arabic Historiography* (London: Routledge).

—— (2001) *Arab Nationalism: A History* (New York: Wiley Blackwell).

Chow, R. (1997) *Ethics after Idealism: Theory – Culture – Ethnicity – Reading*, (Bloomington, IN: Indiana University Press).

Civantos, C. (2006) *Between Argentines and Arabs: Argentine Orientalism, Arab Immigrants, and the Writing of Identity* (New York: State University of New York Press).

Clifford, J. (1994) 'Diasporas', *Cultural Anthropology*, Vol. 9 No. 3, pp. 302–338.

—— (1997) *Routes: Travel and Translation in the Late Twentieth Century* (Cambridge, MA: Harvard University Press).

Cohen, A. (1993) *Masquerade Politics: Explorations in the Structure of Urban Cultural Movements* (Berkeley: University of California Press).

Cohen, A. (1994) *Self Consciousness: An Alternative Anthropology of Identity* (London: Routledge).

Cohen, M. and Kolinsky, M. (1992) *Britain and the Middle East in the 1930s: Security Problems 1935–39* (New York: Palgrave Macmillan).

Cohen, M., Kolinsky, D.M. and Kolinsky, M. (1998) *Demise of the British Empire in the Middle East: Britain's Responses to Nationalist Movements, 1943–55* (London: Routledge).

Cohn, B.S. (1987) *An Anthropologist among the Historians, and Other Essays* (Oxford: Oxford University Press).

Cole, M. (2003) 'Ethnicity, "Status Groups" and Racialization: A Contribution to a Debate on National Identity in Britain', *Ethnic and Racial Studies*, Vol. 26 No. 5, pp. 962–969.

Comaroff, J.L. and Comaroff, J. (2009) *Ethnicity Inc.* (Chicago: University of Chicago Press).

Conklin, B. (1997) 'Body Paint, Feathers, and VCRs: Aesthetics and Authenticity in Amazonian Activism', *American Ethnologist*, Vol. 24 No. 4, pp. 711–737.

Connell, R.W. and Messerschmidt, J. (2005) 'Hegemonic Masculinity Rethinking the Concept', *Gender & Society*, Vol. 19 No. 6, pp. 829–859.

Conquergood, D. (1989) 'Poetics, Play, Process, and Power: The Performative Turn in Anthropology', *Text and Performance Quarterly*, Vol. 9 No. 1, pp. 82–88.

Cooke, M. (1994) 'Arab Women Arab Wars', *Cultural Critique*, Vol. 29 No. 5, pp. 5–29.

—— (2000) 'Women, Religion, and the Postcolonial Arab World', *Cultural Critique*, Vol. 45 (Spring), pp. 150–184.

Corbey, R. (1993) 'Ethnographic Showcases, 1870–1930', *Cultural Anthropology*, Vol. 8 No. 3, pp. 338–369.

Cowan, J. (1990) *Dance and the Body Politic in Northern Greece* (Princeton, NJ: Princeton University Press).

Cubitt, G. (2007) *History and Memory* (Manchester: Manchester University Press).

Cutter, M. (2010) 'Passing as Narrative and Textual Strategy in Charles Chesnutt's "The Passing of Grandison"', in S.P. Wright and E.P. Glass (eds) *Passing in the Works of Charles W. Chesnutt* (Jackson: University Press of Mississippi).

Dahlstedt, M. (2009) 'Parental Governmentality: Involving "Immigrant Parents" in Swedish Schools', *British Journal of Sociology of Education*, Vol. 30 No. 2, pp. 193–205.

Danaher, G., Schirato, T. and Webb, P.J. (2000) *Understanding Foucault* (New York: Sage).

D'Andrea, A. (2006) 'Neo-Nomadism: A Theory of Post-Identitarian Mobility in the Global Age', *Mobilities*, Vol. 1 No. 1, pp. 95–114.

Das, V. (1997) *Critical Events: An Anthropological Perspective on Contemporary India* (New York: Oxford University Press).

Davidson, C.M. (2007) 'Arab Nationalism and British Opposition in Dubai, 1920–66', *Middle Eastern Studies*, Vol. 43 No. 6, pp. 879–892.

Dawisha, A. (2003) *Arab Nationalism in the Twentieth Century: From Triumph to Despair* (Princeton, NJ: Princeton University Press).

Deagon, A. (2002) 'The Image of the Eastern Flaubert's Salome', *Habibi*, Vol. 19 No. 1, available at: http://thebestofhabibi.com/vol-19-no-1-feb-2002/salome/ (accessed June 2014).

—— (2005) 'The Dance of the Seven Veils', in A. Shay and B. Sellers-Young (eds) *Belly Dance: Orientalism, Transnationalism, and Harem Fantasy* (Costa Mesa, CA: Mazda Publishers), pp. 244–273.

Dean, M. (2009 [1999]) *Governmentality: Power and Rule in Modern Society* (New York: Sage).

Debord, G. (2013) *The Society of the Spectacle* (Berkeley, CA: Bureau of Public Secrets).

Deck, A. (1990) 'Autoethnography: Zora Neale Hurston, Noni Jabavu, and Cross-Disciplinary Discourse', *Black American Literature Forum*, Vol. 24 No. 2, pp. 237–256.

Deeb, L. (2006) *An Enchanted Modern: Gender and Public Piety in Shi'i Lebanon*. (Princeton, NJ: Princeton University Press).

Deleuze, G. and Guattari, F. (1987) *A Thousand Plateaus: Capitalism and Schizophrenia* (Minneapolis: University of Minnesota Press).

Denzin, N.K. (1989) *Interpretive Autoethnography* (Los Angeles: Sage).

Derrida, J. (1981) 'Interview with Jean-Louis Houdebine and Guy Scarpetta', in J. Derrida, *Positions* (Chicago: University of Chicago Press), pp. 42–44.

—— (1982) *Margins of Philosophy* (Chicago: University of Chicago Press).

—— (1988) 'Letter to a Japanese Friend (1983)', in D.C. Wood and R. Bernasconi (eds) *Derrida and différance* (Evanston, IL: Northwestern University Press).

—— (1997) *Politics of Friendship* (London: Verso).

—— (2001) *Writing and Difference*, 2nd edn (London: Routledge).

Derrida, J. and Spivak, G.C. (1998) *Of Grammatology* (Baltimore, MD: Johns Hopkins University Press).

Dhingra, P. (2003) 'Being American between Black and White: Second-generation Asian American Professionals' Racial Identities', *Journal of Asian American Studies*, Vol. 6 No. 2, pp. 117–147.

Diamond, E. (1989) 'Mimesis, Mimicry, and the "True-Real"', *Modern Drama*, Vol. 32 No. 1, pp. 58–72.

Djebar, A. (1999) *Women of Algiers in their Apartment* (Charlottesville: University Press of Virginia).

Djebar, A. (2004) *Femmes d'Alger dans leur Appartement* (Paris: Librairie générale française).

Donnan, H. and Magowan, F. (2010) *The Anthropology of Sex* (London: Berg).

Dox, D. (2006) 'Dancing around Orientalism', *Drama Review*, Vol. 50 No. 4, pp. 52–71.

Du Bois, W.E.B., Gibson, D.B. and Elbert, M.M. (1996) *The Souls of Black Folk* (New York: Penguin Classics).

Du Bois, W.E.B. (2007 [1903]) *The Souls of Black Folk* (Oxford: Oxford University Press).

Dunne, B. (1996) *Sexuality and the Civilizing Process in Modern Egypt* (Washington, DC: Georgetown University Press).

Dürrschmidt, J. (1997) 'The Delinking of Locale and Milieu', in J. Eade (ed.) *Living the Global City: Globalization as Local Process* (London: Routledge).

Dwyer, C. and Bressey, C. (2008) *New Geographies of Race and Racism* (Aldershot: Ashgate).

Dwyer, O. and Jones, J.P. (2000) 'White Socio-Spatial Epistemology', *Social & Cultural Geography*, Vol. 1 No. 2.

Eade, J. and Garbin, D. (2002) 'Changing Narratives of Violence, Struggle and Resistance: Bangladeshis and the Competition for Resources in the Global City', *Oxford Development Studies*, Vol. 30 No. 2, pp. 137–151.

Edmunds, J. (1998) 'The British Labour Party in the (1980)s: The Battle Over the Palestinian/Israeli Conflict', *Politics*, Vol. 18 No. 2, pp. 111–118.

Elam, M. (2007) 'Passing in the Post-Race Era: Danzy Senna, Philip Roth, and Colson Whitehead', *African American Review*, Vol. 41 No. 4, pp. 749–768.

El-Guindi, F. (1999) *Veil: Modesty, Privacy and Resistance* (London: Bloomsbury).

Erdman, J. (1996) 'Dance Discourses: Rethinking the History of the "Oriental Dance"', in G. Morris (ed.) *Moving Words: Re-writing Dance* (London: Routledge), pp. 288–305.

Eriksen, T.H. (2000) 'Ethnicity and Culture – A Second Look', in R. Benedix and H. Roodenburg (eds) *Managing Ethnicity: Perspectives from Folklore Studies, History and Anthropology* (Amsterdam: Het Spinhuis).

Eribon, D. (2009) *Retour à Reims* (Paris: Fayard).

Erikson, E.H. (1968) *Identity: Youth and Crisis* (New York: W.W. Norton).

Evans-Pritchard, E.E. (1928) 'The Dance', *Africa*, Vol. 1 No. 4, pp. 446–462.

Eves, R. (2010) 'Engendering Gesture: Gender Performativity and Bodily Regimes from New Ireland', *Asia Pacific Journal of Anthropology*, Vol. 11 No. 1, pp. 1–16.

Fahmy, F. (1987) 'The Creative Development of Mahmoud Reda: A Contemporary Egyptian Choreographer', MA thesis, University of California, Los Angeles.

Fanon, F. (1967a) *Black Skin, White Masks*, trans. C. Markmann (New York: Grove Publishers).

Fanon, F. (1967b) *The Wretched of the Earth* (London: Penguin).

Feldman, G. (2005) 'Essential Crises: A Performative Approach to Migrants, Minorities, and the European Nation-State', *Anthropological Quarterly*, Vol. 78 No. 1, pp. 213–246.

Ferguson, J. (1999) *Expectations of Modernity: Myths and Meanings of Urban Life on the Zambian Copperbelt* (Berkeley: University of California Press).

Finella, G. (2005) *London Country of Birth Profiles: The Arab League* (London: Greater London Authority).

Fisher, J. and Shay, A. (2009) *When Men Dance: Choreographing Masculinities Across Borders* (New York: Oxford University Press).

Fog Olwig, K. (1997) 'Cultural Sites: Sustaining Home in a Deterritorialized World', in K. Fog Olwig and K. Hastrup (eds) *Siting Culture: The Shifting Anthropological Object* (London: Routledge).

Fortier, A. (1999) 'Re-Membering Places and the Performance of Belonging(s)', *Theory, Culture & Society*, Vol. 16 No. 2, pp. 41–64.

Foucault, M. (1972) *The Archaeology of Knowledge: And, The Discourse on Language* (London: Tavistock Publications).

—— (1980) *Language, Counter Memory, Practice* (Ithaca, NY: Cornell University Press).

—— (1983) 'Afterword: The Subject and Power', in H.L. Dreyfus and P. Rabinow (eds) *Michel Foucault: Beyond Structuralism and Hermeneutics* (Chicago: University of Chicago Press).

—— (1984) 'Nietzsche, Genealogy, History', in P. Rabinow (ed.) *The Foucault Reader* (New York: Pantheon).

—— (2000) *Ethics: Subjectivity and Truth.* (New York: The Penguin Press).

Foucault, M. and Bouchard, D. (1980) *Language, Counter-Memory, Practice* (Ithaca, NY: Cornell University Press).

Foucault, M., Senellart, M., Ewald, F. and Fontana, A. (2007) *Security, Territory, Population: Lectures at the Collège de France 1977–1978* (New York: St Martin's Press.

Fraser, M. (1999) 'Classing Queer', *Theory, Culture & Society*, Vol. 16 No. 2, pp. 107–131.

Freud, S. (1922) 'Mourning and Melancholia', *Journal of Nervous and Mental Disease*, Vol. 56 No. 5, pp. 543–545.

Ftouni, L (n.d.) *Dismantling or Reproducing the Orientalist Canon? Neo-Orientalism in Visual Arts*, unpublished PhD thesis, University of Westminster, London.

Gannon, S. (2006) 'The (Im)Possibilities of Writing the Self-Writing: French Poststructural Theory and Autoethnography', *Cultural Studies ↔ Critical Methodologies*, Vol. 6 No. 4, pp. 474–495.

Gardner, K. (2002) *Age, Narrative and Migration: The Life Course and Life Histories of Bengali Elders in London* (London: Berg).

Gardner, K. and Mand, K. (2012) '"My Away Is Here": Place, Emplacement and Mobility amongst British Bengali Children', *Journal of Ethnic and Migration Studies* Vol. 38 No. 6, pp. 969–986.

Geertz, C. (1993) *Local Knowledge: Further Essays in Interpretive Anthropology* (London: Fontana Press).

Geller, P.L. (2009) 'Bodyscapes, Biology, and Heteronormativity', *American Anthropologist*, Vol. 111 No. 4: 504–516.

Gergen, K. (2001) 'Psychological Science in a Postmodern Context', *American Psychologist*, Vol. 56 No. 10, pp. 803–813.

Gessier, V. (2010) 'Islamophobia: A French Specificity in Europe?', *Human Architecture: Journal of the Sociology of Self-Knowledge*, Vol. 8 No. 2, pp. 39–46.

Gilmore, D. (1987) *Honor and Shame and the Unity of the Mediterranean* (New York: American Anthropological Association).

Gilroy, P. (1991) *'There Ain't No Black in the Union Jack': The Cultural Politics of Race and Nation* (Chicago: University of Chicago Press).

—— (1993) *The Black Atlantic: Modernity and Double-Consciousness* (Cambridge, MA: Harvard University Press).

—— (1994) *Small Acts: Thoughts on the Politics of Black Cultures* (London: Serpent's Tail).

—— (1995) 'Roots and Routes: Black Identity as an International Project', in H. Harris, H. Blue and E. Griffith (eds) *Racial and Ethnic Identity: Psychological Development and Creative Expression* (London: Routledge), pp. 15–30.

—— (2000a) *Between Camps: Nations, Culture and the Allure of Race* (London: Allen Lane).

—— (2000b) *Against Race: Imagining Political Culture Beyond the Color Line* (Cambridge, MA: Belknap Press of Harvard University Press).

—— (2001) 'Joined-up Politics and Postcolonial Melancholia', *Theory, Culture & Society*, Vol. 18 No. 2–3, pp. 151–167.

—— (2002) *Against Race: Imagining Political Culture beyond the Colour Line* (Cambridge, MA: Belknap Press of Harvard University Press).

—— (2006) *Postcolonial Melancholia* (New York: Columbia University Press).

—— (2008) *Black Britain: A Photographic History* (London: Saqi Books).

—— (2010) *Darker than Blue: On the Moral Economies of Black Atlantic Culture* (Cambridge, MA: Belknap Press of Harvard University Press).

Ginsberg, E.K. (1996) *Passing and the Fictions of Identity* (Durham, NC: Duke University Press).

Glucksmann, M. (1974) *Structuralist Analysis in Contemporary Social Thought: A Comparison of the Theories of Claude Lévi-Strauss and Louis Althusser* (London: Routledge & Kegan Paul).

Gmelch, G. and Zenner, W. (1996) *Urban Life: Readings in Urban Anthropology* (Long Grove, IL: Waveland Press).

Goffman, E. (1959) *The Presentation of Self in Everyday Life* (New York: Doubleday Anchor Books).

Goldberg, D. (1993) *Racist Culture: Philosophy and the Politics of Meaning* (New York: Wiley-Blackwell).

Goode, J. and Schneider, J. (1994) *Reshaping Ethnic and Racial Relations in Philadelphia: Immigrants in a Divided City* (Philadelphia, PA: Temple University Press).

Gotanda, N. (2011) 'Race, Religion and Late Democracy: The Racialization of Islam in American Law', *Annals of the American Academy of Political and Social Science* Vol. 637, pp. 184–195.

Gottdiener, M. (1995) *Postmodern Semiotics: Material Culture and the Forms of Postmodern Life* (New York: Wiley-Blackwell)

Grau, A. (1999) 'Fieldwork, Politics and Power', in T. Buckland (ed.) *Dance in the Field: Theory, Methods and Issues in Dance Ethnography* (New York: Palgrave Macmillan).

Gross, J., McMurray, M. and Swedenburg, T. (1996) 'Arab Noise and Ramadan Nights: *Rai*, Rap and Franco-Maghrebi Identity', in S. Lavie and T. Swedenburg (eds) *Displacement, Diaspora, and Geographies of Identity* (Durham, NC: Duke University Press), pp. 119–155.

Gupta, S. (2007) *Social Constructionist Identity Politics and Literary Studies* (New York: Palgrave Macmillan).

Guss, D. (2000) *The Festive State: Race, Ethnicity, and Nationalism as Cultural Performance* (Berkeley: University of California Press).

Hackforth-Jones, J. and Roberts, M. (2005) *Edges of Empire: Orientalism and Visual Culture* (New York: Wiley-Blackwell).

Hall, S. (1990) 'The Emergence of Cultural Studies and the Crisis of the Humanities', *October*, Vol. 53, pp. 11–23.

—— (1992) *Culture, Media, Language: Working Papers in Cultural Studies, 1972–79* (London: Routledge).

—— (1996) 'Who Needs "Identity"?', in S. Hall and P. du Gay (eds) *Questions of Cultural Identity* (London: Sage).

—— (1997) 'The Work of Representation', in S. Hall (ed.) *Representation: Cultural Representations and Signifying Practices* (London: Sage).

Halliday, F. (1992) *Arabs in Exile: Yemeni Migrants in Urban Britain* (London: I.B. Tauris).

—— (1996) *Islam and the Myth of Confrontation: Religion and Politics in the Middle East* (London: I.B. Tauris).

Hammond, A. (2005) *Pop Culture Arab World: Media, Arts, and Lifestyle* (Santa Barbara: University of California Press).

Handal, N. (2001) *The Poetry of Arab Women* (Northampton, MA: Interlink Publishing Group).

Hanna, J.L. (1988) *Dance, Sex, and Gender: Signs of Identity, Dominance, Defiance, and Desire* (Chicago: University of Chicago Press).

Hannerz, U. (1969) *Soulside: Inquiries into Ghetto Culture and Community* (New York: Columbia University Press).

—— (1983) *Exploring the City* (New York: Columbia University Press).

—— (1993) *Cultural Complexity: Studies in the Social Organization of Meaning* (New York: Columbia University Press).

—— (1996) *Transnational Connections: Culture, People, Places* (London: Routledge).

—— (2010) *Anthropology's World: Life in a Twenty-First Century* (London: Pluto Press).

Harper, R. (1966) *Nostalgia: An Existential Exploration of Longing and Fulfilment in the Modern Age* (Cleveland, OH: Press of Western Reserve University).

Harrison-Kahan, L. (2005) 'Passing for White, Passing for Jewish: Mixed Race Identity in Danzy Senna and Rebecca Walker', *MELUS*, Vol. 30 No. 1, pp. 19–48.

Hartigan, J. (1999) *Racial Situations: Class Predicaments of Whiteness in Detroit* (Princeton, NJ: Princeton University Press).

Hastrup, K. and Fog Olwig, K. (1997) *Siting Culture* (London: Routledge).

Hatem, M. (1999) 'The Microdynamics of Patriarchal Change in Egypt and the Development of an Alternative Discourse of Mother–Daughter Relations: The Case of A'isha Taymur', in S. Joseph (ed.) *Intimate Selving in Arab Families: Gender, Self, and Identity* (Syracuse, NY: Syracuse University Press).

Hattox, R. (1985) *Coffee and Coffeehouses: The Origins of a Social Beverage in the Medieval Near East* (Seattle: University of Washington Press).

Hayano, D. (1979) 'Auto-Ethnography: Paradigms, Problems, and Prospects', *Human Organisation*, Vol. 38 No. 1 (Spring), pp. 99–104.

Heggy, T. (1998) *Critique of the Arab Mind* (Cairo: Dar Al-Maaref).

Heider, K. (1975) 'What Do People Do? Dani Auto-Ethnography', *Journal of Anthropological Research*, Vol. 31 No. 1, pp. 3–17.

Hermann, E. (2005) 'Emotions and the Relevance of the Past: Historicity and Ethnicity Among the Banabans of Fiji', *History and Anthropology*, Vol. 16 No. 3, pp. 275–291.

Hesse, B. (2000) *Unsettled Multiculturalisms* (London: Zed Books).

Hirsch, A. (1983) *Making the Second Ghetto: Race and Housing in Chicago, 1940–1960* (Santa Barbara: University of California Press).

Hirschmann, N. (1999) 'Eastern Veiling, Western Freedom?', in F. Dallmayr (ed.) *Border Crossings: Toward a Comparative Political Theory* (Lanham, MD: Lexington Books), pp. 39–59.

Ho, P. (2003) 'Performing the "Oriental": Professionals and the Asian Model Minority Myth', *Journal of Asian American Studies*, Vol. 6 No. 2, pp. 149–175.

Hollinger, D. (1995) *Postethnic America: Beyond Multiculturalism* (New York: Basic Books).

hooks, b. (1999) *Black Looks: Race and Representation* (New York: South End Press).

Horne, G. (2006) *The Color of Fascism: Lawrence Dennis, Racial Passing, and the Rise of Right-Wing Extremism in the United States* (New York: New York University Press).

Hourani, A. (1947) *Minorities in the Arab World* (Oxford: Royal Institute of International Affairs Oxford University Press).

—— (1962) *Arabic Thought in the Liberal Age, 1798–1939* (London: Oxford University Press).

—— (1970) *The Ottoman Background of the Modern Middle East* (Harlow: Longmans for the University of Essex.)

—— (1980) *Europe and the Middle East* (London: Macmillan).

—— (1981) *The Emergence of the Modern Middle East* (London: Macmillan in association with St Antony's College, Oxford).

—— (1991) *A History of the Arab Peoples* (London: Faber & Faber).

Hubel, T. and Brooks, N. (2002) *Literature and Racial Ambiguity* (New York: Rodopi Press).

Hutnyk, J. (2000) *Critique of Exotica: Music, Politics and the Culture Industry* (London: Pluto Press).

Ignatiev, N. (1995) *How the Irish Became White* (London: Routledge).

Inglehart, R., Moaddel, M. and Tessler, M. (2006) 'Xenophobia and In-Group Solidarity in Iraq: A Natural Experiment on the Impact of Insecurity', *Perspectives on Politics*, Vol. 4 No. 3, pp. 495–505.

Jacobs-Huey, L. (2006) 'The Arab Is the New Nigger', *Transforming Anthropology*, Vol. 14 No. 1, pp. 60–64.

Jameson, F. (1984) 'The Politics of Theory: Ideological Positions in the Postmodernism Debate', *New German Critique*, Vol. 33, pp. 53–65.

Jarmakani, A. (2008) *Imagining Arab Womanhood: The Cultural Mythology of Veils, Harems, and Belly Dancers in the U.S.* (New York: Palgrave Macmillan).

Jawad, S. (2005) *Dirāsāt Fī Al-Mas alah Al-Qawmīyah Al-Kurdīyah* (Bayrūt: al-Dār al-Arabīyah lil-Ulūm).

Johnston, R., Poulsen, M. and Forrest, J. (2007) 'The Geography of Ethnic Residential Segregation: A Comparative Study of Five Countries', *Annals of the Association of American Geographers*, Vol. 97 No. 4, pp. 713–738.

Joseph, S. (1993) 'Gender and Relationality among Arab Families in Lebanon', *Feminist Studies*, Vol. 19 No. 3, pp. 465–486.

—— (1994) 'Brother/Sister Relationships: Connectivity, Love, and Power in the Reproduction of Patriarchy in Lebanon', *American Ethnologist*, Vol. 21 No. 1, pp. 50–73.

—— (1999) *Intimate Selving in Arab Families: Gender, Self, and Identity* (Syracuse, NY: Syracuse University Press).

Joyce, M. (2003) *Ruling Shaikhs and Her Majesty's Government, 1960–1969* (London: Routledge).

Juda, B. and Bennett, J. (1998) *The Passing Figure: Racial Confusion in Modern American Literature* (New York: Peter Lang).

Kabbani, R., Tromans, N. and Mernissi, F. (2008) *The Lure of the East: British Orientalist Painting* (New Haven, CT: Yale University Press).

Kaeppler, A. (1970) 'Tongan Dance: A Study in Cultural Change', *Ethnomusicology*, Vol. 14 No. 2, pp. 266–277.

—— (1999) 'The Mystique of Fieldwork', in T. Buckland (ed.) *Dance in the Field: Theory, Methods and Issues in Dance Ethnography* (London: Palgrave Macmillan).

—— (2000) 'Dance Ethnology and the Anthropology of Dance', *Dance Research Journal*, Vol. 32 No. 1, pp. 116–125.

Kalmar, I. (2004) 'The Hookah in the Harem: On Smoking and Orientalist Art', in S. Gilman and X. Zhou (eds) *Smoke: A Global History of Smoking* (London: Reaktion Books).

Kapchan, D. (2011) *Gender on the Market: Moroccan Women and the Revoicing of Tradition* (Philadelphia, PA: University of Pennsylvania Press).

Kapoor, N. (2013) 'The Advancement of Racial Neoliberalism in Britain', *Ethnic and Racial Studies*, Vol. 36 No. 6, pp. 1028–1046.

Karayanni, S. (2004) *Dancing Fear and Desire: Race, Sexuality, and Imperial Politics in Middle Eastern Dance* (Waterloo, ON: Wilfrid Laurier University Press).

—— (2006) 'Moving Identity: Dance in the Negotiation of Sexuality and Ethnicity in Cyprus', *Postcolonial Studies*, Vol. 9 No. 3, pp. 251–266.

Karayanni, S. (2009) 'Native Motion and Imperial Emotion: Male Performers of the "Orient" and the Politics of the Imperial Gaze', in J. Fisher and A. Shay (eds) *When Men Dance: Choreographing Masculinities Across Borders* (New York: Oxford University Press).

Karmi, G. (1991) 'The Arab Community and British Public Life', in R. El-Rayyes (ed.) *Arabs in Britain* (London: Riad El-Rayyes Books).

—— (1994) 'Migration and Health: Profile of a North African Community in London', *Journal of the Society for Moroccan Studies*, Vol. 1 No. 1, pp. 99–107.

—— (1997) *The Egyptians of Britain: A Migrant Community in Transition* (Durham, NC: Centre for Middle Eastern and Islamic Studies).

Karmi, G. (2005) 'A Case of Early Migration and the Problems of Adjustment and Integration', in A. Shiblak (ed.) *The Palestinian Diaspora in Europe* (Ramallah and Jerusalem: Shaml and the Institute of Jerusalem Studies), pp. 101–115.

Karmi, G., Afshar, H. and Maynard, M. (1993) 'The Saddam Hussein Phenomenon and Male–Female Relations in the Arab World', in H. Afshar (ed.) *Women in the Middle East: Perceptions, Realities and Struggles for Liberation* (London: Palgrave Macmillan), pp. 146–158.

Kayali, H. (1997) *Arabs and Young Turks: Ottomanism, Arabism, and Islamism in the Ottoman Empire, 1908–1918* (Berkeley: University of California Press).

Keith, M. (1993) *Race, Riots and Policing: Lore and Disorder in a Multi-racist Society* (London: Routledge).

Keith, M. (1995) 'Making the Street Visible: Placing Racial Violence in Context', *New Community*, Vol. 21 No. 4, pp. 551–565.

—— (2004) 'Racialization and the Public Spaces of the Multicultural City', in K. Murji and J. Solomos (eds) *Racialization: Studies in Theory and Practice* (Oxford: Oxford University Press).

—— (2005) *After the Cosmopolitan? Multicultural Cities and the Future of Racism* (new edition) (London: Routledge).

Keresztesi Treat, R. (2002) 'Writing Culture and Performing Race in Mourning Dove's *Cogewa, The Half Blood* (1927)', in T. Hubel and N. Brooks (eds) *Literature and Racial Ambiguity* (New York: Rodopi).

Khaldun, I., Rosenthal, F. and Dawood, N. (1969) *The Muqaddimah, An Introduction to History* (Princeton, NJ: Princeton University Press).

Khalidi, R. (1991a) 'Arab Nationalism: Historical Problems in the Literature', *American Historical Review*, Vol. 96 No. 5, pp. 1363–1373.

—— (1991b) *The Origins of Arab Nationalism* (New York: Columbia University Press).

Khattak, S. (2008) *Islam and the Victorians: Nineteenth-century Perceptions of Muslim Practices and Beliefs* (London: Tauris Academic Studies).

Khemir, M. and Benjamin, R. (1997) *Orientalist Aesthetics: Art, Colonialism, and French North Africa, 1880–1930* (Berkeley: University of California Press).

Khemir, S. (1993) *Waiting in the Future for the Past to Come* (London: Quartet Books).

Knadler, S. (2003) 'Traumatized Racial Performativity: Passing in Nineteenth-Century African-American Testimonies', *Cultural Critique*, No. 55, pp. 63–100.

Kobayashi, A. (1994) 'Coloring the Field: Gender, "Race," and the Politics of Fieldwork', *The Professional Geographer*, Vol. 46 No. 1, pp. 73–80.

—— (2000) 'Racism out of Place: Thoughts on Whiteness and an Antiracist Geography in the New Millennium', *Annals of the Association of American Geographers*, Vol. 90 No. 2, pp. 392–403.

—— (2008) 'Racism in Place: Another Look at Shock, Horror, and Racialization', in P. Moss and K. Falconer el-Hindi (eds) *Feminisms in Geography: Rethinking Space, Place and Knowledges* (Lanham, MD: Rowman and Littlefield).

Kobayashi, A. and Peake, L. (1994) 'Unnatural Discourse, "Race" and Gender in Geography', *Gender, Place & Culture*, Vol. 1 No. 2, pp. 225–243.

Kolankiewicz, L. (2008) 'Towards an Anthropology of Performance(s)', *Journal of the Performing Arts*, Vol. 13 No. 2, pp. 8–24.

de Koning, A. (2009) *Global Dreams: Class, Gender, and Public Space in Cosmopolitan Cairo* (Cairo: American University in Cairo Press).

Korom, F. (2013) *The Anthropology of Performance: A Reader* (New York: John Wiley & Sons).

Koutsouba, M. (1999) '"Outsider" in an "Inside" World, or Dance Ethnography at Home', in T. Buckland (ed.) *Dance in the Field: Theory, Methods and Issues in Dance Ethnography* (London: Palgrave Macmillan).

Kramvig, B. (2005) 'The Silent Language of Ethnicity', *European Journal of Cultural Studies*, Vol. 8 No. 1, pp. 45–64.

Kumar, K. (2003) *The Making of English National Identity* (Cambridge: Cambridge University Press).

Kundnani, A. (2007) *The End of Tolerance: Racism in 21st-Century Britain* (London: Pluto Press).

Lane, J. (2012) 'From "*Amor Fati*" to "disgust": Affect, Habitus, and Class Identity in Didier Eribon's *Retour À Reims*', *French Cultural Studies*, Vol. 23 No. 2, pp. 127–140.

Larsen, N. (2004) *Passing* (Lafayette, IN: Courier Dover Publications).

Lave, J. (1988) *Cognition in Practice: Mind, Mathematics and Culture in Everyday Life* (Cambridge: Cambridge University Press).

Lawless, R (1995) *From Ta'izz to Tyneside: Arab Community in the North-east of England in the Early Twentieth Century* (Exeter: University of Exeter Press).

Leatherdale, C. (1983) *Britain and Saudi Arabia, 1925–1939: The Imperial Oasis* (London: Routledge).

Lefebvre, H. (1991) *The Production of Space* (New York: Wiley).

Lejeune, P. (1989) *On Autobiography* (Minneapolis: University of Minnesota Press).

Lewin, E. and Leap, W. (2002) *Out in Theory: The Emergence of Lesbian and Gay Anthropology* (Champaign: University of Illinois Press).

Lewis, A. (2003) *Race in the Schoolyard: Negotiating the Color Line in Classrooms and Communities* (New Brunswick, NJ: Rutgers University Press).

Lewis, R. (1995) *Gendering Orientalism: Race, Femininity and Representation* (London: Routledge).

Lincoln, B. (1991) *Emerging from the Chrysalis: Rituals of Women's Initiation* (New York: Open University Press USA).

Linville, S. (2000) '"The Mother of All Battles": Courage under Fire and the Gender-Integrated Military', *Cinema Journal*, Vol. 39 No. 2, pp. 100–120.

Lloyd, M. (1999) 'Performativity, Parody, Politics', *Theory, Culture & Society*, Vol. 16 No. 2, pp. 195–213.

Loizos, P. and Papataxiarchis, E. (1991) *Contested Identities: Gender and Kinship in Modern Greece* (Princeton, NJ: Princeton University Press).

Low, S. (1996) 'The Anthropology of Cities: Imagining and Theorizing the City', *Annual Review of Anthropology*, Vol. 25 No. 1, pp. 383–409.

—— (1999) *Theorizing the City: The New Urban Anthropology Reader* (New Brunswick, NJ: Rutgers University Press).

Low, S. and Lawrence-Zúñiga, D. (2003) *Anthropology of Space and Place: Locating Culture* (New York: Wiley).

Lowe, L. (1994) *Critical Terrains: French and British Orientalisms* (Ithaca, NY: Cornell University Press).

—— (1996) *Immigrant Acts: On Asian American Cultural Politics* (Durham, NC: Duke University Press).

Lyons, A. and Lyons, H. (2011) *Sexualities in Anthropology: A Reader* (New York: Wiley).

Lyotard, J.-F. (2004 [1990]) *Libidinal Economy* (London: A. & C. Black).

Mac an Ghaill, M. (1994) *The Making of Men: Masculinities, Sexualities and Schooling* (Milton Keynes: Open University Press).

MacKenzie, J. (1995) *Orientalism: History, Theory and the Arts* (Manchester: Manchester University Press).

Mahmood, S. (2004) *Politics of Piety: The Islamic Revival and the Feminist Subject* (Princeton, NJ: Princeton University Press).

Mahtani, M. (2006) 'Challenging the Ivory Tower: Proposing Anti-Racist Geographies within the Academy', *Gender, Place & Culture*, Vol. 13 No. 1, pp. 21–25.

—— (2014) 'Toxic Geographies: Absences in Critical Race Thought and Practice in Social and Cultural Geography', *Social & Cultural Geography*, Vol. 15 No. 4, pp. 359–367.

Makdisi, S. (1992) 'The Empire Renarrated: "Season of Migration to the North" and the Reinvention of the Present', *Critical Inquiry*, Vol. 18 No. 4, pp. 804–820.

—— (1995) '"Postcolonial" Literature in a Neocolonial World: Modern Arabic Culture and the End of Modernity', *Boundary 2*, Vol. 22 No. 1, pp. 85–115.

—— (1998) *Romantic Imperialism: Universal Empire and the Culture of Modernity* (Cambridge: Cambridge University Press).

Makhoul, S. (1998) 'Unveiling North African Women, Revisited: An Arab Feminist Critique of Orientalist Mentality in Visual Art and Ethnography', *Anthropology of Consciousness*, Vol. 9 No. 4, pp. 39–48.

Malikki, L. (1992) 'National Geographic: The Rooting of Peoples and the Territorialization of National Identity among Scholars and Refugees', *Cultural Anthropology*, Vol. 7 No. 1, pp. 24–44.

Mamdani, M. (2002) 'Good Muslim, Bad Muslim: A Political Perspective on Culture and Terrorism', *American Anthropologist*, Vol. 104 No. 3, pp. 766–775.

Marchart, O. (2003) 'Bridging the Micro–Macro Gap: Is There Such a Thing as a Post-Subcultural Politics?', in D. Muggleton and R. Weinzierl (eds) *The Post-Subcultures Reader* (Oxford: Berg).

Marcus, G.E. (1995) 'Ethnography In/Of the World System: The Emergence of Multi-Sited Ethnography', *Annual Review of Anthropology*, Vol. 24 No. 1, pp. 95–117.

Martínez, L. (2000) *The Algerian Civil War, 1990–1998* (London: C. Hurst & Co.).

Massey, D. and Denton, N. (1993) *American Apartheid: Segregation and the Making of the Underclass* (Cambridge, MA: Harvard University Press).

Mason, J. (1975) 'Sex and Symbol in the Treatment of Women: The Wedding Rite in a Libyan Oasis Community', *American Ethnologist*, Vol. 2 No. 4, pp. 649–661.

Matthews, J. (2007) 'Eurasian Persuasions: Mixed Race, Performativity and Cosmopolitanism', *Journal of Intercultural Studies*, Vol. 28 No. 1, pp. 41–54.

Maybin, S. (2001) 'Language, Struggle and Voice: The Bakhtin/Volosinov Writings', in M. Wetherell (ed.) *Discourse Theory and Practice: A Reader* (London: Sage).

McClintock, E. (2010) 'When Does Race Matter? Race, Sex, and Dating at an Elite University', *Journal of Marriage and Family*, Vol. 72 No. 1, pp. 45–72.

McDermott, R. (1987) 'The Explanation of Minority School Failure, Again', *Anthropology & Education Quarterly*, Vol. 18 No. 4, pp. 361–364.

McDonough, S. (1995) 'The Impact of Social Change on Muslim Women', in J. Morny, J. Eva and K. Neumaier-Dargyay (eds) *Gender, Genre and Religion: Feminist Reflections* (Waterloo, ON: Wilfrid Laurier University Press), pp. 125–141.

McDowall, D. (1992) *Minorities in the Middle East* (London: Minority Rights Group).

McGown, R.B. (1999) *Muslims in the Diaspora: The Somali Communities of London and Toronto* (Toronto: University of Toronto Press).

McKittrick, K. and Woods, C. (2007) *Black Geographies and the Politics of Place: Between the Lines* (Toronto and Cambridge, MA: Between the Lines Press and South End Press).

McRobbie, A. (1989) *Zoot Suits and Second-Hand Dresses: An Anthology of Fashion and Music* (London: Macmillan).

Mead, M. (1949) *Male and Female* (New York: Morrow).

—— (1963) *Sex and Temperament in Three Primitive Societies* (New York: Morrow).

Meeker, M. (1979) *Literature and Violence in North Arabia* (Cambridge: Cambridge University Press Archive).

Menicucci, G. (1998) 'Unlocking the Arab Celluloid Closet: Homosexuality in Egyptian Film', *Middle East Report*, No. 206, pp. 32–36.

Mickolus, E., Sandler, T. and Murdock, J. (1988) *International Terrorism in the 1980s: A Chronology of Events, 1980–1983* (Ames: Iowa State University Press).

Miller, D. (2009) *The Comfort of Things* (London: Polity Press).

Mills, C. (2000) 'Efficacy and Vulnerability: Judith Butler on Reiteration and Resistance', *Australian Feminist Studies*, Vol. 15 No. 32, pp. 265–279.

Miron, L. and Inda, J. (2000) 'Race as a Kind of Speech Act', *Cultural Studies a Research Annual*, No. 5, pp. 86–99.

Mitchell, J. (1959 [1956]) *The Kalela Dance: Aspects of Social Relationships Among Urban Africans in Northern Rhodesia* (Manchester: Manchester University Press).

Mitra, D. (2008) 'Punjabi American Taxi Drivers: The New White Working Class?', *Journal of Asian American Studies*, Vol. 11 No. 3, pp. 303–336.

Modood, T. (2005) *Multicultural Politics: Racism, Ethnicity, and Muslims in Britain* (Minneapolis: University of Minnesota Press).

Modood, T., Berthoud, R. and Nazroo, J. (2002) '"Race", Racism and Ethnicity: A Response to Ken Smith', *Sociology*, Vol. 36 No. 2, pp. 419–427.

Modood, T., Triandafyllidou, A. and Zapata-Barrero, R. (2006) *Multiculturalism, Muslims and Citizenship: A European Approach* (London: Routledge).

Monroe, P. (1981) *Britain's Moment in the Middle East, 1914–1971* (Baltimore, MD: Johns Hopkins University Press).

Moore, H. (1986) *Space, Text, and Gender: An Anthropological Study of the Marakwet of Kenya* (New York: Guilford Press).

Morris, R. (1995) 'All Made Up: Performance Theory and the New Anthropology of Sex and Gender', *Annual Review of Anthropology*, Vol. 24 No. 1, pp. 567–592.

—— (2007) 'Legacies of Derrida: Anthropology', *Annual Review of Anthropology*, Vol. 36, pp. 355–389.

Murji, K. and Solomos, J. (2004) *Racialization: Studies in Theory and Practice* (Oxford: Oxford University Press).

Naber, N. (2006) 'Arab American Femininities: Beyond Arab Virgin/ American(ized) Whore', *Feminist Studies*, Vol. 32 No. 1, pp. 87–111.

Naff, A. (2000) 'Growing up in Detroit: An Immigrant Grocers Daughter', in N. Abraham and A. Shryock (eds) *Arab Detroit: from Margin to Mainstream* (Detroit: Wayne State University Press).

Nagel, C. (2001) 'Hidden Minorities and the Politics of "Race": The Case of British Arab Activists in London', *Journal of Ethnic and Migration Studies*, Vol. 27 No. 3, pp. 381–400.

—— (2002a) 'Geopolitics by Another Name: Immigration and the Politics of Assimilation', *Political Geography*, Vol. 21 No. 8, pp. 971–987.

—— (2002b) 'Constructing Difference and Sameness: The Politics of Assimilation in London's Arab Communities', *Ethnic and Racial Studies*, Vol. 25 No. 2, pp. 258–287.

—— (2005) 'Skilled Migration in Global Cities from "Other" Perspectives: British Arabs, Identity Politics, and Local Embeddedness', *Geoforum*, Vol. 36 (Spring), pp. 197–210.

Nagel, C. and Staeheli, L. (2008a) 'Being Visible and Invisible: Integration from the Perspective of British Arab Activists', in C. Dwyer and C. Bressey (eds) *New Geographies of Race and Racism* (Aldershot: Ashgate).

—— (2008b) 'Integration and the Negotiation of "Here" and "There": The Case of British Arab Activists', *Social and Cultural Geography*, Vol. 9 No. 4, pp. 415–430.

—— (2008c) 'To Be or Not to Be "British Muslim": British Arab Perspectives on Religion, Politics, and "the Public"', in P. Hopkins and R. Gale (eds) *Muslims in Britain: Race, Place, Identities* (Edinburgh: Edinburgh University Press).

Nance, S. (2009) *How the Arabian Nights Inspired the American Dream, 1790–1935* (Chapel Hill, NC: University of North Carolina Press).

Nehme, M. (2009) *Fear and Anxiety in the Arab World* (Gainsville: University Press of Florida).

Newton, E., Lewin, E. and Leap, W. (2002) *Out in Theory: The Emergence of Lesbian and Gay Anthropology* (Champaign: University of Illinois Press).

Niedermüller, P. (2000) 'Urban Ethnicity between the Global and the Local', in R. Bendix and H. Roodenburg (eds) *Managing Ethnicity: Perspectives from Folklore Studies, History and Anthropology* (Amsterdam: Het Spinhuis).

Nelson, L. (1999) 'Bodies (and Spaces) Do Matter: The Limits of Performativity', *Gender, Place & Culture: A Journal of Feminist Geography*, Vol. 6 No. 4, pp. 331–54.

Nguyen, T. (2005) *We Are All Suspects Now: Untold Stories from Immigrant America After 9/11* (Boston, MA: Beacon Press).

Nochlin, L. (1989) 'The Imaginary Orient', in *The Politics of Vison: Essays in Nineteenth-century Art and Society* (New York: Harper & Row).

—— (1987) 'The Political Unconscious in Nineteenth-Century Art', *Art Journal*, Vol. 46 No. 4, pp. 259–260.

—— (1989) *The Politics of Vision: Essays on Nineteenth-Century Art and Society* (New York: Harper & Row).

O'Donnell, M. and Sharpe, S. (2000) *Uncertain Masculinities: Youth, Ethnicity, and Class in Contemporary Britain* (London: Routledge).

ONS (Office for National Statistics) (2012) 'Ethnic Group, Local Authorities in England and Wales (Table No. KS201EW)', in *2011 Census* (Fareham, Hants: ONS).

Osella, C. and Osella, F. (1998) 'On Flirting and Friendship: Micro-politics in a Heirarchical Society', *Journal of the Royal Anthropological Institute*, Vol. 4 No. 2, pp. 189–206.

—— (2006) *Men and Masculinities in South India* (Delhi: Anthem Press).

Panayi, P. (2009) *An Immigration History of Britain: Multicultural Racism Since 1800* (London: Pearson Longman).

Patthey-Chavez, G. (1993) 'High School as an Arena for Cultural Conflict and Acculturation for Latino Angelinos', *Anthropology & Education Quarterly*, Vol. 24 No. 1, pp. 33–60.

Peristiany, J. (1966) *Honour and Shame: The Values of Mediterranean Society* (Chicago: University of Chicago Press).

Peters, C. (1992) *Collateral Damage: The New World Order at Home and Abroad* (Cambridge, MA: South End Press).

Peterson Royce, A. (1977) *The Anthropology of Dance* (Bloomington: Indiana University Press).

Phelan, P. (1988) 'Feminist Theory, Poststructuralism, and Performance', *Theatre and Dance Review*, Vol. 32 No. 1, pp. 107–127.

—— (1993) *Unmarked: The Politics of Performance* (London: Routledge).

Piper, A. (1992) 'Passing for White, Passing for Black', *Transitions*, Vol. 58, p. 4.

Portes, A. and Stepick, A. (1993) *City on the Edge: The Transformation of Miami*. (Berkeley: University of California Press).

Potuoğlu-Cook, Ö. (2006) 'Beyond the Glitter: Belly Dance and Neoliberal Gentrification in Istanbul', *Cultural Anthropology*, Vol. 21 No. 4, pp. 633–660.

Pratt, M. (1992) *Imperial Eyes: Travel Writing and Transculturation* (London: Taylor & Francis).

Pulido, L. (2000) 'Rethinking Environmental Racism: White Privilege and Urban Development in Southern California', *Annals of the Association of American Geographers*, Vol. 90 No. 1, pp. 12–40.

Rabi, U. (2006) 'Oil Politics and Tribal Rulers in Eastern Arabia: The Reign of Shakhbut (1928–1966)', *British Journal of Middle Eastern Studies*, Vol. 33 No. 1, pp. 37–50.

Racy, A. (1996) 'Heroes, Lovers, and Poet-Singers', *Journal of American Folklore*, Vol. 109 No. 434, pp. 404–424.

Radhakrishnan, R. (2003a) 'Ethnicity in an Age of Diaspora', in J. Braziel and A. Mannur (eds) *Theorizing Diaspora: A Reader* (New York: Wiley-Blackwell).

—— (2003b) *Theory in an Uneven World* (Malden, MA: Wiley-Blackwell).

Ramadan, T. and Nassef, A. (2004) 'An Interview with Tariq Ramadan', *The American Muslim*, 9 September. Available at: http://www.theamericanmuslim.org/tam. php/features/articles/interview_with_tariq_ramadan/ (accessed September 2014).

Ramm, C. (2010) 'The Muslim Makers', *Interventions*, Vol. 12 No. 2, pp. 183–197.

Rasmussen, A. (2005) 'An Evening in the Orient'. In A. Shay and B. Sellers-Young (eds) *Belly Dance: Orientalism, Transnationalism, And Harem Fantasy* (Costa Mesa, CA: Mazda Publishers).

Reed-Danahay, D. (1997) *Auto/Ethnography: Rewriting the Self and the Social* (London: Berg).

Reinelt, J. (1989) 'Feminist Theory and the Problem of Performance', *Modern Drama* Vol. 32, pp. 48–57.

Rosaldo, M. (1974) *Woman, Culture, and Society* (Stanford, CA: Stanford University Press).

Rosenthal, D. (1982) *Orientalism, the Near East in French Painting, 1800–1880* (Rochester: Memorial Art Gallery of the University of Rochester).

Roth, W. (2000) 'Sol Bloom, the Music Man', *Chicago Jewish History*, Vol. 24 No. 3.

Rottenberg, C. (2004a) 'Passing: Race, Identification, and Desire', *Criticism*, Vol. 45 No. 4, pp. 435–452.

—— (2004b) 'Race and Ethnicity in "The Autobiography of an Ex-Colored Man" and "The Rise of David Levinsky": The Performative Difference', *MELUS*, Vol. 29 Nos 3/4, pp. 307–321.

—— (2004c) 'Salome of the Tenements: The American Dream and Class Performativity', *American Studies*, Vol. 45 No. 1, pp. 5–29.

Sabry, T. (2005) 'Emigration as Popular Culture', *European Journal of Cultural Studies*, Vol. 8 No. 1, pp. 5–22.

—— (2010) *Cultural Encounters in the Arab World: On Media, the Modern and the Everyday* (London: I.B.Tauris).

—— (2011) *Arab Cultural Studies: Mapping the Field* (London: I.B. Tauris).

Said, E. (1978) *Orientalism* (London: Vintage Books).

Salhi, Z. and Netton, I. (2006) *The Arab Diaspora: Voices of an Anguished Scream* (New York: Routledge).

Salih, S. (2002) *Judith Butler* (London: Routledge).

Salih, S. and Butler, J. (2004) *The Judith Butler Reader* (London: Wiley-Blackwell).

Ṣaliḥ, Ṭ. (1991 [1966]) *Season of Migration to the North* (London, Heinemann).

Sánchez, M. and Schlossberg, L. (2001) *Passing: Identity and Interpretation in Sexuality, Race, and Religion* (New York: New York University Press).

Sangster, J. (1994) 'Telling Our Stories: Feminist Debates and the Use of Oral History', *Women's History Review*, Vol. 3 No. 1, pp. 5–28.

Sarroub, L. (2005) *All American Yemeni Girls: Being Muslim in a Public School* (Philadelphia, PA: University of Pennsylvania Press).

Savigliano, M. (1995) *Tango and the Political Economy of Passion* (Boulder, CO: Westview Press).

Sawalha, A. (2014) 'Gendered Space and Middle East Studies', *International Journal of Middle East Studies*, Vol. 46 No. 1, pp. 166–168.

Sayyid, S. (2003) *A Fundamental Fear: Eurocentrism and the Emergence of Islamism* (London: Zed Books).

—— (2006) *A Postcolonial People: South Asians in Britain* (London: C. Hurst & Co.).

Ṣayigh, Y. (1997) *Armed Struggle and the Search for State: The Palestinian National Movement, 1949–1993* (Oxford: Oxford University Press).

Schechner, R. (2005) *Performance Studies: An Introduction* (London: Routledge).

Schein, L. (1999) 'Performing Modernity', *Cultural Anthropology*, Vol. 14 No. 3, pp. 361–395.

—— (2000) *Minority Rules: The Miao and the Feminine in China's Cultural Politics* (Durham, NC: Duke University Press).

Scheper-Hughes, N. (1995) 'The Primacy of the Ethical: Propositions for a Militant Anthropology', *Current Anthropology*, Vol. 36 No. 3, pp. 409–440.

Schiesari, J. (1992) *The Gendering of Melancholia: Feminism, Psychoanalysis, and the Symbolics of Loss in Renaissance Literature* (Ithaca, NY: Cornell University Press).

Schmitt, N. (1990) 'Theorizing about Performance: Why Now?', *New Theatre Quarterly*, Vol. 6 No. 23, pp. 231–234.

Schwartzman, L. (2002) 'Hate Speech, Illocution, and Social Context: A Critique of Judith Butler', *Journal of Social Philosophy*, Vol. 33 No. 3, pp. 421–441.

Searle, C. and Shaif, A. (1991) '"Drinking from One Pot": Yemeni Unity, at Home and Overseas', *Race & Class*, Vol. 32 No. 4, pp. 65–81.

Semmerling, T. (2006) *'Evil' Arabs in American Popular Film: Orientalist Fear* (Austin: University of Texas Press).

Senna, D. (2002) *Caucasia* (Madison, WI: Demco Media).

Shaheen, J. (1984) *The TV Arab* (Bowling Green, OH: Bowling Green State University & Popular Press).

—— (1997) *Arab and Muslim Stereotyping in American Popular Culture* (Washington, DC: Georgetown University Press).

—— 2008. *Guilty: Hollywood's Verdict on Arabs After 9/11* (Northampton, MA: Olive Branch Press).

—— (2009) *Reel Bad Arabs: How Hollywood Vilifies a People* (Northampton, MA: Olive Branch Press).

Shain, F. (2003) *The Schooling and Identity of Asian Girls* (Stoke-on-Trent: Trentham).

Shain, Y. (1996) 'Arab-Americans at a Crossroads', *Journal of Palestine Studies*, Vol. 25, pp. 46–59.

Sharabi, H. (1970) *Arab Intellectuals and the West: The Formative Years, 1875–1914* (Baltimore, MD: Johns Hopkins University Press).

Sharma, S., Hutnyk, J. and Sharma, A. (1996) *Dis-orienting Rhythms: The Politics of the New Asian Dance Music* (London: Zed Books).

Shay, A. (2000) 'The 6/8 Beat Goes On: Persian Popular Music from Bazm-e Qajariyyeh', in W. Ambhurst (ed.) *Mass Mediations* (Berkeley: University of California Press).

—— (2002) *Choreographic Politics: State Folk Dance Companies, Representation, and Power* (Middletown, CT: Wesleyan University Press).

—— (2005) 'The Male Oriental Dancer', in B. Sellers Young and A. Shay (eds) *Belly Dance: Orientalism, Transnationalism, and Harem Fantasy* (Costa Mesa, CA: Mazda Publishers).

—— (2006) *Choreographing Identities: Folk Dance, Ethnicity and Festival in the United States and Canada* (Jefferson, NC: McFarland & Co.).

—— (2008) *Dancing across Borders: The American Fascination with Exotic Dance Forms* (Jefferson, NC: McFarland & Co.).

Shay, A. (2009) 'Invented Hypermasculinity: Colonial Influences on Dance Styles in Egypt, Iran, and Uzbekistan', in J. Fisher and A. Shay (eds) *When Men Dance: Choreographing Masculinities Across Borders* (New York: Oxford University Press).

Shay, A. and Sellers-Young, B. (2003) 'Belly Dance: Orientalism: Exoticism: Self-Exoticism', *Dance Research Journal*, Vol. 35 No. 1, pp. 13–37.

—— (2005) *Belly Dance: Orientalism, Transnationalism, and Harem Fantasy* (Costa Mesa, CA: Mazda Publishers).

Sikh Federation UK (2010) *Can the Office of National Statistics be Trusted with the (2011) Census?* Available at: http://www.sikhfederation.com/pdf/SikhsCensusJan2010.pdf (accessed December 2010).

Silverman, K. (1988) *The Acoustic Mirror: The Female Voice in Psychoanalysis and Cinema* (Bloomington: Indiana University Press).

Silverman, M. (1992) *Deconstructing the Nation: Immigration, Racism, and Citizenship in Modern France* (London: Routledge)

Silverman, M. and Yuval-Davies, N. (1999) 'Jews, Arabs and the Theorization of Racism in Britain and France', in A. Brah, M. Hickman and M. Mac an Ghaill (eds) *Thinking Identities: Ethnicity, Racism and Culture* (Basingstoke: Macmillan).

Silverstein, P. (2004) *Algeria in France: Transpolitics, Race, and Nation* (Bloomington: Indiana University Press).

Singer, C. (2002) *The Middle East in London* (London: Stacey International).

Sivanandan, A. (2008) 'Catching History on the Wing', conference speech at the Institute of Race Relations, London.

Skellington, R. and Morris, P. (1996) *'Race' in Britain Today* (London: Sage in association with the Open University).

Smith, G. (2010) 'Reconsidering Gender Advertisements: Performativity, Frame and Display', in M. Jacobsen (ed.) *The Contemporary Goffman* (New York: Routledge).

Smith, K. (2002) 'Some Critical Observations on the use of the Concept of "Ethnicity"', *Sociology*, Vol. 36 No. 2, pp. 399–417.

Smith, R. (1985) 'Rule-by-Records and Rule-by-Reports: Complementary Aspects of the British Imperial Rule of Law', *Contributions to Indian Sociology*, Vol. 19 No. 1, pp. 153–176.

Smith, V. (1994a) 'Reading the Intersection of Race and Gender in Narratives of Passing. *Diacritics*, Vol. 24 No. 2/3, pp. 43–57.

Spencer, P. (1985) *Society and the Dance: The Social Anthropology of Process and Performance* (Cambridge: Cambridge University Press).

Spivak, G. (1985) 'Can the Subaltern Speak? Speculations on Widow-Sacrifice', *Wedge* Vol. 7 No. 8, pp. 120–130.

—— (1987) *In Other Worlds: Essays in Cultural Politics* (New York: Methuen).

St John, G. (2008) *Victor Turner and Contemporary Cultural Performance* (Oxford: Berghahn Books).

Stavrou, S. (2002) 'The Ghaziya and the Khawaja', *The Best of Habibi*, Vol. 19 No. 1, available at: http://thebestofhabibi.com/vol-19-no-1-feb-2002/the-ghaziya-and-the-khawaja/ (accessed June 2014).

Steet, L. (2000) *Veils and Daggers: A Century of National Geographic's Representation of the Arab World* (Philadelphia, PA: Temple University Press).

Strathern, M. (1987) 'An Awkward Relationship: The Case of Feminism and Anthropology', *Signs*, Vol. 12 No. 2, pp. 276–292.

Straw, M. (2008) 'Traumatized Masculinity and American National Identity in Hollywood's Gulf War', *New Cinemas: Journal of Contemporary Film*, Vol. 6 No. 2, pp. 127–143.

Tambiah, S. (1985) *Culture, Thought and Social Action: An Anthropological Perspective* (Cambridge, MA: Harvard University Press).

Tannous, I. (1988) *The Palestinians: A Detailed Documented Eyewitness History of Palestine Under British Mandate* (New York: IGT Co.).

Tapper, R. and O'Shea, M. (1992) *Some Minorities in the Middle East* (London: Centre of Near and Middle Eastern Studies, SOAS, University of London).

Tarlo, E. (1996) *Clothing Matters: Dress and Identity in India* (London: C. Hurst & Co.).

Tarlo, E. (2010) *Visibly Muslim: Fashion, Politics, Faith* (Oxford: Berg).

Tarr, C. (2005) *Reframing Difference: Beur and Banlieue Filmmaking in France* (Manchester: Manchester University Press).

Taylor, J. (1976) *The Half-Way Generation – A Study of Asian Youths in Newcastle Upoon Tyne* (Windsor: NFER).

Thompson, M. (1974) 'The Second Generation – Punjabi or English?', *Journal of Ethnic and Migration Studies*, Vol. 3 No. 3, pp. 248–278.

Tibi, B. (1981) *Arab Nationalism: A Critical Enquiry* (London: Macmillan).

Trienekens, S. (2002) '"Colourful" Distinction: The Role of Ethnicity and Ethnic Orientation in Cultural Consumption', *Poetics*, Vol. 30, pp. 281–298.

Trinh, T.M. (2009) *Woman, Native, Other: Writing Postcoloniality and Feminism* (Bloomington: Indiana University Press).

Troeller, G. (1976) *The Birth of Saudi Arabia: Britain and the Rise of the House of Sa'ud* (London: Routledge).

Turner, V. (1969) *The Ritual Process: Structure and Anti-Structure* (Chicago: Aldine).

Turner, V. (1986) *The Anthropology of Performance* (New York: PAJ Publications).

Turner, V. and Turner, E. (1986) *On the Edge of the Bush: Anthropology as Experience.* (Tucson: University of Arizona Press).

Ulrich, B. (2009) 'Historicizing Arab Blogs: Reflections on the Transmission of Ideas and Information in Middle Eastern History', *Arab Media and Society* (Spring).

Valassopoulos, A. (2007) '"Secrets" and "Closed Off Areas": The Concept of *Tarab* or "Enchantment" in Arab Popular Culture', *Popular Music and Society*, Vol. 30 No. 3, pp. 329–341.

Van Maanen, J. (ed.) (1995) *Representation in Ethnography* (Thousand Oaks, CA: Sage).

Veblen, T. (2008 [1899]) *The Theory of the Leisure Class* (New York: Oxford University Press).

Vermeulen, H. and Govers, C. (1994) *The Anthropology of Ethnicity: Beyond 'Ethnic Groups and Boundaries'* (Amsterdam: Het Spinhuis).

Vertovec, S. (2007) 'Introduction: New Directions in the Anthropology of Migration and Multiculturalism', *Ethnic and Racial Studies*, Vol. 30 No. 6, pp. 961–978.

Wacquant, L. (1993) 'Urban Outcasts: Stigma and Division in the Black American Ghetto and the French Urban Periphery', *International Journal of Urban and Regional Research* , Vol. 17 No. 3, pp. 366–383.

—— (1994) 'The New Urban Color Line: The State and Fate of the Ghetto in Postfordist America', in C. Calhoun (ed.) *Social Theory and the Politics of Identity*. Oxford: Basil Blackwell, pp. 231–276.

Wacquant, L. and Wilson, W. (1989) 'The Cost of Racial and Class Exclusion in the Inner City', *Annals of the American Academy of Political and Social Science*, Vol. 501 No. 1, pp. 8–25.

Wald, G. (2000) *Crossing the Line: Racial Passing in Twentieth-Century U.S. Literature and Culture* (Durham, NC: Duke University Press).

Ware, V. (2007) *Who Cares About Britishness? A Global View of the National Identity Debate* (London: Arcadia Books).

Warren, J. (2001) 'Doing Whiteness: On the Performative Dimensions of Race in the Classroom', *Communication Education*, Vol. 50 No. 2, pp. 91–108.

Watson, J. (1977) *Between Two Cultures: Migrants and Minorities in Britain* (Oxford: Blackwell).

Weeks, E. (1998) 'About Face: Sir David Wilkie's portrait of Mehemet Ali, Pasha of Egypt', in J. Codell and D. Macleod (eds) *Orientalism Transposed: The Impact of the Colonies on British Culture* (Aldershot: Ashgate).

Weston, K. (1993) 'Lesbian/Gay Studies in the House of Anthropology', *Annual Review of Anthropology*, Vol. 22 No. 1, pp. 339–367.

Whitehead, N. (2009) 'Post-Human Anthropology', *Identities*, Vol. 16 No. 1, pp. 1–32.

Williams, T.K. (2004) 'Racing and Being Raced: The Critical Interrogation of "Passing"', in J. Ifekwunigwe (ed.) *'Mixed Race' Studies: A Reader* (New York: Routledge).

Willis, P. (1977) *Learning to Labor: How Working Class Kids Get Working Class Jobs* (New York: Columbia University Press).

Wilson, J. (2005) *Nostalgia: Sanctuary of Meaning* (Lewisburg, PA: Bucknell University Press).

Wilkinson, L. (2002) 'The Harem: Contrasting Orientalist and Feminist Views (by Latifa)', *Habibi*, Vol. 19 No. 1, available at: http://thebestofhabibi.com/vol-19-no-1-feb-2002/the-harem/ (accessed June 2014).

Yúdice, G. (2003) *The Expediency of Culture: Uses of Culture in the Global Era* (Durham, NC: Duke University Press).

Index